How to Say It™

TO YOUR

THE RIGHT WORDS TO SOLVE PROBLEMS, SOOTHE FEELINGS & TEACH VALUES

Dr. Paul Coleman

PRENTICE HALL

Library of Congress Cataloging-in-Publication Data

Coleman, Paul W.
    How to say it to your kids. / Paul Coleman.
       p. cm.
    Includes index.
    ISBN 0-13-030884-6 — ISBN 0-7352-0177-3 (pbk.)
     1. Parent and child.   2. Communication in the family.   3. Parenting.
   4. Miscommunication.   I. Title.
    HQ755.85.C629 2000
    649'.1—dc21

                                        00-033995
                                           CIP

Acquisitions Editor: *Tom Power*
Production Editor: *Sharon L. Gonzalez*
Formatting/Interior Design: *Robyn Beckerman*

Grateful acknowledgment is made to the following for permission to reprint previously published material:

From *Getting to the Heart of the Matter*, copyright 1994 by Paul Coleman.
Reprinted by permission from Adams Media, Holbrook, MA.

Printed in the United States of America

10 9 8 7 6 5 4 3 2 1

ISBN 0-13-030884-6 (PPC)

ATTENTION: CORPORATIONS AND SCHOOLS

Prentice Hall books are available at quantity discounts with bulk purchase for educational, business, or sales promotional use. For information, please write to: Prentice Hall Special Sales, 240 Frisch Court, Paramus, New Jersey 07652. Please supply: title of book, ISBN, quantity, how the book will be used, date needed.

PRENTICE HALL
Paramus, NJ 07652

On the World Wide Web at http://www.phdirect.com

To my wife, Jody,
and our three children, Luke, Anna, and Julia.
I cherish you all.

And to the memory of my wonderful father, George Coleman.
I no longer hear your words,
but I do live by them.

Acknowledgments

First and foremost, I wish to thank my literary agents, Mike and Patricia Snell. They always have an idea, an encouraging word, and a cheery willingness to listen. A writer should be so lucky.

I wish to thank the following people who also made helpful contributions:

Tom Power, senior editor at Prentice Hall, for his faith in my work;

Sharon L. Gonzalez, production editor, and Rose Ann Ferrick, copy editor, who helped make the manuscript shine;

John Coleman, my brother and assistant principal at J.F.K. Middle School in Enfield, Connecticut, for his insights into school safety and teaching issues;

Kristen Fandl, C.S.W., my colleague. Although much of the time we just pass each other in the hall, I'm always glad to have you around;

Gary Blum and Master Robert Blum at *Just for Kicks Martial Arts* for their assistance in rounding up stories for the book. And to Master Joseph Klee for his comments and insights on sportsmanship;

Donna Berrios for her well-thought-out ideas;

Robert and JoAnne Van Scoy, as well as Luanne and Tony Nappi, for their suggestions as we sat overlooking the lake;

Paul Varricchio for his enthusiastic comments and sheer brilliance;

Claire, Ann Marie, Jane, Debby, and John for always being there;

My wife, Jody, and our children, Luke, Anna, and Julia, for their suggestions and tolerance while I was busy writing;

And my parents, George and Frances Coleman. I love you and am forever grateful.

Contents

The difference between the right word and a word
is like the difference between lightning and a lightning bug.

—MARK TWAIN

Smart Talk:
The Six Ways We Speak
to Our Kids

Kathy glanced at the wall clock. Only fifteen minutes until the school bus arrived! Her two children were dawdling, trying to delay the inevitable moment when they must grab their belongings and head down the driveway for their first day back at school.

"Mark!" Kathy cried. "Why aren't your supplies in your book bag where they're supposed to be?"

Before he could respond, eight-year-old Jenny dropped a box of cereal on the floor, scattering its contents.

Kathy sighed loudly. "Jenny, aren't you finished with your breakfast? The bus will be here any minute!" She yelled to her ten-year-old son, "Mark, I need you to help your sister clean up. I'll get your book bag ready. Hurry!"

"But I didn't spill anything," he protested.

"I never said you did. Just help her, please. Now!"

Mark made a face and walked over to his younger sister. While she was bent over scooping up the cereal, he hit her just hard enough behind her knee to cause her to fall. "Mom," Jenny called. "Mark pushed me!"

"I did not!"

"Then why am I on the floor?"

Mark whispered back, "Because I hit you. But I didn't push you."

Kathy huffed back into the kitchen and stood over her arguing children. She felt like screaming. She just wanted her kids to be ready on time, and she wanted them to be in a reasonably good mood for school. The vision she'd had of giving them warm hugs before they left had vanished. The only wish that would come true now was that they would make it to the bus with seconds to spare. But she'd have to act like a drill sergeant to make it happen.

What could she possibly have said to improve the situation?

THE THREE OUTCOMES OF ALL COMMUNICATION

Talking to your kids isn't hard. But talking *smart* takes some forethought and a little practice. Communicating with children is an essential and important job of parents. Done well, it can bind a family together and prevent or heal many problems. Not done well, family life can be tense and confusing, and the child will venture into the world inadequately prepared to cope with all life has to offer.

Most parents overestimate the amount of meaningful conversation they have with their grade-school children. Recent findings at the University of Michigan showed that household conversation (just sitting and talking with children) had dropped nearly 100 percent in 1997 compared to 1981. One reason was that kids spent more time at before- and after-school activities, and family mealtime declined by an hour per week. Also, the time kids spent visiting with friends or talking on the phone tripled.

If you're like most busy parents, chatting with your children is brief and usually begins with one of the following:

"How did you sleep?" *("Fine . . .")*

"How was your day?" *("Fine . . .")*

"Where are you going?" *("Outside . . .")*

"When will you be back?" *("Later.")*

"What did you do at school today?" *("Nothing.")*

"Did you finish your homework?" *("I didn't have any.")*

"Stop that!" *("But she started it!")*

"How many times have I told you . . ." *("Oh, Mom!")*

For many parents these comments and others just like them make up the bulk of conversation on most days. Whether parents realize it or not, any communication attempt will have one of three consequences:

1. It will bring them closer to their children.
2. It will start an argument.
3. It will lead to avoidance or withdrawal.

Be honest. Do the majority of your conversations encourage closeness with your kids? Arguments are sometimes unavoidable, but they need not be poisonous to the relationship. As often as not they can end positively or at least without one or both sides feeling frustrated.

In too many families, conversations with children have a neutral effect at best. No harm was done, but neither was anything accomplished. The goal is to talk so that the parent-child relationship is enhanced, discipline is more effective, and your children will want to talk to you—not avoid you—when they have a problem. By knowing all six ways of communicating (instead of relying on just one or two) you can achieve those goals.

THE **TENDER** APPROACH TO COMMUNICATION

Kathy, the exasperated mom who was worried that her kids would miss the school bus, used—or, rather, misused—three of the six approaches to communication. Yes, she was able to get them to the bus on time, but at a high emotional price. She, Jenny, and Mark felt angry and put upon. What a way to start the school year. Had she used the approaches properly or in the right combination (a few seconds of forethought was all she needed), it still might have resulted in a mad dash for the school bus—but without the irritation and bad feelings that tainted everything.

The **TENDER** ways of speaking are **TEACHING** (criticism is a negative form of teaching), **EMPATHIZING, NEGOTIATING, DO'S & DON'TS** (commands, household rules), **ENCOURAGING** (including praise), and **REPORTING** (neutral comments, statement of facts, reporting your thoughts and feelings). When stressed, overtired, or preoccupied, parents are prone to responding to their children in limited ways. For example, four hours into a six-hour road trip, weary parents of bickering children might understandably yell, "Knock it off!" or, if trying to sound adultlike, they might say, "Must you fight like that!" (**DO'S & DON'TS** command). Will it work? Anyone who has been there will probably say, "Not for long." The main problem is that parents instinctively select a response without considering the alternatives, which are usually more effective. In fact, most stressed parents overuse some styles of talking (commands and criticism) and underuse others (especially **EMPATHIZING**). Even when not stressed, parents may be unsure of how to respond to a child's question or handle a predicament, and so they fall back on standby clichés and hope the child gets the point. One father, surprised when his son didn't win a trophy in a martial arts competition, didn't know how to console his son. "Life's not always fair," he finally said. Chances are that if the father knew more about the six ways of communicating, he would have come up with a more effective response.

When Kathy, the frazzled mom, said to Mark, "Why aren't your supplies in your book bag where they're supposed to be?" she was not really asking a question. She was criticizing Mark for his dawdling. The criticism was justified, but it complicated Kathy's situation in two ways. First, Mark thought she was being unfair, and he got angry. He'd intended to get his supplies together, but why did it have to be on his mother's timetable? Second, Kathy was not being clear about what she wanted. She really wasn't interested in *why* his book bag was still empty. She wanted it filled, but she didn't say that. Similarly, when she said to Jenny, "Aren't you finished with your breakfast?" she gave the appearance of asking a simple question (**REPORTING**) but in fact it was a veiled criticism. Imagine if instead she had said, "I'm sorry, Jenny, but we're running late. I know you are still hungry, but you can't have a second bowl of cereal. Grab an apple if you'd like." That would have been a clear statement of what Kathy wanted Jenny to do, and it would have been without the criticism.

When Kathy told Mark to help his sister clean up the spilled cereal, she was issuing a command (**DO'S & DON'TS**). Commands are fine and important, but in this case it only added to the tension that Kathy feared was already spoiling the morning. **EMPATHIZING** or praising ("You're a big help to me, Mark") might have taken the sting out of her command. Furthermore, and perhaps just as important, her choice of words might have lessened Kathy's irritation, too.

The more aggravated our speaking tone and the more harsh our words, the more upset we will become. The more we can speak calmly and pleasantly, the less upset we will become.

So if Kathy had used **REPORTING** to express her concern about being late for the school bus, without criticizing, and if she had balanced her commands (**DO'S & DON'TS**) by empathizing or encouraging, then the first-day-back-to-school blues might have been avoided.

INCREASING YOUR **TENDER** REPERTOIRE

At first glance you might believe that you regularly use all six communication styles. After all, what parent hasn't praised or empathized or taught or negotiated with their child, right? Guess again. When you run through the following list of common expressions that exemplify each of the six approaches, you may discover that you favor one or two approaches more than others. While it is easy to shift from one style to another when all is calm and the household is happy, people under stress tend to overuse certain styles. They might criticize more or bark out commands, or they might be overly sympathetic and lenient and not inclined to enforce rules. Interestingly, some couples balance each other out: One spouse emphasizes two or three styles while the other emphasizes the remaining styles. Together they are a complete set, but alone they lean to the left or right and then blame the other when matters get out of hand.

TEACHING

The "T" in **TENDER** stands for **TEACHING**. It is a rare day that parents don't teach their children. Teaching can be a warm, meaningful experience that bonds grown-ups with kids, such as when a parent patiently instructs her child how to ride a two-wheeler or tie a lure to a fishing line or scoop up ground balls. And children ask many questions that allow parents an opportunity to explain the ways of the world.

But teaching can degrade into lectures or nagging, and the message may get lost. Some parents feel comfortable teaching but uncomfortable showing much affection. Those same parents often get uneasy when their child is very emotional. They try to overcome their uneasiness by trying to get their child to understand the logic of the situation. They get impatient when logic doesn't help their child. ("Elizabeth, if you would just listen to what I am saying, then you would know how to do your math homework. Crying won't help!") Like each of the six styles, teaching has its benefits and its limitations. Is teaching a common style for you?

How to Say It

- "Let me explain . . ."
- "Watch how I do it, then you try."
- "Let's see if we can figure this out together."
- "Interesting choice. Why did you pick that answer?"
- "The answer is . . ."
- "I'm not sure what the answer is. Let's look it up."

- "Do it this way."
- "How would you feel if someone did that to you?"
- "When you told your sister she couldn't use your baseball glove, how do you think that made her feel?"
- "Making mistakes is one of the ways we learn things."
- "I want you to do this because . . ."
- "The reason you can't go is . . ."

Of course, tone of voice is key. Saying "Do it this way!" in a gruff, exasperated tone will be taken as a criticism. In fact, parents often slip into a critical teaching mode. It is not fatal, and used sparingly it may get the child's attention, but usually it adds to stress and lessens the likelihood your child will want you to help with problems.

How Not to Say It

- "I can't believe you did that!"
- "That's stupid!"
- "Never mind, I'll do it!"
- "If that's the way you're going to be, then you can take care of this by yourself."
- "That answer is wrong. I thought you said you studied for this test?"
- "You're acting like a baby!"
- "Why can't you be like your sister?"

Put-downs, name-calling, and comparisons are the worst kinds of statements you can make. Parents who use a critical teaching mode seldom use **EMPATHIZING**. Learning to speak more empathetically can actually help parents feel more patient.

The best time to use teaching is when:

anxiety or frustration (for either parent or child) is low;

children calmly ask questions;

children are not preoccupied with other things;

you are not likely to be critical.

EMPATHIZING

The first "E" in **TENDER** stands for **EMPATHIZING**. Empathy is important when your child is experiencing strong emotions. A child who calmly asks, "What is the capital of Kentucky?" will do fine with a straightforward answer. But if the child wads up his homework into a ball and yells, "I can never remember this stuff! Who cares what the capital of Kentucky is!" a little empathy may go a long way. "I don't blame you for being frustrated," a parent might say. "It's hard when you study your notes but still can't remember everything."

Parents trip up when it comes to showing genuine empathy. It's difficult to empathize when you're upset or angry or reeling from something your child has just said. Sometimes parents confuse empathy with encouragement and say things like, "Don't worry, I'm sure you'll do just fine." Sympathetic pep talks are encouraging, but they are not empathic. When you make an empathic response, you are not trying at that moment to solve problems or heal wounds. Instead, you are trying to understand your child's pain and talk about it in a way that helps the child realize you truly do understand.

When Annie came home crestfallen because a boy playmate preferred the company of another boy, her mother wanted Annie to feel better. She said, "Your sister will be home soon, and you can play with her." Mom was trying to be encouraging, but to show empathy she might have said, "That must make you feel sad and maybe a little angry, too." Annie would know that her feelings were being heard, not dismissed. That might have been sufficiently soothing, or it might have prompted Annie to talk even more about how she feels ("That happens to me at school sometimes, too"). Then Mom may have realized that her daughter's concerns were worth examining.

How to Say It

- "You're feeling sad [or mad or nervous or glad] about . . ."
- "It bothers you that your brother got to go on a class trip and you didn't."
- "I know you're feeling scared about . . ."
- "You wish Grandpa was here with you, don't you?"
- "You missed the goal, and you're worried you let your team down. Do I have that right?"

- "It feels good when you finally make friends at a new school."
- "The way you hung up the phone makes me think you're upset about something."
- "It's frustrating and sad when you look forward all week to the ball game but then get sick and have to stay home."
- "You're really excited about the class trip to the aquarium."

A true empathic response is like holding up a mirror to someone. What they hear you say is a reflection of how they feel. Empathic comments are without judgment. They do not contain solutions to a problem, but solutions fall more easily into place if you can empathize because you understand the problem better. When you are showing empathy, your child will likely talk more. It's easier for a child to reveal her concerns when someone can accurately describe her feelings. If your child looks troubled but refuses to talk, asking "Why won't you tell me?" is not empathic and probably won't help. Say instead, "You seem worried [or hurt or angry or sad, etc.] about something. I'd like to talk about it with you, but maybe you'd rather think about it by yourself for a while." That may gently coax your child to respond.

Clues that you are not being empathic (when you think you are):

You rush in with answers or solutions.

You find yourself debating with your child about how she should be feeling.

You are providing reassurances before you've clearly expressed your understanding of your child's concerns.

You want to get the conversation over with.

You are very angry.

How Not to Say It

- "I know how you must feel." (The feeling is not described.)
- "I understand." (Understand what?)
- "I still love you." (But is that your child's concern right now?)
- "You'll be fine." (Reassurance is not empathy.)
- "It's not as big a problem as you're making it." (You're telling your child he is wrong to feel the way he does.)

- "Life does that to you sometimes. The important thing is to think about something positive." (Your intent is to make her feel better, but this is not empathy.)

The best time to use empathy is:

when your child is emotional and not likely to listen to reason (this is also the hardest time);

when you're not sure what the real problem is (empathy can draw your child out);

if your child is sensitive by nature;

if you want your child to understand her emotions.

NEGOTIATING

The "N" in **TENDER** stands for **NEGOTIATING**. It should be used less often than parents realize. **NEGOTIATING** begins when your growing child requests more freedoms (choosing which clothes to buy, staying up later, etc.). You can then discuss with her the responsibilities that accompany those freedoms. Children are not your peers. They haven't the right—as do adults in contract disputes—to break off negotiations. Parents have the final say. Still, your children benefit when you hear them out, understand their reasons for wanting something, and sometimes negotiate an agreement with them.

When eleven-year-old Danny wanted to own an expensive pair of in-line skates, his father had two concerns. First, he wanted Danny to appreciate the value of money. Second, since his son tended to postpone getting his homework done by playing too much, the new skates would add to that problem. Dad expressed those concerns. Danny said he would do extra chores to earn the money. His father liked the idea, but the expensive skates would require a lot of chores. Dad really wanted the garage painted, but it wasn't a very big job because the first coat was nearly finished. Additional chores were required. Danny suggested they buy a cheaper pair of used skates so that extra chores would not be necessary. Dad agreed. Then Dad said that if Danny spent extra time playing and didn't finish his homework by nine o'clock, he would not be able to play the next day. Danny agreed. Obviously, Dad held all the cards in this negotiation. But because he believed his son would learn a valuable lesson, he took his son's ideas seriously.

The mistake parents make is when they negotiate out of desperation (that is also known as "bribery"). Maybe they are worried that their kids will misbehave during an important event, so they beg them to be good and promise them ice cream later. Or a mother screams, "Okay, you can have a new video game. Just stop yelling!" That situation is different from one where Mary must go grocery shopping and has to pull her two kids away from Nintendo to accompany her. She can start out by **EMPATHIZING** and saying, "I know it's no fun to go shopping when you'd rather play. But I promise I'll hurry, and if you two promise not to complain when we are in the store, we can have pizza for dinner tonight." Mary is not desperate. She wants to reward her kids for good behavior. If she also praises them once or twice in the supermarket for their pleasant behavior, she will increase the odds that her kids will cooperate even more in the future.

How to Say It

- "I know you've done a lot of work already, but we still have some more to do. I really appreciate your effort. Is there anything special you'd like to do later?"
- "I know you want to go to the lake today with your friend and her family. I think that would be nice but I have these concerns. . . . Any suggestions?"
- "Before I can consider what you want, I need these things to happen…"
- "Before we leave for the ball game, I want you to tidy up the house. Which rooms do you want to start with?"
- "I cannot agree to that. Is there something else you want instead?"

The parent who negotiates in the best way is a benevolent dictator. She is willing to make accommodations to her child's wishes because she believes it is deserved or that it is in her child's best interest. A benevolent dictator never loses sight of who is in charge.

How Not to Say It

- "Okay, you can sleep over your friend's house tonight, but remember you have a paper to write for school." (This is fine if your child is very responsible, but it is better to have an agreement ahead of time about your expectations. Kids are experts at putting fun ahead of responsibilities.)

- "Will you promise to be home on time if I let you play at the neighbor's?" (Of course your child will promise. If it is important that he not be late, discuss what the consequences will be if he is late.)
- "All right, all right. If you just be quiet for the next half hour, we'll go to McDonald's for dinner." (Using blackmail is a bad habit to get into.)

The best time to negotiate is when:

you are not desperate;

you want your child to take on more responsibilities;

you want to teach your child the art of negotiation and compromise and the consequences of keeping or breaking agreements.

DO'S & DON'TS

The "D" in **TENDER** stands for **DO'S & DON'TS**. Listen to Charlie and his mom:

"Charlie, put your coat on if you're going outside. You'll get cold."

"No, I won't get cold, Mom."

"Yes, you will. You'll freeze. Put your coat on."

"But Mom . . ."

"I don't like it when you don't wear a coat."

"But *I* like it!"

Mom is making two mistakes. First, she's confusing **DO'S & DON'TS** with **TEACHING**. If she absolutely wants Charlie to wear a coat, she should say that without explaining why. Rules and orders are not requests. When a parent gives a rationale for her command, the implication is that if the child can outwit her with logic, then the rule can be put aside. If you think that explaining your rule is important (**TEACHING**), feel free to do so. But if a debate begins, you must be ready to enforce the rule or open up negotiations. More explanations will not help.

Mom's second mistake was stating that she doesn't like it when Charlie goes outside without a coat. Again, that is *not* only not a command (she is **REPORTING** her opinion), but it gives Charlie an opportunity to whittle away Mom's resolve ("But *I* like it!").

Every parent has rules. While rules can be changed or even negotiated, they are meaningless if parents do not enforce them. When children are younger and the rules are being introduced, parents may use a teaching style to explain them ("No eating food on the couch because . . ."), but when kids are a little older, explaining the rule invites discussion ("But, Dad, I promise I'll be careful not to drip jelly on the new furniture") when discussion is not necessary. Children need the structure that rules provide. And the most important, nonnegotiable rules involve moral values and safety. When your eight-year-old refuses to wear a seatbelt, you do not negotiate. You may give an explanation, but chances are your child knows the reasons. It is better to say, "Until you wear your belt, we will not go to the mall."

Sometimes enforcing rules is best done when accompanied by an empathic statement. Telling your child sincerely that you know he is disappointed or angry can soften the blow a little. It is bad enough when a child feels he does not get what he wants, but it is worse when he also feels that his parent doesn't understand him—or care to understand.

How to Say It

- "Stop pushing each other right now."
- "Stop throwing a ball in the living room. That's not allowed."
- "I know that you don't agree, but the rule is . . ."
- "Hitting your sister is very wrong."
- "We made an agreement, and you have to stick by it. Thank you."
- "Bedtime is in five minutes. Brush your teeth now."
- "Turn off the television now. It's dinnertime."
- "You can ride your bike as far as the end of the block, but no farther."

The best rules are clear and concise. When stating a rule, ask yourself if it is really a teaching moment (giving reasons why) or if the rule is simply to be enforced. Also ask yourself if you are willing to negotiate. If not, stick to your guns.

How Not to Say It

- "What did we just talk about?"
- "How many times have I told you . . ."

- "What do you think you are doing?"
- "What's going on here?"
- "I don't like it when you talk back to me."
- "How much longer do I have to wait before you clean your room?"
- "Don't do that." "Stop it." "That's not allowed." (Don't do what? Stop what? Be specific.)

None of those comments is clear, and they invite irrelevant discussion. They will only aggravate you and your children. Be straightforward and clear when stating **DO'S AND DON'TS**. If you get angry or loud when enforcing a rule, you may be frustrated or upset by more things than just your child. The more confident you are about your parenting, the less you need to yell.

Rule of Thumb: Saying "please" not only models politeness, it actually can help aggravated parents to feel more in control of their emotions.

The best time to state **DO'S AND DON'TS** is when:

you have your child's full attention;

your child is causing or risking harm;

you are clear about what you want to happen;

you are capable of enforcing the rules.

ENCOURAGING

The second "E" in **TENDER** stands for **ENCOURAGING** (which also includes praising and reassuring). A common mistake parents make is that they infrequently praise good behavior and are quick to criticize bad behavior. Criticizing bad behavior is not helpful if parents don't show the child a desirable alternative. Also, many parents undermine their praise by following it with a criticism ("Yes, you stopped fighting, but only after I scolded you").

Praising effort, self-control, and thoughtful gestures will reap rewards for you and your child.

How to Say It

- "Remember how you practiced hard for the concert and performed so well? I bet you can practice just as hard this year, too." (Reminding of past efforts and successes.)

- "I'm happy and proud of the way you behaved today. I know it wasn't easy." (Praise followed by an empathic comment.)
- "Great job! I especially liked it when you . . ." (Being specific.)
- "You could have gotten mad at your sister and pushed her, but you didn't. That shows self-control, and you made me very happy." (Praising desirable behavior.)
- "I noticed you shared your pretzels with your friends. That was very thoughtful. Some children wouldn't have done that." (Praising desirable behavior.)

How Not to Say It

- "I'm sure you'll do fine." (Have you taken time to really understand your child's concerns? If not, your reassurances will not help.)
- "Nice job." (This is okay, but what specifically did you like? Elaborate. Don't miss an opportunity to praise your child's effort or self-control.)
- "Everybody loses once in a while." (She knows that. It's better to simply make empathic comments before offering a pep talk.)
- "You did okay, but you could have done better." (Be careful. Will such a comment actually discourage your child instead?)
- "That was incredible! Amazing! Unbelievable!" (Exaggerations are fine on occasion. Kids like to know you are enthused. But such overly exuberant commentary will have more impact when said infrequently. Besides, what will you say when they accomplish something that really is amazing?)
- "Yes, you did fine, but I expect you to act that way." (Faint praise is worse than no praise at all. Why miss an opportunity to help your child feel even better about his accomplishment?)

Growing children crave parental praise and encouragement. Done wisely, it will help shape desirable behaviors and improve esteem.

The best time to encourage, praise, or reassure is:

as soon as possible;

as often as possible;

when you see good effort, self-control, or thoughtful behavior.

REPORTING

The "**R**" in **TENDER** stands for **REPORTING**. This refers to:

> statements of fact ("We're going to Grandma's today");
>
> common questions ("How was school?");
>
> personal opinion ("I like going to the lake . . .");
>
> expressing feelings ("I'm annoyed that . . .");
>
> making requests ("Please empty the dishwasher").

Typically, well-meaning parents use **REPORTING** as a poor substitute for some of the other approaches. Saying "I don't like it when you fight in the car" is reporting a feeling. But if the parent means "Stop fighting," she should say that. Parents caught up in New Age thinking assume they are showing respect to a youngster when they use sweet phrases like "We don't do that in this house, Kenny. Remember what I told you before?" The more words you use to get your point across to a child, the more likely you are being vague, confusing your child, and undermining your authority.

Sometimes a concerned parent talks about her own feelings and mistakes it for empathy ("I'm so sad that you hurt yourself"). Generally, normal everyday conversation includes a lot of **REPORTING** that fills in the gaps between opportunities to teach, praise, command, or empathize with your child. But don't confuse **REPORTING** with any of the other **TENDER** approaches. Otherwise, the message your child hears will not be the message you intend.

How to Say It

- "Tell me what you learned at your swimming lesson." (Make a statement instead of asking open-ended questions like "How was your swimming lesson?" You are more likely to get an informative response.)

- "We were late getting to the ball game and you missed seeing the home run. That's frustrating. I'm sorry." (Reporting a statement of fact as a preface to an empathic comment.)

- "Take off your headphones, please. I like it better when you are part of the family during dinner." (Reporting your preference after telling your child what to do.)

- "I love you."
- "I forgive you."
- "I'm sorry."

How Not to Say It

- Reporting that you like or dislike something when you really mean "Stop doing that!"

If your communication efforts have been less than satisfying, you've probably overused one or more of the **TENDER** approaches. Try your hand at a different approach or use some in combination. You will likely get better results.

1

Adoption

Michelle and Bill felt uneasy when their twelve-year-old adopted son, Brian, began asking if he would ever meet his birth parents.

"As far as I know the records are sealed, and he may never meet them," Michelle said. "I don't feel threatened, not really. But why am I so uncomfortable?"

Every week approximately thirteen hundred children are adopted in the United States. There are two common reasons why some adoptive parents are uncomfortable discussing adoption with their children. First, many parents decide to adopt because of infertility. Infertility can be a long, despairing process as the couple seeks treatment and tries for years to become pregnant to no avail. Thus, the decision to adopt is at least in the beginning a second-best choice. They then fear that their child will view his adoptive status as second-rate. Second, adoptive parents sometimes discover that their own parents are less enthusiastic about having a grandchild that is not of their bloodline. It is an attitude that certainly changes over time but nonetheless can create uncomfortable feelings.

By age five or six an adopted child should already know he is adopted. The task for parents is to answer the more detailed questions the child might have as he gets older. But another issue is what to say to the older brother or sister (who might not be adopted) when parents decide to adopt a child.

Things to Consider

➤ Adoption is not only legal, it has become a normal and quite beautiful way to bring a child into a loving family. If you talk about adoption with the attitude that it is normal and beautiful, there is nothing to be nervous about.

➤ Despite the previous point, it is not necessary to speak excessively about the fact that your child is adopted. He is your child, plain and simple. There isn't a need to draw a distinction between adopted children and children born to a family except to help your child initially understand. How a child gets to your family is not nearly as important as the fact that he is—and always will be—part of the family.

➤ Adopting an older child is a big adjustment to the children already in the family. Patience and understanding will be necessary.

How to Say It

- **REPORT** the basic facts. "You were born like any other child. A woman gave birth to you. But she was not able to take care of you, and she wanted you to live with people who could love you and take care of you. We were the lucky family you came to live with."
- "You are our real child. You belong to this family. We will always be your mother and father."
- "Sometimes adopted children have questions about their birth parents. If you ever have any questions, I'll answer them as best I can."
- If your child is furious one day and yells, "I wish you never adopted me!" say something like: "Well, I love you, and I'll always be happy you became my child."
- Reassure. "Once you are adopted, you are my child forever. I will never give you to another family."

How Not to Say It

- "Your birth mother was a drug addict . . ." Such a condemnation, even if true, is done to make yourself sound more loving and devoted than the birth parent. What insecurity do you have that warrants such a remark? It is far better to comment on the birth parents' circumstances (they were teenagers, they had no money, etc.) than to attack their character.
- "Your natural parents . . ." or "Your real parents . . ." You are the real and natural parent at this point—legally and emotionally. The term "birth mother," or "birth parents," is accurate and doesn't detract from your status.

If you already have an older child in the house and you decide to adopt, listen to questions and concerns your child might have, but do not give her the idea that her opinion will sway you one way or the other. The decision to adopt—like the decision to become pregnant—is the parents'.

What to Say to the Older Sibling

- "It sounds as if you're wishing you never had a younger brother. All children feel that way at times. Tell me what worries or saddens you."

- "I love your mom, but that doesn't mean I love you any less. I love both of you. And I am beginning to love your new brother, and that means I won't love you or Mom any less."

- "Your new brother may wonder if we love him as much as we love you. What do you think he is feeling? Any suggestions on how we might help him feel better?"

- "I liked the way you played with your new sister. You showed her what having an older brother can be like."

Smart Talk

A recent study involved 715 families with adopted children. The children had been adopted before their first birthday, and information was taken when the children were between twelve and sixteen years of age. Results showed a slight increase among some adoptees to engage in delinquent behavior compared with their nonadoptive siblings. There was also a slight increase among some adoptees to be more socially outgoing and helpful. The final conclusion was that adopted and nonadopted children are much more similar than they are different.

2

Angry Child

When kids get very angry, you might hear them yelling:

"I hate you, Mommy!"

"No, I won't stop, and you can't make me!"

"I don't have to listen to you! You're just my stepfather!"

"I won't love you anymore!"

"I don't want to talk about it!"

Younger children don't possess all the skills necessary to control their emotional outbursts (many adults don't, either). Parents and caretakers therefore need to uncover what is bothering the angry child, and they need to teach alternative ways to express anger. It can get confusing because if the child's anger is out of hand or obnoxious, parents don't always know what to focus on first—the underlying problem or the anger.

Rule of Thumb: Common sense says that if you address the problem that is causing your child's anger, the anger will diminish. However, the angrier or more out of control your child is, the less likely you will be able to discuss his underlying problem. In that case, calming the child down is necessary before any discussion can take place.

Things to Consider

➢ If you or your spouse has trouble controlling anger, your child will have a more difficult time controlling his. The old adage, "Physician, heal thyself," makes sense.

➢ When your child is very angry, speak in a conversational tone; otherwise, you run the risk of yelling.

➤ If your child is not breaking things or hurting anyone, be patient if she is unwilling to talk about what's bothering her just yet. Let her know you are very interested and available.

➤ According to psychiatrist David Viscott in his book *The Language of Feelings,* behind anger is hurt and sadness. Think about what is hurting your child instead of focusing on his anger, and you may hit pay dirt. People feel hurt when they lose their sense of being loved (or lose someone they love), when they suffer a loss of esteem or competence, or if life seems unfair or less in their control.

How to Say It

EMPATHIZING is usually your best bet for openers. Calmly **REPORTING** your observations or your reaction can also help.

- "When you're angry like that, I know you must be sad about something. Tell me what happened."
- "It hurt your feelings when your brother knocked your new bike over on purpose."
- "If you're angry, you must have a pretty good reason. Please tell me what it is."
- "When you're yelling, it is hard for me to concentrate. Please lower your voice."
- "You just slammed the door. That tells me you're hurt about something. I'd like you to tell me what's wrong."
- "I remember saying that to my father when I was a kid. I felt a lot better when we talked about it."
- "I can't force you to talk about it if you don't want to. I just hope you change your mind because talking usually helps. Besides, I hate to see you feeling so bad."

When your child is calmer, it is a good idea for each of you to sit while talking. Standing up increases the chances of another angry outburst or walking away prematurely. As the discussion nears the end, be **ENCOURAGING**. Praise your child for talking to you more calmly.

- "Even though you felt hurt and angry, I liked it much better when you talked more calmly. It made it easier for me to listen."
- "I noticed it when you started to speak more softly and with less anger. Good job. It isn't always easy to do that when you're upset."

Any **TEACHING** about how to handle angry emotions is best done in a friendly way when you are less annoyed. Role-playing is a good idea if you can make a game out of it.

- "Remember show-and-tell? When you are really angry or sad or upset about something, please tell me how you feel, but don't show it by yelling or calling people names or by stomping your feet or throwing things."
- "Let's pretend you are very mad at me about something. Can you say, 'Dad, I'm real mad right now,' instead of yelling at me?"
- "A friend of mine didn't know what to say when his son was very angry about something. What advice should I give him?" By referring to a third party, you make the topic less personal. That might make it easier for your child to offer his opinion.

How Not to Say It

- "Don't you talk to me in that tone of voice!" You may be right to feel angry (see the chapter on defiance and disrespect), but first consider what your goal is. Will a comment like that prompt your child to be more polite, or will it add fuel to the fire? It is very important to discuss the issue of disrespect, but that is best done a little later when the immediate problem is solved.
- "How dare you!" Same as above.
- "Don't you know how that makes me feel?" Trying to teach your child to empathize with your feelings is a good idea—but not as the first item. Your child is more concerned with her feelings, not anybody else's. Save that comeback for a little later in the conversation.
- "I refuse to talk to you as long as you're in that mood." Unless you are pretty sure that your child will change his tone, you run the risk that he will decide it is simply not worth talking to you. Then you've eliminated any way for either of you to approach the other without losing

face. It would be better to comment first that your child must be hurt about something and that you are available to talk. Or say something like "I want to hear about what's bothering you, I really do. But you'll have to change your tone a little bit. It's hard for me to pay attention when you're so mad."

- "You sound very angry." In their book *What Did I Just Say!,* Denis Donovan and Deborah McIntyre insightfully point out that validating a child's anger but not the hurt or sadness behind it can sometimes encourage more angry behavior. Telling a child he is angry may stir him up even more. Telling him he is sad is also accurate but more likely to lower aggressiveness.

3

Apologies

Karl and Pete were sitting on the back porch while their kids played. Pete's eight-year-old son, Joey, came out wearing his father's sport coat. It went down to his knees.

"I'm going to work now," Joey said.

"Don't spill anything on that jacket," Pete called out.

The boy went into the yard, and Karl chuckled. "I remember wearing my old man's stuff when I was a kid," he said. "Try walking down the stairs with a pair of size elevens!" He reached into a bowl of pretzels. "Of course, my father never liked me doing that. All I ever heard from him was complaints. And I never once heard him apologize. He never admitted to making mistakes. Not ever."

Kids yearn for their parents' love and approval. They like dressing up, pretending to be their mom or dad. They want their parents—especially their same-sex parent—to be proud of them. So when a parent makes mistakes and doesn't apologize, children feel deep down that they are unworthy. As they get older, they'll resent it. It's not enough for parents to teach their children to say they're sorry. Parents must admit when they are wrong and not feel ashamed to apologize to their kids when necessary.

Things to Consider

➤ Some parents show anger a lot. They are least likely to apologize and most likely to instill a sense of inadequacy in their children.

➤ While arguments and misunderstandings between a parent and child do happen, any negative effects are greatly diminished when there is positive closure. Not apologizing can leave the matter hanging and a child may believe his parent is still angry long after the incident has passed.

➤ You will not undermine your status or authority by apologizing. On the contrary, children are more likely to respect your authority and be less likely to rebel later.

How to Say It

REPORTING your apology and perhaps EMPATHIZING are called for.

- "I'm sorry. I shouldn't have yelled at you that way. Please forgive me."
- "I left for the store without asking if you wanted to come with me. Now you're upset. I'm sorry. Next time I'll remember to ask if you want to join me."
- "I probably should have apologized before now. I'm sure I hurt your feelings by waiting so long."
- "I was wrong to get so upset with you over such a small thing. I apologize."
- "I bet you're very hurt over what I said. I made a mistake. I was wrong, and I hope you'll forgive me."

How Not to Say It

- "I'm sorry, but I wouldn't have yelled at you in front of your friends if you'd done what I'd asked." That is more accusatory than remorseful.
- "Don't be so upset. You know I didn't mean it." If she's that upset, she did take it personally. Don't tell her she's wrong. Apologize.

When trying to get kids to apologize to you or someone else, don't insist they sound sincere. They probably won't sound sincere, at least not right away. The first thing they need to learn is that they were wrong to have done what they did. Later, when emotions are not so intense, help them to think about how they hurt someone else's feelings and what they might do to make amends.

How to Say It

- "This problem will not go away until you say you're sorry."
- "You broke your brother's toy on purpose. Tell me how you think he felt when you did that."

- "I know you were mad when you said those hurtful things, but that doesn't excuse what you did. It is important for you to apologize." (**EMPATHIZING** can soften his defensiveness.)
- "I heard you tell your sister you were sorry. That meant a lot to me. Good for you."
- "It's not like you to be this hurtful. Usually you are more kind. You need to apologize; otherwise, people's feelings will stay hurt." (It is always a good idea to balance complaints or criticisms with a positive remark.)
- "Don't apologize right this minute. I don't think you're ready. I'd like you to think about it for a while." This can be helpful if you sense your child will defy your request for an apology and you'd rather not butt heads. If your child wants to defy you, it allows her the chance to do so by not waiting to apologize but apologizing right away.

How Not to Say It

- "If you don't apologize, you can forget going swimming tomorrow." Applying an arbitrary punishment won't get you what you ultimately want—a child who is sincerely willing to apologize for being hurtful and who will try to avoid being hurtful in the future. It is better to say something like "I don't intend for us to be in the car together when you two haven't worked things out. I won't drive you anywhere when I know you'll just argue." That shows how not apologizing can have a natural consequence that might best be avoided by saying one is sorry.

A recent study in the journal *Child Development* showed that when parents tried to help their children empathize with the person who was hurt, as opposed to simply forcing their child to get along, the children did score higher on empathy and on the tendency to engage in positive social acts. The more often you ask your children to consider how they might have affected others, the more likely they will be better-acting kids.

4

Arguments
Between Two Adults

Katie often overheard her mother and grandmother arguing. She felt sad about it and tried to cope by occupying her mind with other things such as television or music. She was usually glad when the fighting stopped.

Bobbie overheard his parents arguing. Sometimes he would get in the middle and tell them to stop. Sometimes he'd start acting silly and giddy. Other times he'd get angry or aggressive.

Each child's style is different. Katie is concerned but uninvolved. If her caretakers argue frequently or if there are many unresolved fights (and certainly if there is violence), she is at risk for behavioral or emotional problems. Bobbie is already showing signs of disturbance. When a child intervenes in an adult argument, it is a sign that the arguing is of long standing and the child is overly involved. His occasional giddiness is not happiness but physical arousal that he cannot control. He is at high risk for acting out and developing more serious behavioral problems as he gets older.

Arguments between parents or caretakers happen, but their impact on a child depends on several factors, including how the adults respond to the child's concerns.

Things to Consider

➤ Prolonged conflicts or unresolved arguments between parents are damaging to a child's sense of security. It is not the arguing or yelling per se that is harmful, it is the child's belief that his security is threatened and that his environment is not trustworthy.

➤ Open hostility between parents is more likely to lead to behavioral problems in children than marital dissatisfaction without hostility.

➤ About one-half of all children are fearful when their parents argue.

➤ Children who witness spousal abuse engage in the same kinds of behavioral disturbances as do children who are victims of parental abuse.

➤ Children's anxiety is immediately lessened once they believe that their parents have resolved their argument. If parents who argue are observed smiling and holding hands later, the kids will breathe a sigh of relief and develop a sense of optimism that fighting won't lead to disaster.

How to Say It

- If you think your child overheard an argument you had with your mate, **EMPATHIZE** with her concerns. "I bet it made you worried or a little nervous."
- "Maybe you felt a little afraid."
- "I'm sorry you had to hear that. I'm sure it upset you."
- **REPORT.** Let your child know if matters have improved. He doesn't need to know the details but he needs to know if the situation has resolved. "I know you overheard that argument. You'll be happy to know that your mom and I have settled our differences, and we're not upset anymore."
- "Sometimes your mom and I get mad at each other, but we don't stay that way for very long. We still love each other very much."
- If your arguments remain unresolved, and especially if there is hostility, your child will feel insecure. Telling her that all is okay won't work. She'll know the truth by observing how you and your mate act toward each other. It is better to make any reassuring comment you can than say nothing. "Your dad and I are still upset with each other, but we're trying to work it out. I hope it will be soon. If this continues to trouble you, we'll talk about it."

How Not to Say It

- "That argument you overheard didn't bother you, did it?" Sometimes parents ask leading questions, using subtle tones and body language to make their children respond the way the parent wants to hear. If you really want to know how your child feels, make an **EMPATHIC** comment ("You must be upset over what you heard") instead of asking a question ("Did that argument bother you?")

- "I can't believe your mother!" Criticizing a mate to a child will not alleviate his anxiety; it will heighten it.

- "Don't look at me like that! I'm angry with you, too. When was the last time you cleaned your room!" Spillover effects can happen, but yelling at a child because you are upset with your mate only adds to the misery.

Rule of Thumb: Your children will eventually know how well you and your mate get along. You can't hide the truth. The issue is whether or not your children will feel worried and insecure about it.

Bed-wetting

Elliot is one of the 7 percent of eight-year-olds who wets his bed. He feels embarrassed and won't attend sleepovers or let his friends sleep at his house. While he has had many dry nights, the unpredictability of his bed-wetting haunts him and exasperates his parents. He has tried halting fluid intake after 7 P.M., but that has proved an inconvenience on hot summer nights. His pediatrician recommends a line of medication known as tricyclic antidepressants. His parents don't know what to do or how to console their son.

Things to Consider

➢ Bed-wetting is considered a problem if the child is at least five years of age and wets the bed twice a month or more.

➢ Eighty percent of bed-wetters have never achieved six months of continuous nighttime continence. That is called primary enuresis.

➢ Children who achieved continence for six months or more but then resumed wetting the bed (secondary enuresis) usually took longer to have dry nights and have more stress.

➢ About 3 percent of bed-wetters will continue this problem into early adulthood.

➢ By far the most successful treatment method is the urine alarm. The alarm goes off at the first sign of wetness and allows the child to interrupt the bed-wetting and use the toilet. Research is clear that this method far surpasses the use of medication. Tricyclic medications can have cardio-toxic effects if overdose occurs. Try the urine alarm before you try medications.

➢ Children over five who wet their pants during the day while awake are slower to improve.

How to Say It

- **TEACH** that the problem occurs in about one in fourteen children (age eight or under) and that it is treatable. **EMPATHY** is crucial. "I know you are very upset about this problem. You should know that you are not alone. There is probably one other child in your class with this problem. The good news is that you can stop having this problem with the urine alarm treatment."

- Reassure. "I'm glad we are tackling this problem. I know you'll feel so much better in time."

- After the bed is wet: "Okay, you pull off the sheets, and I'll get a fresh set. I'll help you make the bed." It is fine if your child prefers to make the bed alone. It is also fine if you tell the child he is to make it by himself (you are tired or busy). However, making the bed should not be viewed as a punishment. Your tone should not be scolding. Having to make a bed will not motivate your child to overcome the enuresis.

Rule of Thumb: Don't think your child will outgrow the problem. It is overcome by treatment and is likely to persist without treatment. Only 15 percent of eight-year-old bed-wetters stopped wetting within a year without treatment.

How Not to Say It

- "Can't you control yourself? You're nine years old already!" Scolding won't help, and it will definitely hurt. Your child feels bad enough as it is. If you find yourself scolding him, apologize soon. "I'm so sorry. I know it isn't your fault. I just wish you could feel better, and I think I took my frustrations out on you."

- "I'm not washing those smelly sheets. You do it." The critical tone is inappropriate. You are adding to your child's sense of shame.

- "Just try to sleep over at a friend's house. You might have a great time." Don't push it. Your child will feel humiliated if he wets the bed at a friend's house. Get the urine alarm and work on his training at home first.

6

Bossy or Domineering Child

Carol watched her daughter playing outside. The nine-year-old girl had her hands on her hips and was clearly bossing her friends. A few minutes later the girl came in the house.

"They didn't want to play with me anymore," the girl said.

Carol was not surprised.

To some extent bossiness can be part of a child's temperament. Shy, withdrawn children are less likely to try to dominate their peer group. Outgoing children can be bossy but often they are merely exuberant or filled with ideas and strategies. They are not so interested in taking charge but are willing to take the lead.

Bossy children are not leaders. They are rulers. They want things their way, and they think their way really is the best way. Bossy children may prefer playing with younger kids because it is easier to get their way. But domineering children run the risk of being rejected by their peers. To com-. pensate, they may become even bossier.

Things to Consider

➢ Bossy, domineering behavior is probably being reinforced. The first place to look is the home. Is the bossy child one who has many responsibilities? A single-parent home or a home with an alcoholic or dysfunctional parent often relies on older children to abandon some of their childhood and join the ranks of the adults. Expecting these kids to do extra chores and look out for their younger siblings but not to be bossy with their peers may be expecting too much.

➢ Is the bossy child one who is frequently dominated at home? If so, he may be trying to balance the scales by dominating his playmates. If the way the siblings treat him is changed, the bossiness might take care of itself.

➤ Does the child show signs of perfectionism? If she is easily frustrated by her mistakes, afraid to take risks for fear of failing, or engages in compulsive rituals such as cleaning excessively or counting, she may have an anxiety disorder and should be examined by a professional.

How to Say It

A straightforward command that he stop being bossy and let his friends have their way probably won't work for long. Many reminders will be needed. Realize that this pattern of bossiness gives your child a sense of mastery or esteem and that alternative ways to achieve those ends are required. You may first want to help your child open up more.

- "I noticed you got upset when your friends didn't want to do things your way. Tell me more about that."

- "What is it like when somebody else wants things to go their way?"

- "When you told Jeremy that you wouldn't play with him unless he followed your rules, how do you think that made him feel?"

- "Would you want to play with someone who always had to get his way? No? Well, I'm worried that your friends won't want to play with you because you always want your way."

Plan ahead with your child. If you know he will be playing with friends, rehearse ways he can act more fairly and less bossy. Reward his efforts with praise and hugs.

- "I watched you agree to play soccer when you wanted to play dodge ball. That was terrific. I'm proud of you for letting other kids get their fair chance to have their way."

- "I saw you doing rocks, scissors, and paper. That was a very fair way to decide who goes first in the game. Good for you."

- "I think you like to be in charge with your friends because you also have a lot of responsibilities here at home. What could happen at home that would give you less work and more time for fun?" Be willing to negotiate. Children need responsibilities, and they also need to be children.

How Not to Say It

- "Nobody likes a bossy friend." First, that isn't always true. Some kids don't mind being led. Second, you don't want to suggest that being liked is the most important thing. Kids often make poor decisions just so they will be liked. It is better to say, "Kids who like you probably won't have fun playing with you unless they get to do what they want sometimes."

- "How was school? Did you try to cooperate more with your friends?" It is important to follow up when helping a child modify his behavior. But this question is vague (are you sure your child knows exactly what you mean by the word *cooperate*?), and it is a question that can be answered by yes or no and may therefore be uninformative. Be specific: "Tell me how you tried to be more fair and less bossy with your friends today." Ask how difficult or easy it was and exuberantly praise any improvements.

7

Bullies

Danny had been moody and lethargic for a few days. Ordinarily a happy eleven-year-old, something was the matter. It was only when he complained about going to school that his parents had their first clue. Finally, when Danny said he had lost his lunch money, his parents put two and two together. An older boy on the school bus had been bullying him. What began as mild teasing escalated to loud put-downs that got the attention of the other kids and finally resulted in forcefully taking Danny's lunch money. Danny was afraid and embarrassed. Like many children, especially pre-teens, he felt awkward about telling his parents.

Conservative estimates are that 75 percent of children will be bullied at some point in their school career. There is more violence in schools today than a generation ago. A study of fifty-three randomly selected middle schools in North Carolina showed that 3 percent of the students had carried a gun and over 14 percent had carried a knife or club. Consequently, the rules for dealing with bullies need to be modified.

Things to Consider

➤ Fighting back is risky given the prevalence of weapons. Think twice about teaching your child to use fists as a way to dissuade bullies. Also, many schools have a zero-tolerance policy for fighting, and children who are trying to defend themselves are still punished even though they did not start the fight.

➤ Phoning the bully's parents can help but do so only if you know the parents (even casually). The home life of the bully may not be ideal, and he or she may be a victim of abuse or living in a home where abuse is tolerated.

➤ Always get the school involved. Have a meeting with the principal, teachers, and any counselor. They need to know what is happening and are likely to have more clout.

➤ Some children are more vulnerable to being bullied. Children who are physically smaller than average, who cry easily, or who possess poor social skills (unable to effectively initiate conversation or less likely to offer help or kindness) are more frequently the prey. Teaching them assertiveness can help.

➤ Some bullying is physical (shoving, hitting, preventing movement), some is verbal, and some is nonverbal (obscene gestures, staring).

➤ Follow up by asking your child several weeks later if matters have improved. Don't presume the situation is fully resolved.

How to Say It

If you suspect a bully problem, **REPORTING** your observations and suspicions straightforwardly is best. Then you need to find out the details.

- "I think you are dealing with a bully. That happens to most kids, and it can be very upsetting. There are things that can be done to make it stop."
- "Tell me exactly what happened and when."

If your child tells you how he feels, an **EMPATHIC** response will help him feel understood and he will talk more.

- "So it's scary to play at recess now. A lot of kids know how that feels."
- "You feel embarrassed when you get teased in front of your classmates. I remember when I got teased like that."

An older child may be too humiliated to go into details. Empathizing by telling him he feels embarrassed to talk may actually make him more self-conscious. It is better to use general terms when trying to be empathic.

- "I bet it bothers you a lot. No one likes putting up with bullies."
- "It can really ruin a guy's day when a bully is around."

Finally, **TEACH** by role-playing with your child the various ways he might respond to being bullied. Rehearsing their response will improve their confidence in coping. There are no sure-fire formulas for dismissing a bully. However, experts agree that the most successful strategy involves two steps:

1. A brief, firm, and confident rebuff such as "I don't have to take this from you . . ." or "I don't have to put up with this!" (Rehearse this several times.)
2. Walking away with shoulders straight and head held high.

If your child has a capacity for entertainment and enjoys humor, he can respond by poking fun at himself after being taunted by a bully. "You're right! I am a freak! Aaagh!"

Bullies are more apt to stop their bullying if they are not getting a strong fear response from the other children. Ask your child to recall who witnessed the bullying and to report the bullying to a school official or you.

How Not to Say It

- "Just ignore him. He'll go away eventually." It is impossible to ignore a bully unless you spend your time in hiding. Fear is best overcome by teaching assertiveness.

- "But you're so tall and strong! You don't have to be pushed around by anyone." Size and strength are less a factor than your child's personality. Shyer or more sensitive children can be easily intimidated. It is better to coach him in effective responses and praise that performance.

- "You're getting older now. I can't solve all your problems for you. I'm sure you can figure this one out." The consequences of being bullied can be devastating. At best, kids are humiliated. At worst, they harbor deep resentments and may take matters into their own hands by finding a weapon. Your child needs your full support, the support of the school, and sensitivity to the feelings of humiliation or anger that can result.

- "He didn't hit you, he just called you names" or "He didn't tease you, he just stared at you." Don't underestimate how intimidating non-physical forms of bullying can be.

8

Cheating

Billy and Sam were stationed in front of the television playing their favorite video racing game. Every so often Billy would press the pause button and interrupt the game for a split second before restarting it. It had the effect of distracting Sam just enough to give Billy the edge he wanted.

"Stop doing that. It messes me up!" Sam said.

"Okay, okay," Billy said. But when it appeared that Sam would win the game, Billy pressed the pause button and managed to eke out a victory.

Most children will cheat at something. While parents understand that, it is a bothersome trait as the child gets older. Parents view it as a form of dishonesty similar to lying, and they don't want it encouraged. Plus, parents are aware that in order to get along with others, children must learn how to play fairly.

Things to Consider

➤ Sometimes children cheat merely to aggravate their opponent. It is a way of teasing a sibling; for example, a child may blatantly cheat and then watch the little sister get angry and hurt. If teasing is the motivation, address that instead.

➤ On average, cheating at games tends to diminish as the child gets older. The more pronounced it is for a child over ten, the more other areas of concern need to be probed. Are there upsetting things going on in the child's life?

How to Say It

- **REPORTING** your observation should come first, followed by a **DO & DON'T** reminder. "I just saw you switch cards. That's called cheating. Let's agree not to do that."

- "I saw you cheating again. I don't enjoy playing when you cheat. I'm going to stop playing now and we'll try again later."
- **ENCOURAGING** or praising noncheating behavior should be done periodically. "We've been playing this game for fifteen minutes, and you have played by the rules. That's great. I have much more fun when we play by the rules."
- "You just scored a point and you played by the rules. I bet that feels really good to know you accomplished something."
- Teach and encourage **EMPATHY.** "I wonder how your friend felt when you kept cheating at the game."
- "Sometimes you'll break the rules just to get that good feeling when you win. But that doesn't make it right."

How Not to Say It

- "You're a cheater. Nobody likes a cheater." Labels are unnecessary, much too critical, and not likely to help you achieve your goal. Besides, your child does not cheat all the time, so the label is wrong. Criticize the behavior, not the child's character.
- "We played a game, and you didn't cheat!" This is not a terrible thing to say and your intent is good—to praise your child for being honest—but whenever possible, praise what the child did that was positive (he was honest, he played by the rules) instead of praising the fact that he didn't do something (he didn't cheat). Teaching a child *not* to do something is not the same as teaching her an appropriate alternative.
- When you tell your child that she cheated, odds are that she will deny it. Don't say, "You're lying! Don't lie to me!" While her dishonesty may trouble you, stick to the issue at hand (see the chapter on lying for more advice). It is better to say, "I saw you move my piece on the game board. Maybe you don't think that is cheating, but I don't want to play with you when you move my pieces like that."
- Model appropriate self-talk during the game when you are excited or frustrated by your score in the game. In other words, teach tolerance and self-control. "I'm losing this game, and I want to win. I know I could try to cheat, but I don't want to win that way. If I lose, I'll try harder next time."

9

Chores

"How many times do I have to tell you to tidy up this room?" Dad said. He was feeling exasperated. The kids always have time for the computer, friends, and outside activities, but they never seem to have time to clean up after themselves.

"But I made my bed," six-year-old Anthony said.

"Yes, you did. Thank you," Dad said. "But that was last Friday."

It took them all of five minutes to tidy up.

"See how easy that was," Dad said. "Why do I have to tear my hair out to get you guys to help around here?"

Why, indeed.

Things to Consider

➤ Chores can be divided into two types. "Self tasks" involve activities that pertain to the person in question, such as making one's own bed, washing one's dishes, or cleaning up after oneself. "Family tasks" are those that benefit the family as a whole, such as mowing the lawn, doing laundry, feeding the dog, or shoveling the driveway. It's a good idea to have your children do both types, especially as they get older.

➤ Some parents have a managerial style. They assign chores and expect the child to take responsibility for getting it done. Other parents make requests and expect the child to help out when asked. Again, as they get older, children should bear responsibility for doing some chores without being asked.

➤ One study showed that adolescents who did family tasks were also more likely to be helpful to others in various contexts. Learning to clean up only after oneself may not teach about doing for others.

➤ Boys and girls do the same amount of self tasks, while girls do more family tasks.

➤ When chores don't get done, parents are usually inconsistent in enforcing the rules.

How to Say It

- **REPORT** accurately what you expect to be done, by whom, and when. "Before we leave at two o'clock I want you to pick up everything on the family room floor that doesn't belong there. Please throw away the things that are broken."

- "I want the leaves swept out of the garage. Tony, you do that. You can do it right after breakfast. It should take you ten minutes."

- You do not need to threaten punishments, but there can be natural consequences that would work to your advantage. "If you're not finished by two o'clock, we won't go to the party until it is finished. It's your choice."

- "If it's not done by nine tonight, you'll have to stop whatever you're doing then and get it done."

- "I've asked you to put away your papers and hang up your clothes, and you haven't done it. In five minutes the computer will be turned off, and it will stay off until those jobs get done."

- **NEGOTIATE.** Give kids age-appropriate choices. "Tommy, the dog needs to be exercised and given a bath. Also, the leaves need raking and the gutters need to be cleaned out. Which of those would you be willing to do today?"

- "I'd like you to do some regular chores. If you had your pick, which would you choose?"

- **EMPATHIZE** when your child seems disgruntled. "I know it isn't fun having to put your boots on to take the garbage out. But thanks for doing it."

- **ENCOURAGE** responsible behavior. "It helps out so much when you do your chores. I'm very grateful."

How Not to Say It

- Eliminate any vague commands such as "Clean up your room," "Tidy up the kitchen," and "Clean the countertop." According to whose standards? Your child's version of a clean room may be different from yours.

- "How many times have I asked you . . ." If you talk like that, it is a strong clue that you need to enforce the rules more consistently. You've probably allowed your child to get away with dawdling in the past. Give reasonable time limits and enforce them.

- "What am I, your servant?" What parent hasn't felt that way? Clarify with your child your expectations about what needs to be done and when. Then calmly but firmly enforce those expectations.

- "If you don't get your chores done, you can kiss the birthday party good-bye." If this works, it is only because your child has detected that you are losing your patience. The neat thing about clear expectations and clear consequences is that the consequences speak for you. You don't have to yell or get exasperated. Also, if you make threats you won't enforce, you are only whittling away your authority.

10

Initiating Conversation

Ed and his son, Ray, were driving home. It was raining and the streets were crowded with cars.

"Some weather, isn't it, Ray?" Ed said.

"Yeah."

"What did you say?"

"I said yeah."

"Oh." Ed continued to drive but was feeling self-conscious about the lack of real conversation. It wasn't for lack of trying. His son just tended to be closemouthed about a lot of things. Not always, but a lot of the time.

"Did you finish your homework, Ray?"

Ray stared out the window and said nothing.

"Ray, did you hear what I just said? Did you finish your homework?"

"Yeah."

"When?"

"This afternoon."

"What subject was it?"

"English."

Ed knew he'd have to pull teeth. He decided not to ask any more questions for the remainder of the ride home.

Some kids are not prone to conversation. Some tips might help.

Things to Consider

➤ Sometimes kids don't talk much to their parents because they already know what their parents will say. If your child was troubled or frustrated about something, would you have a standard comeback? Would you try to solve the problem? Would you say not to worry? Would you say something like "That's what happens when you don't follow rules"? If your responses are prepackaged, you are not truly listening to your child.

➤ Preteen and teen boys are prone to mulling things over before they discuss them. What looks like stonewalling is their effort to handle matters on their own. While that can be a strength, it is intensified for boys whose fathers are not as physically or psychologically available (due to overwork, divorce, etc.). These boys don't want to discuss some things with their mothers, so they have no one else to turn to for advice.

➤ When trying to draw out a quiet child, do something different. Talk about something new and exciting, change your verbal approach (use the **TENDER** guidelines), or change the environment (kids who do not open up in a car or the family room may do so at a restaurant or on a walk).

➤ Don't try to get your child to open up if you are busy doing something else or she is busy. Neither of you is sending a signal that you are ready to really listen to each other.

➤ If you talk to your child only when *you* feel like talking, don't be surprised if conversations are infrequent and less than satisfying.

How to Say It

- Ask questions that cannot be answered in one or two words. "What were some of the questions on your history test today?"

- If your usually not-too-verbal child asks or tells you anything, respond with comments that will invite more discussion, not shut it down. Usually, the best response is one where you show empathy or reflect back your child's feelings about something.

"I can't wait until Saturday."

"Oh, you're excited about going rafting."

"Yeah."

"If you had to convince someone to go rafting, what would be your three best reasons?"

- Ask your child to teach *you* something that you know she is interested in. "Tell me more about the exercise your teacher used in acting class. I always wanted to learn more about acting."

- If your child is brooding and feeling self-critical, don't automatically challenge her beliefs. She may just think you don't understand. **EMPATHIZE** first. "You put on makeup today, and none of your friends were impressed. Now you're telling me you feel ugly." That comment will probably invite more conversation. Telling her she is beautiful may make you feel better, but it may not be what she needs to hear just yet.

- Make the lull in conversation *your* problem and ask your child for help. "You know, I sometimes want to make conversation but don't always know how to keep it going. Could you help me by bringing up topics?"

- Praise any openness. "I like it when we can talk about these things. Everything that goes on in your life means a lot to me."

- Talk about something that excites you. Your enthusiasm might possibly be infectious, and your child will want to know more. "Wouldn't it be great if we could build an addition to the house? I've always wanted a large sunroom."

- If you try to respond effectively to a child's comment but her body language tells you that you missed the boat, let her know you really want to understand. "What you're telling me sounds really important, but I don't think I understand yet. Help me to understand. Has something I've said troubled you?"

- If you continue to feel frustrated that your child doesn't talk to you much, it's okay to ask if you are doing something wrong. Humility never hurts, and it might help. "Every time I try to talk to you it seems I say something wrong. Can you help me with this problem? What things do I say that turn you off?"

How Not to Say It

- "What am I? A head of lettuce? Why won't you talk to me?" This can work if your child enjoys your sense of humor, but if said with antagonism, you may get nowhere.

- "I hate it when I have to drag things out of you." This is a bit strong and has an accusatory tone. If children think they will be accused or criticized, they will definitely withhold conversation unless they have to. Talk using softer words. "It means a lot when we can have a conversation. I have a harder time when you give me short answers."

- "Why can't you be like your sister?" You've just increased the odds that he will talk even less.

- "Have you done something wrong? Is that why you don't talk much?" Don't make him feel paranoid or self-conscious.

11

Dawdling

"Lizzie, we should have left five minutes ago. Where are your shoes?"

"I can't find them."

"Then why were you watching television when you should have been searching for your shoes? You'll be late for your ballet class!"

A few minutes later the shoes were found, but Lizzie still wasn't ready to leave. First she had to brush her hair, then use the bathroom, then . . .

"Lizzie, you just have to be more organized from now on," her mom complained in the car. "I'm tired of running around at the last minute."

Tired, sure. But it will happen again and again. Lizzie's Mom is making two fundamental errors when she tries to get her daughter organized in the morning:

1. The words she uses are ineffective yet she keeps using them.
2. The only consequence to dawdling is that Lizzie must put up with a frustrated parent. Any kid can handle that.

Things to Consider

➤ Children who dawdle in the morning may be overtired. Children do not require eight hours of sleep per night; they require ten to twelve hours. Poor sleep habits will cause sluggishness in the morning.

➤ Teaching a child to be more organized and on time must usually be done for each and every situation. A child who no longer dawdles before school may dawdle before bedtime or as he prepares for an extracurricular activity such as dance or karate lessons.

➤ A child who awakens the first morning in Walt Disney World doesn't dawdle. He is motivated to be ready on time. Children are not always that motivated to hurry for school or shopping. Rewarding on-time behavior with check marks or stars that can be exchanged for something desirable (such as extra time at Nintendo) can help motivate a child. Praise is essential and ultimately more powerful than tangible rewards.

How to Say It

- Let the more rewarding morning activities (eating breakfast, watching TV) occur after your child has gotten himself better organized. "I'll be happy to serve you breakfast after you get your shoes on and put all your books in your bag."

- "This is your two-minute warning. In two minutes you have to stop everything you're doing and get ready to leave."

- Praise desirable behavior. "You got dressed before coming downstairs to breakfast. Good for you. That will give you more time to relax before school."

- "Right now I need you to do . . . [list the specific behaviors]. Any questions?"

- "You can take your time if you want, but if you miss the school bus you will have to pay me gas money from your allowance [or you'll have to clean the bathroom or do some other pre-agreed chore]." Under such circumstances you do not have to yell at your child to hurry up. Let the consequences be sufficient.

How Not to Say It

- Don't say "Put on your shoes!" when you mean to say "Stop everything and put your shoes on right now." When you ask a child to do something and then repeat it ten minutes later, your child often responds, "I was going to do it!" You were probably not specific about when you wanted the task completed.

- "Why are you never ready when it's time to go?" It simply wasn't that important to him. It would be better to ask yourself how you can speak more clearly to the kids and enforce your rules calmly but strictly.

- "Do I have to yell at you every day in order for you to be organized?" If you have to ask that question, the answer is yes. Your kids have learned the fine art of distinguishing between those moments when they can ignore your request and when they must obey. They've learned not to take you seriously until you get ballistic. Speak clearly, calmly, and firmly. Turn off all distractions. Reward efficiency and be willing to let your children deal with the natural consequences of being late.

- Teach them a lesson when you are disorganized. "See? I have to pay a late fee because I didn't pay this bill on time. It was hidden under all these other papers. If I was better organized, that would not have happened."

Smart Talk

In a study conducted at Rhodes College in Memphis, researchers concluded that children who procrastinate are more likely to have parents who do the same. These parents also procrastinated when they were youngsters. If your child is a slowpoke when it comes to organization and efficiency, first modify your own shortcomings. Are you sometimes late picking them up? Do you always sign their papers or report cards at the last minute? Do the kids overhear you complaining about bills that are overdue? Do you promise to do something only to say later, "I was too busy," "I didn't have time," or "I forgot . . ."?

The apple doesn't fall far from the tree when it comes to procrastination.

12

Death of an Adult Family Member

Maryanne and the kids had just turned into their street when the cell phone rang. She knew it was her mother. Her mom had called twice a day every day for the past week, ever since Maryanne's husband, Adam, had to be rehospitalized for cancer. She and the children had just visited him. He looked awful but his eyes shimmered in the presence of his wife and kids. They would return later in the day after their oldest son Scott's soccer game. A win would tie his team for the league lead. The boy loved soccer, and his parents wanted his daily life to be as familiar and routine as possible despite his father's setback.

"Hi, Mom," Maryanne said with a smile. "You could have left a message on the machine at home. You know I would have called you right back."

But it wasn't her mother; it was the hospital. Maryanne stopped the car just two houses away from her driveway, trying to grasp the full meaning of the message. Adam had died quite suddenly, not ten minutes after she had last seen him.

"Mom?" Scott said, looking wide-eyed at his mother.

Maryanne turned and looked at her son. The other two kids were now silent in the backseat, waiting. She knew she had to tell them, but how? Would things ever be the same again?

Things to Consider

➤ Some children between five and seven do not fully understand the finality of death. They may have to be retold that because a loved one has died, she will not be returning.

➤ Children will take their cue from their caretakers about how to mourn. If the adults cope with stoicism and unexpressed sadness, children will learn that showing feelings or asking questions is not allowed. They will then have to grieve alone somehow.

➤ Anticipate that the children will act out or withdraw emotionally if the deceased was very close and important to them. They may become argumentative, be less conscientious about schoolwork, or isolate themselves from pleasurable activities.

➤ If the death was unexpected or violent, children may suffer nightmares or other more intense forms of distress.

➤ Rituals can be crucial to the healing process. A memorial service, a wake, or a funeral helps to reinforce the reality that the loved one has indeed died. It also offers a clearer line of demarcation to help people move on.

➤ Reminisce. Look through photos or videos. While painful at first, a vital component of healing is allowing the happier memories to act as a warm blanket to the cold, sad reminders of loss. Children may always miss a loved one, but over time they can smile at the memory instead of cry.

➤ Experts agree that there is no "normal" length of time to grieve. Even when it appears that a child is faring well, there will be many moments of overwhelming sadness—especially during the first year. Holidays, birthdays, and anniversaries of special family times can trigger sadness.

How to Say It

- Be direct but sensitive. Let your nonverbal language convey that your child's response matters to you. "I have very sad news. Grandpa died this morning."

- If the children have questions, answer them honestly. Details that are frightening or grisly should be left out. "Remember that Grandpa had heart surgery? Well, he developed an infection called pneumonia. Pneumonia can usually be treated but Grandpa was so weak the medicines didn't work and he died."

- Children will worry about your safety and possibly their own. If a child asks whether he will die or whether you are going to die, it's okay to reassure her that you will live a long time and she will, too. "Everybody dies someday. But most people live to be very old. By the time I die you will be all grown up and living in your own house with your own children."

- Some children will be overprotective of you. They may worry when you are sick with a cold or when you are driving in bad weather. Make **EMPATHIC** comments and then *reassure* them that you are taking proper care of yourself. "You sound worried that I might die just as Daddy did. Those are scary thoughts. But you and your brothers are the most important things in my life, so you need to know that I take very good care of myself and always drive with my seatbelt on and very carefully."

- *Reassure* them by pointing out the other times they worried and everything turned out well. "Remember how last week you got worried when I had to take antibiotics for my bronchitis? But I got all better, didn't I?"

- Comment when you know your child is feeling sad but isn't saying anything to you. "Here we are having dinner, and Mommy isn't here. I miss her, too."

- Reinforce any religious beliefs. They can be a comfort. "I know Mommy is with God. And I truly believe she is watching us right now. She just can't talk to us. And every time you pray for her she will hear you. She died, but she didn't stop loving you."

- Most young children are capable of handling a wake and funeral. Take your cue from them. If they seem very frightened at the idea of viewing a dead body, let them know it is adults who mostly attend wakes and it is not necessary for them to go. Performing a ritual with them may be helpful—say a prayer together, send a balloon off "to heaven,"* or write a short letter to the deceased and then bury it.

- If your child is going to attend a wake, explain what he will see. "Daddy will be lying in a casket. His hands will be folded. He might not look exactly the way you remember because when we die our appearance changes a little. Everybody there will want to kneel down next to Daddy and say a prayer for him. If you want, you can do that,

---

Where the Balloons Go by Paul Coleman is a story that helps children cope with loss. It is published by The Centering Corporation, a not-for-profit organization with an extensive and remarkably helpful list of books and brochures on the topic of loss. For a catalogue call 402-553-1200.

too. Or you can pray for him standing up." Explain how long you will spend at the funeral home.

- If your child sees you crying or upset even months later, don't pretend nothing was wrong. "I was thinking about Grandma and got very sad. Some days I miss her a lot."

How Not to Say It

- "I know how you feel, but Mommy would want you to be happy [or eat your supper . . .]." Any remark that tells a child he is wrong to feel the way he does can cause confusion, at the least. At the worst, he may feel guilty for not acting the way his dead relative would want him to act. It is better to say, "Mommy understands that you are sad now. She understands that you are not hungry. I understand, too. But I also believe that Mommy is looking forward to the day you can begin to feel less sad and more happy. But she knows it takes time."

- "Grandpa is taking a beautiful journey everyone takes one day." "Grandma is asleep forever." Children younger than eight or nine think in literal terms, not abstractions. Using words other than *dead* or *died* may confuse a child. He may never want to go on a *journey* or may be afraid to fall *asleep.*

- "Grandma died after she went to the hospital." "Grandma died because of an accident." Children go to hospitals sometimes, and all children have accidents. Don't imply that death commonly follows after such events. Instead, let your child know that the accident was severe and that accidents or routine hospitalizations don't usually cause death.

- "Grandma was sick . . ." Kids get sick, too. State that Grandma was extremely sick, and medicines that ordinarily work did not because she was so severely ill.

- "Don't worry, I will never die." But how do you explain that Daddy did? It is better to say that you don't expect to die until you are very old. If a child wonders what would happen to him if both you and your spouse died, you can explain the plans you made for providing a guardian. At the same time, reassure him that you don't expect it to happen.

- "It's been two years since Grandpa died. Everyone else feels better now, so why are you still upset?" The best way to forget is to remember. As contradictory as that seems, people are more able to move on from a loss when they have the freedom to remember the person who died and to feel sad. If your child surprises you by showing more sadness than you expected, use **EMPATHIC** comments to help you understand. Perhaps a friend's relative died, and it brought back sad memories. There could be many reasons. Say instead, "It's normal to have sad moments like this. What specifically were you thinking about that made you feel sad?"

Recovering emotionally from the death of a loved one can take time. Children who fare the best have caretakers who are supportive, who are able to provide for the children's ongoing needs, and who know how to offer comfort, reassurance, and a willingness to listen at all times.

13

Death of a Sibling

The death of a child is tragic to adults. For surviving brothers and sisters it can also be a disturbing reality because the child realizes she is not protected from death simply by being young. A deceased sibling was probably also a playmate, roommate, and everyday companion. Siblings share secrets and come to rely on one another in handling life's ups and downs. So when a sibling dies, a child can be truly lost, bewildered, and frightened. And that occurs at a time when the parents are themselves grieving a horrible, untimely loss. When talking to a child about a sibling's death, there are special considerations.

Things to Consider

➤ As with adults, children often go through stages of grief. The first is shock, then hurt and anger, and finally acceptance. These stages can overlap and take place over the course of many months or even longer. Yet, on a day-to-day basis, children seem to be able to grieve one minute and play ball the next.

➤ Parents tend to overprotect a surviving child. While understandable, it may inadvertently teach the child that life is fragile and death could happen to him at any moment.

➤ Some children cope with family tragedy or hardship by taking on adult responsibilities—even if it is just in their mind. They might feel they have to make a sad parent feel better, or they may want to be a "perfect" child so as not to make their parents any more upset. While learning compassion and responsibility is a good thing, children do best when they do not have to "grow up quickly."

➤ A surviving child may want to sleep with his parents for a while. That is fine.

How to Say It

- Encourage visits with the dying child. "Your brother loves it when you spend time with him. Even though he tires easily, it means so much."

- If a child is dying, you can let siblings know early enough so they have time to ask questions and make some preparations. "The doctors say that Jeremy may not live much longer. We will hope that he does live, but we are also sad thinking that he might die soon."

- According to psychologist and grief expert Dr. David Crenshaw, children often need to be told that one's body stops functioning after death. They may not understand that concept on their own. "Your sister's body completely stopped working. She feels no pain now. She does not feel hot or cold."

- A surviving child may feel guilty for past fights with the deceased. Don't automatically tell him he's wrong to feel that way. Be **EMPATHIZING** first; hear the details of the concern and then offer reassurance. "You're telling me you feel bad for all the times you fought with your brother. It's normal to feel that way. I felt bad for all the times I punished him. But you know what? I punished him because that's what parents do sometimes. And sometimes brothers fight. I don't feel bad for being a parent, and you don't have to feel bad for being a brother."

- "You feel bad about the times you and your sister didn't get along. But I remember that your sister still played with you afterward. You got over being mad, and she got over being mad because you loved each other."

- "You want to sleep with Mom and Dad tonight? It can be difficult sleeping on your own at a time like this. You won't feel the need to sleep with us every night, but for now it's okay." (A cot in the parents' room is also fine, as is any other arrangement that helps in the early days after a sibling's death.)

- "Looking at your brother's toys reminds you of him. Some days it can be easy to play with those toys, but some days you won't feel like it. Either way it's okay."

- Some children will feel guilty for having fun and feeling joyful when their parents are still grieving. "It brings joy to your mom and me that you can have fun. The sadness and grief of a child should not be the same as a parent's grief."

- "Today looks like a great day for sledding. How about getting your snowpants on and we'll go out." Grief expert David Crenshaw recommends that parents give children permission to have fun and take a break from grieving; otherwise, children can feel guilty for having fun.

- In the days or weeks after a child's death, quieter siblings might be encouraged to talk. "Let's take turns saying something about Tony. It can be whatever you like—some memory that makes you smile, something about your sadness, or any questions you might have."

- Use your religious beliefs to help provide consolation. "I don't understand why God let your sister die. But I believe she is very happy with God and will ask God to help us when we need help."

- "We will all be together in heaven one day, but we must live our lives as fully as we can in the way God would want us to."

How Not to Say It

Don't avoid discussing the deceased child on special days such as birthdays, family vacations, or holidays. In fact, have a special remembrance by saying a family prayer or bringing up pleasant memories of past holidays. Tell stories about the person. You need not dwell on the memory but the absent child should be acknowledged and everyone should be allowed to express feelings. Make specific plans ahead of time about how the child (or other deceased family member) will be remembered. Perhaps one sibling can recite a prayer, another place a memorial ornament on the Christmas tree, and so forth.

- "I can't imagine this family being happy ever again." Life will never be the same, but it can be beautiful and meaningful. There will be days you will all laugh. Reassure the surviving children that life will go on, that you will be involved in their school work and activities, that there will be vacations and fun times.

- "Your brother, God rest his soul, never gave me a hard time when I asked him to do chores. Why do you?" Don't make unfavorable comparisons—ever.

- "We'll discuss your brother's death later." Be willing to stop whatever you are doing to respond to your child's questions or comments.

Smart Talk

If your child is grieving, how should classmates welcome her back to school? According to experts David Crenshaw and Phyllis Rubin, in their videotape *Grief: How to Help Children Feel, Deal, and Heal,* you should take your cue from your child. Some children may feel too self-conscious if classmates make a big presentation. Other children might feel better knowing their grief is acknowledged and that they can talk about it to friends. Once you have an idea, discuss it with your child's teacher. Perhaps the class could make a card. Maybe students will be taught how to express their sadness to your child. Knowing that their classmates care can make a difference to many grieving children.

14

Death of a Pet

When Chance the golden retriever died, nine-year-old Mark was devastated. His sister was sad, too. But somehow Mark was particularly grieved. Mark's father recalled how at bedtime Mark's habit was to spend at least five minutes lying next to Chance and petting him. Chance seemed to look forward to it, too. (All Mom and Dad got was a good-night peck on the cheek from Mark if they were lucky.)

It was Mark who insisted that Chance be buried in their backyard. His parents agreed, but the request made them a little uneasy. They worried that a gravesite might be a constant reminder to Mark and would keep him feeling sad.

Often, a child's first experience with death happens when a pet dies. It can be a time when children learn about death and that life is precious, and discover that however sad such a loss can be, they can feel better over time. Talking to a child about death involves some of the same concepts and phrasings mentioned in the other chapters. But the death of a pet can have its own, unique aspects as well. In fact, since a pet was there every day, a child may have stronger emotional ties to the family dog than to a relative who visits less often.

Things to Consider

➤ A pet such as a dog or cat is as likely to die from an accident as it is from old age. A sudden, cruel death can be more upsetting than an expected death.

➤ Putting an animal to sleep, while humane, may not be understood by children. They may think you killed the animal or were willing to have it die because you no longer wanted to care for it.

➤ The death of a pet can be more difficult to cope with if it comes on the heels of some other death or loss.

➤ Don't replace the pet right away. Give your child several months to get used to the loss and to grieve.

➤ Don't presume that the death of a pet is either devastating or no big deal to your child. Find out, and take your time doing so. Overreacting or underreacting won't be as helpful to your child.

How to Say It

- When informing a child of a pet's unexpected death, use simple but clear words. Give the details if asked. "I came home from work today and found Pokey on the side of the road. A car had hit him, and he died." If the body is available, a child may wish to see the pet. Unless the body is badly mutilated, a child can handle seeing it. (Younger children might also handle it well but may not fully comprehend the meaning of death.) A blanket covering most of the body might be appropriate to hide some of the wounds.

- If the pet was brought to a veterinarian for disposal, a child may or may not be upset that he did not get a chance to see the body. If the child is upset, say, "I wanted to take Pokey to the veterinarian as soon as I could. Nothing could be done to save him." If it would be helpful for your child, ask the veterinarian to show your child where his pet was examined and how the animal was cared for.

- Putting an animal to sleep should be an adult decision, not a child's. The child may never want the animal to be put to sleep or may agree to the procedure only to feel guilty later on. Discuss as far ahead of time as possible that you intend to have the dog put to sleep. Explain your reasons. Empathize whenever possible. "The doctor said that Pokey cannot live much longer. While Pokey is alive, he is in a lot of pain, so the doctor will give Pokey a special medicine that only animals get. That medicine will make Pokey fall asleep, and then after a few minutes he will die. That way he does not have to suffer any more pain. I feel very sad that Pokey will die, but I'm glad we can help him so that he does not feel any pain."

- Use the death of a pet as a springboard for a discussion about death. "Tell me your understanding of what death means." "Do you have any questions about death?"

- You may want to remind your child what happens to a body at death. "Pokey's body has stopped working. He doesn't feel anything, not pain or heat or cold."

- Replacing a pet immediately might seem like a good idea, but it may not be necessary (the child may not be that upset by the loss or may not want a new pet). And sometimes it can backfire. The child might resent the pet, comparing it unfavorably with the dead one. Besides, it is best that children take time to grieve a loss without trying to cover those emotions with a new pet. "I like the idea of having another pet. It was fun playing with Pokey and taking care of him. But I want to wait awhile and remember Pokey. I also want to save up some extra money because it is important to have our new pet examined by a veterinarian and have shots."

How Not to Say It

- "It was just an animal." Maybe to you, but to your child the pet may have been a companion, a protector, a best friend.

- "If we get a new cat, I expect you to take more care of this one than you did with Mopsy." Now is not the time to suggest to your child that he was an inadequate caretaker.

- "If we go to the animal shelter to look for a new pet, will that make you happy?" A new pet will not necessarily make your child happy. It takes time to grieve for a beloved pet. Also, don't be too quick to get your child to feel better. Grief is natural and should be given its due. This is a sad but wonderful opportunity to connect to your child in a meaningful way over the loss.

- "If we get another pet, that one will die eventually, too. We shouldn't bother." If you absolutely do not want a new pet, you have that right. But don't suggest to a child that it is of no value loving something because it is not permanent. It is better to state your genuine reasons for not wanting a pet—particularly reasons your child is familiar with. "I decided not to get another pet. Remember how I worried about having enough money to pay the expenses?"

15

Comforting the Dying Child

Timmy's father walked into the boy's bedroom and opened the blinds. The leaves of the huge maple outside the window were a blazing orange, the same color as the pumpkins that dotted the front porches in the neighborhood in preparation for Halloween.

"How's my boy?" the father whispered, walking toward the twin bed.

Timmy smiled but was too weak to say anything. His father sat on the bed and began gently massaging his son's bony shoulders.

"It's a beautiful day, son. Would you like to sit on the porch with me later? Mom and your sister are going to pick apples before lunch. That means applesauce later on for you and me." The father smacked his lips comically, hoping to nudge a smile from his son.

"Yeah," Timmy said. Then he looked his father square in the eyes. "Dad, I'm going to die, aren't I?"

There may be nothing more heart wrenching than a child dying. Sadly, every year thousands of parents have to suffer what is arguably the most painful type of grief. For many of these parents there will be time to talk to their dying child about death and to say good-bye. To the very end, parents want to protect their children from any unnecessary suffering. Trying to decide how much a dying child should be told about his situation may seem confusing. Will it add to the child's fears? Will it make him more depressed? Will he lose the will to fight his illness? According to the research, families are usually better off when death can be discussed openly with the dying child. It is hard, but it can make an important difference in the final days of a child's life.

Things to Consider

➤ One purpose of the discussion is to alleviate fears, not enhance them. Your child will have many questions about death and the afterlife. This is an opportunity to put his mind at ease.

➤ The discussion will happen more than once. The first time will probably be the hardest.

How to Say It

- You may still be holding out hope for survival and don't want to upset your child unnecessarily. But if the odds of survival truly are diminishing, it is best to acknowledge the possibility of death. "Some children with your problem have died, but some haven't. The doctors still want to help you. They haven't quit."

- When it is clear that death is certain and you haven't spoken about that yet, do so honestly. You may want to emphasize what will happen to ensure his comfort. "At this point there is nothing more that can be done to help you get better. Yes, the doctors say you will die. But we will all be here with you and make you as comfortable as possible."

- *"Will dying hurt?"* "There are medicines that will make you feel comfortable. If you have pain, we can give you more medicine to take that pain away."

- *"I'm afraid. . . . I don't want to die."* "Nobody wants you to die. We all love you and will miss you. But when you die, you will not feel fear anymore. Your body will not feel pain anymore. [Here you can discuss religious beliefs.] You will be with God. While that is hard to understand, I believe with all my heart you will be happier than you've ever been. You will have no more pain and not be afraid at all."

- *"But you won't be with me."* "I will someday. I believe that in heaven a long time can feel like a very short time. You will be in heaven for what feels like a little while, and then I will join you and everybody you love will join you."

- *"What if there isn't a heaven?"* "There is. I know it, and I'm so glad that you will be in such a happy, wonderful place."

- *"Will I see Grandma?"* "Yes, Grandma is in heaven, and you will see her."

- *"Will I become a ghost?"* "Not the way you might think. We all have spirits that will leave our body after we die and go to see God. Your spirit is who you really are. Your body is like clothing. You won't be like ghosts you see on TV. You will be able to watch us from heaven, though."

How Not to Say It

- "You will be fine." When a child is seriously ill and death is probable, the odds are high she already has an inkling she is dying. If you tell her she will be fine, she may not believe other things you say about dying.
- "There is nothing to worry about, I'll take care of you." If your child has concerns, she needs those concerns addressed. Listen to her worries and answer them as honestly as you can.
- "You shouldn't be asking such questions. Save your energy to get better." Your child needs to ask those questions and have them answered. If you do not wish to let him talk, what other choice does he have? Don't suggest to him that he could be working harder to get better. He doesn't have that kind of power.

Dying at Home or in the Hospital

Researchers at the Medical College of Wisconsin studied families of children with a terminal illness. They wanted to know if it made a difference if parents chose to have their child die at home (in a home-care program) or in the hospital. Parents who cared for their dying child at home did suffer less depression and physical ailments after the child died. Spouses also got along better and tended to be less socially withdrawn. The siblings of the dying child also showed less fear and withdrawal after their brother or sister died.

If there is a choice, parents may want to consider having their dying child spend his last days at home. If that is not possible, anything the parents can do to make the hospital room more homelike might help. Regardless, it is always helpful and healing when family members have time to say their good-byes in an atmosphere of warmth and closeness.

16

Defiance and Disrespect

All children disobey. They sneak cookies, "forget" to clean a room, and play computer games when they promised Mom they would do homework. From a parent's viewpoint, disobedience is often similar to a minor driving infraction: It happens to the best of people, and it is hoped they learn something from it. But when children act defiantly, parents know that a line has been crossed. Defiant children are not simply disobeying but are challenging a parent's authority.

Defiance is disobedience with attitude.

Defiance, like beauty, is also in the eyes of the beholder. Imagine a boy who was teased on the bus by a classmate. Later that night the boy refuses to attend a birthday party, adamantly yelling, "No, I won't go, and you can't make me!" A perceptive parent might wonder if the boy is acting this way because he is afraid or anticipates further embarrassment. Was the boy acting defiantly? Technically, yes. But the parent who is aware of the boy's recent troubles might treat the situation with more concern and compassion.

Defiance becomes a problem for most parents when they attribute the defiant act to willful disrespect. When a twelve-year-old scoffs at a request to turn off the television at bedtime and responds contemptuously, "No. You can't tell me what to do!" a parent hears disrespect and sees red. In such a case, no alternative explanation for the defiance is obvious, so it is attributed to bold insolence. However, that does not mean alternate explanations don't exist.

Things to Consider

➢ Is this a new behavior or one that has been repeated often? If it is a recurrent problem, then any communication style you used before probably won't be effective this time, either. Try a different approach using the

TENDER guidelines. If this is a new problem, the suggestions in the How to Say It section are a good first step.

➤ Disrespect for authority is a serious issue. Don't be reluctant to have a follow-up discussion at a time when you are less angry and your child is likely to be more receptive. One father, stunned by his ten-year-old daughter's belligerent back talk, yelled at her immediately but was too tired to have a lengthy argument. The next day after school he invited her to play catch and then discussed his concerns during that time.

➤ Is it willful disrespect, or could your child be reacting to something else? Haven't you said things you didn't mean because you were frightened, ill, worried, or generally overstressed? Disrespect should not be excused, but it shouldn't prevent a parent from trying to understand.

➤ Keep in mind that many children today are dealing with divorce, something that can increase their anger at authority. Some children have to take on added responsibilities because they are living in a single-parent household or in a two-career family where parents are not always home when the children are. These children might view themselves as more grown up. There is also a misguided tendency among many adults to let their children's friends call them by their first name. Raising children to adult status like that gives them a mixed message when we also expect them to obey authority.

Smart Talk

Stressed parents may sometimes misinterpret bad behavior on the part of their child. In a 1994 research study, depressed parents were more likely to describe their children in negative, emotionally laden terms than were nondepressed parents. A parent's poor mood can interfere with the parent's ability to view his or her children more positively. Depressed parents in therapy were able to change the descriptions of their children to more positive ones.

How to Say It

If a disrespectful retort by your child is not part of your list of DO'S & DON'TS, it should be. Children will be dealing with authority figures throughout their school career and during their adult years. They need to learn how to *state* their upset feelings, not act them out.

Your first response most likely should be a **REPORTING** of your strong dislike for the way your child just spoke to you, and a firm reminder that such actions are unacceptable. (Exception: If your child is clearly distraught, then something deeper is bothering him. It is better to show some empathy and inquire what's wrong before sounding too strict. Say, "This isn't like you. Something is troubling you. Let's talk about it.")

Some opening responses you might try:

- "I am your mother [father, grandmother, etc.] and will not tolerate being spoken to that way."

- "What you just said makes me very angry."

- "You can be upset with me, you can disagree with me, you can be furious with me, but I won't put up with being spoken to like that. Now, can you think of a way to rephrase what you just said?"

- "We have two problems to discuss now: the fact that I won't let you go to your friend's house when you still have homework to complete and the fact that you just yelled at me and showed disrespect. Do you want to choose which topic to discuss first, or should I?"

- "What you just said has hurt me deeply. I expect you to think about your actions and come to me later with an apology. Then we'll discuss this further. Until then, don't expect me to feel as proud of you as I did before this."

- "Do you realize you just broke one of the Ten Commandments? When you talk back to me like you just did you are showing dishonor instead of honor."

Keep in mind that while you may be understandably furious and have good reason to raise your voice, this is also an opportunity to model for your child how to express anger and hurt in a clear, firm manner without treating him as he treated you. Otherwise, he may learn that showing disrespect is appropriate when one also possesses power and control.

What Else to Say

After first stating that you are angry and that the defiant behavior was not acceptable, exploring reasons why your child acted so defiantly may reveal some interesting concerns. **EMPATHY** helps here. Children are not as adept as adults at uncovering issues that are bothering them. Even if they are aware of what's bothering them, they may not be capable of reporting it adequately. A calmer tone of voice by the parent and a willingness to make some guesses might result in a new perspective on the child's motivations. After any discussion of problems with your child, you will believe one of two things: that your child is basically good but immature and bothered by some other stress or concern, or that your child is basically bad and must be kept in line. Be careful. Research has repeatedly shown that opinions adults have of children often become self-fulfilling. Here are some ideas of what else to say:

- "What you just did [defiant act] is not like you. My hunch is that something else is bothering you. Let's talk about that."
- "I've watched you be angry before without being so disrespectful. I know you can do better."
- "You're angry and you feel like lashing out. Everybody feels that way sometimes. Are you angry about something that happened today or earlier this week?"
- "I'm wondering if the fight you had with your sister has anything to do with why you just acted so disrespectfully and mean to me?"
- "Sometimes we say or do things that are wrong and hurtful. My guess is that you already realize you shouldn't have done what you did."
- "I get the sense that something else is bothering you but you don't want to discuss it now. I'll ask you again later. If you change your mind, I'm available."
- "I still don't like the way you treated me, but I'm beginning to understand you had a lot on your mind."
- "I know you've watched your father [or Grandma, Uncle Pete, etc.] speak to me [or someone else] that way. That must make it harder for you to realize it is always a wrong thing to do."

As you can see, the above comments are softer in tone, increasing the odds that some positive resolution of the problem will occur. They reflect a purposeful shift in goals. The original goal was to clarify that defiance and disrespect are unacceptable. The current goal is to change the atmosphere from hot to warm and allow for a meaningful dialogue. Don't wait until you feel less angry to say these things. The very act of trying to become more empathic can have a calming, warming effect on you.

Rule of Thumb: Research shows that when you are angry and speak in a tone louder than normal, you just get angrier. Having the presence of mind to speak in a tone *lower* than normal conversation can actually reduce your anger in a matter of seconds.

How Not to Say It

- Comments such as "Who do you think you are?" and "How dare you!" or "Never in my life have I heard such a thing!" may not do any harm if they are short and sweet. Tirades and long lectures are likely to be tuned out. Then you'll be angry about that ("You look at me when I'm talking to you. Do you hear me?"), and the all-important topic of defiance and disrespect may get buried. If you yell often, it won't get a child's attention, but speaking slowly and softly will. If you rarely yell, an initial outburst will get the child's attention, but don't belabor it.

- Don't administer impulsive and arbitrary punishments such as "You can forget about going to the sleepover this weekend." It is better to tell your child you will think about an appropriate punishment rather than lock yourself into something your child will argue is unfair and you cannot modify without losing face. (Punishments should fit the crime. Having a child write you a letter explaining why the behavior was wrong may have more impact. Or, temporarily add to the child's chores, thereby making your day easier.)

Be sure you notice and then **ENCOURAGE** your child every time he could have acted defiantly but did not.

- "I know you didn't like it when I told you no, but it meant a lot to me that you didn't speak to me disrespectfully."

- "Do you realize what you just did? You were angry, but you told me you were angry. You didn't show it by yelling at me. I'm impressed."

- "I've watched you all day [all week], and not once did you act defiantly even though you might have felt like it. That makes me feel wonderful."

Finally, when all is calm and everyone is in a better mood, many younger children enjoy a game of role-playing where they act out the right and wrong ways to talk to their parents. Children need more than being told what to do; they need an opportunity to practice it. (The last "**R**" in **TENDER** can also mean **REPEAT!**)

Divorce:
Telling the Children

"Well, when do you expect us to tell them, Jane? After I've left? Don't you think they should be given some warning?"

Jane cleared away the dinner dishes from the table and plopped them on the kitchen counter. "Of course they should be told sooner rather than later. But what do you intend to tell them? I doubt you'll speak the truth. Maybe they should know that their father is a middle-aged carouser."

Jack stood up from his seat. "The details are unimportant. The point is we fell out of love a long time ago."

"Let me get this straight. You want me to accompany you to the living room where we both will sit together and calmly explain to our children that we are getting a divorce. And you don't want me to tell them that I want to remain married or that the divorce is all your idea."

"I've been unhappy with you for years. Why didn't you do something about my concerns three years ago when I told you where things were heading?"

"The bottom line is that you decided to have an affair and leave your family. Now you want me to make it easy for you to tell them. Don't hold your breath."

Unfortunately, Jack and Jane's argument is common among couples planning a divorce. Often, one person does not want a divorce and wants to punish the spouse. Each holds the other more accountable. When bitter feelings emerge, it becomes easier to demonize a spouse—exaggerating his or her faults and character flaws. Not cooperating with the other in parenting then becomes easier to justify.

Nevertheless, when a separation or divorce happens, the children will be told something. What—and how—they are told can make a difference between adjustment and maladjustment later on.

Things to Consider

➤ Ideally, parents should inform the children together. That guards against their hearing two different versions of events. More important, according to experts, it helps preserve the children's sense of trust in the parental relationship at a time when the marital relationship is dissolving.

➤ Don't assassinate your partner's character. Unless your spouse has a history of harming your children, he or she will continue to have a relationship with the kids. They should not have to listen to derogatory comments about a person they still love.

➤ Children's immediate concerns will be how the divorce affects their life. Be prepared to tell them what their day-to-day life will be like.

➤ Divorce always affects children. They may feel depressed, blameworthy, or out of sorts at the disruption in their life. Some children fare better than others. The best predictors of positive adjustment are two factors: whether the children have adequate time with each parent (especially the father) and whether the parents get along as well as can be expected post-divorce (cooperate in parenting).

➤ When responding to kids' questions, anticipate having to repeat yourself over the course of weeks or even months. Children often have strong fantasies that parents will reunite.

How to Say It

- "For a long time Mom and Dad have not been getting along. We have tried in different ways to make our marriage happier, but we still are not happy. We have decided not to live together and to get a divorce."

- Children will likely protest and ask for more details. It is best to provide reasons that your children are already aware of rather than tell them things they know nothing about. "You've heard us fighting many nights." "You saw how unhappy we were during our last vacation." "You've noticed that Daddy has been spending less time at home and more at work."

- If your children are aware of specific personal problems that a parent might have, such as alcoholism or gambling, there is no use pretending they were not factors in the decision to divorce. However, demonizing a spouse can create more anxiety for your kids and may even backfire. Children often come to the defense of a parent they feel is being overcriticized. "Yes, your mother's drinking problem affected my decision to get a divorce. But it is more than that. We simply agreed we cannot live together any longer."

- If one parent wishes that the divorce would not happen but it clearly is going to happen, it is not worth blaming the divorce on the other spouse. The decision to divorce is not the cause of a divorce. People divorce for many complex reasons, and in most cases the decision is not impulsive but evolves over time. "It is true that your father does not believe we can work things out, and I would like to try a little longer. Still, the reason we are getting a divorce is that we cannot live together and be happy. And we have tried to make it work."

- If you are separating but may not divorce, try to give the children as much information as possible on the length of the separation. "We plan to live apart for the next six months. We will each see you practically every day, and nothing else in your life will change. At the end of six months we will decide if we want to stay separated or not."

- Children need to be reminded that they are not the cause of the breakup. "Your mom and I love you and will always love you. Our reasons for divorcing have nothing to do with you. We simply could not be happy together."

What Else to Say

- After the initial shock has worn off, be prepared for a full range of reactions from your children. They may be spiteful, uncooperative, depressed, withdrawn, or a combination of those. Their school performance may decline, but doing well in school may not be a sign that all is well. Some children cope by suppressing feelings and diverting attention to safe pursuits like schoolwork. However, they may be quietly suffering, unwilling to add to the family's pain by calling attention to themselves. Make **EMPATHIC** comments whenever possible. If your child makes hostile remarks ("You don't care about us!"), don't automatically defend yourself. "You sound real hurt and sad. You feel as if I've let you down."

- "It's been a few days since you've spoken about the divorce. I'm imagining you might be feeling sad and a little scared."

- "It's hard getting used to the idea that we all won't live together."

How Not to Say It

- "It's your father's fault." If your children will have a relationship with their father, it is harmful to make him the culprit and yourself a victim. Your children will cope much better if each parent supports—and doesn't sabotage—the other parent's relationship with them.

- "We don't know when we will actually separate." Until you do know, don't tell the children.

- "Mommy will need you to be the man of the house." A few extra responsibilities appropriate to a child's age will not be a problem, but do not rely on your children for more than that. You are the adult; they are the children.

- "Was I really that horrible to live with?" Never put your children in the middle. Never put them in a position where being loyal or helpful to you will make them feel disloyal to the other parent.

- "The divorce is for the best." Your child probably doesn't see it that way. Your task is to try to understand their feelings and *show* them (not simply tell them) that the divorce will work out fine. You do this by providing a loving home and by cooperating with your spouse in parenting.

Rule of Thumb: Rehearse telling the children about the divorce with your spouse. Anticipate their questions and how they will be answered. Otherwise, you run the risk of turning a difficult moment for all into an angry free-for-all.

It's okay to tell the kids you don't know all the answers to their questions but will tell them as soon as you can.

18

Divorce:
Introducing Your Child
to Your New Partner

Sabrina waltzed into her mother's house after spending the day with her father.

"Daddy's got a girlfriend," she announced.

Her mother quickly ended the phone conversation she was having and stared at her daughter. "What makes you say that?" she said, trying not to sound concerned.

"Because I met her today at the park. We had lunch together."

"Oh? What did she look like?"

"She was kind of pretty. She's a schoolteacher, and she knows lots of songs because she likes music."

"Oh."

An hour later Sabrina's mom and dad were arguing on the telephone. Why didn't he talk to her before about his girlfriend? Shouldn't they have discussed when it would be appropriate to introduce the new woman to their daughter?

In fact, Sabrina's dad did make mistakes in his approach. In this case it may have turned out all right, but he took some big and unnecessary risks.

Things to Consider

➤ Introduce your new partner only when you are sure you are in a committed relationship. Children should not have to grow attached to a new adult only to go through another loss if the relationship breaks up.

➤ You may be curious to know if your new friend will get along with your children. Don't let that curiosity force you into premature introductions. If you have any reservations about your new friend's qualifications to be a stepparent, then he or she may not be the best choice for a mate.

➢ Understand your motivations for introducing your children to your new friend. Some parents do so because it makes it easier to see both the friend and the children at the same time. Otherwise, one relationship may interfere with time for the other. It is better to sacrifice time with your new friend than risk introducing your children to someone who may not remain part of their lives.

➢ Do you want to irritate your ex-spouse by introducing your new friend to the kids? Don't.

➢ Don't surprise your children. A few weeks before the introduction you can inform your kids what you are planning. That gives you time to understand their concerns and feelings. If they sound positive about the meeting, don't presume they will always feel that way.

➢ If you have a child who is not yet a teenager but has begun puberty, you and she may be entering similar phases of life. Just as she is contemplating relationships with the opposite sex and may actually have started to talk on the phone with boys, you are now in the dating scene. Obviously, the dating rules for divorced adults are different for adolescents, but your child will be watching closely. Modeling virtue may never be more important than it is now.

How to Say It

- **REPORT** your wishes. "As you know, I have been seeing a woman from time to time since your mother and I divorced [separated]. This woman has become very special to me. Because she is special, I thought it was time for you to meet her. Tell me what you think about that."

- Either repeat back your child's words, or make an **EMPATHIC** comment if you detect underlying feelings that your child is not verbalizing. "You're saying that it is fine, but I'm wondering if it makes you feel kind of funny inside, maybe a little sad" or "You sound excited to meet her. What about it makes it seem exciting?"

- Give details about the upcoming meeting. "I thought she could visit us next Saturday, and then we would all go to the amusement park together. Do you like that idea?"

- "We'll talk about this again. Please come talk to me if you have any questions or concerns."

- If your child asks if you plan to marry this person, tell the truth. "We don't have definite plans just yet, but we both want to marry each other. As soon as we decide for sure, we'll let you know."

If your child does not want to meet the other person, try to understand why. Probably, she is still hurt and sad over the divorce and does not want to give up hope for a reconciliation. Also, your child may be concerned that she is being disloyal to her other parent.

- "You do not have to meet my friend just yet if it is going to be upsetting. But I want you to know that I will continue to spend time with her and that she is very special to me. I hope you'll change your mind soon about meeting her." It's okay to tell your child about times you spend with your friend. It can reaffirm the hard fact that the marriage is over and that you are moving on with your life.

Smart Talk

Do you plan to cohabit with your new friend? You may want to do it for companionship or convenience, but think twice if you think it will improve the odds of success in a remarriage. Researchers from the University of Nebraska discovered that cohabitation does not improve subsequent marriage quality or mate selection. In fact, cohabitors are more likely to eventually divorce their new mate compared with couples who did not cohabit before marriage. Researchers at the University of Wisconsin found that 40 percent of cohabitors end their relationship before marriage. Once married, couples who lived together prior to marriage have close to a 75-percent divorce rate. *More disturbing is that 64 percent of child abuse perpetrated by a nonparent is done by boyfriends. A child left alone with a boyfriend is statistically at risk for potential abuse.*

How Not to Say It

- "Don't you think she's wonderful?" "Isn't he nice?" "Aren't you happy I found him?" You can report how you feel ("I think he's nice . . ."), but don't suggest to your children that they should feel the same way. They probably don't, at least not yet. It is better to wait until the children spontaneously report their own positive feelings.

- "Don't tell Daddy that you met my friend." Never put your kids in the middle like that.

- "Look who's sitting over there, sweetheart—someone I've wanted you to meet. What a surprise!" Prepare your children ahead of time. It is a thoughtful thing to do for all parties involved.

- "I will be spending every weekend with her. If you want to see me, you will have to spend time with her, too." Your kids come first. Spend time alone with them. If you remarry, your children will have to adjust to that fact, although spending some time alone with your kids is still a good idea.

19

Divorce:
Saying Good-bye
After a Visit

"I simply hate it," Don said. He was the father of two boys. "I feel sad and miserable, and it sometimes takes me a day or two to get over it."

Saying good-bye to your kids after a weekend or a vacation together is something many separated or divorced parents never adjust to. They want to end the visit on an upbeat note, so they try to sound happy, but inside they feel like crying. Children, too, can get moody or downcast after returning from a visit with a parent. There is no way to take away the pain, but there are things to say that may help.

Things to Consider

➤ It can take a long time to adjust to visitation. Pace yourself.

➤ If at all possible, try to live close enough to your children that they can bike to your place. Knowing they can pop in at any time or that you can be with them on a few minutes' notice will definitely ease the separation pain.

➤ If you did not want the divorce, dropping your children off at your ex's will likely be more difficult than if you had wanted the divorce.

➤ If you and your ex argue a lot, drop-offs will also be more problematic. Your kids are best served when their parents are civil and reasonably cooperative with each other.

How to Say It

• Don't pretend you feel great when you feel awful. Your children sense how you really feel and they may get the message that unhappy feelings are not allowed. It's best to **REPORT** any sad thoughts well before the actual drop-off so that there is time for feelings to be discussed or at least acknowledged. "We'll be getting ready to leave in a few hours. I always feel sad around this time because I start to miss you. I wonder if you feel the same way."

- "The hardest part is right after I say good-bye. I feel better later, though, and I always look forward to your next visit."

- **TEACH** about mixed feelings. "Even though I'm sad I won't see you for a while, I get excited thinking about what we'll do when we're together next time. So I feel sad and excited at the same time."

- When the pain of separation is less raw, you can make a game out of everyone's feelings. "Here we are, the four dwarfs. Who wants to be Gloomy? Who wants to be Miserable? Is anybody Excited? No one try to be Sleepy or you'll miss dinner."

How Not to Say It

- "There's no need to cry. We'll be together on Wednesday night, and I'll call you tomorrow." Evidently there is a need to cry. It is better to acknowledge that their sadness is okay and understandable. Don't make them think it's wrong to feel the way they do. You can remind them of things to look forward to.

- "I'd better get you home on time. You know how your mother gets when I'm just five minutes late." Criticizing their mother will only add to the tense feelings.

- "Oh, next Saturday I won't be able to see you. I'll be away on business." Inform them of such things when you have time to discuss it.

- "You haven't been upset the last few times I've dropped you off. You guys are brave and strong." Don't praise them for not showing any emotional distress. They will learn that in order to please you they will have to pretend about their feelings. If they have begun handling the situation well, just let them know that you've noticed it's getting easier.

Picking up your children for a weekend or evening together can sometimes be awkward. Leaving one parent to be with the other is a reminder of the realities of divorce. Some days they may wish they could have stayed at home and been with their friends. Then they might feel guilty. What could you say?

How to Say It

- Sounding upbeat when you first greet them is fine but pay attention to the emotional undertone. If the kids seem tired or a bit depressed or if there are awkward silences in the car, it's best to comment on those reactions by normalizing them. "I'm thinking you might feel weird some days when we get together. Even though you want to see me, I'm sure there are times when you're tired or busy with other things. On those days you might even wish Mom and Dad didn't get divorced."

- Older children (preteen and teen) may want to spend time with their friends on days or nights they are with you. "Since we have to schedule our visits, I bet there are times when you want to be somewhere else but you can't because the schedule says we have to be together. Sometimes we can work around that. Maybe we can figure a way to get together at a different time so you can then be with your friends. What do you think?"

- "I still want to be with you as often as I can. But I understand there will be times when you'll want to be with friends."

How Not to Say It

- "Your mom was in a bad mood as usual when I picked you up." Don't put the kids in the middle.

- "You can see your friends instead of me." Don't make it sound as if you are eager to get rid of them. If they want to see their friends, try to be flexible when possible, but don't push aside your relationship with them. Make arrangements with the custodial parent so that you can get extra time with the kids if an important function interferes with your visitation.

20

Divorce:
When One Parent
Abandons the Children

Charlie sat by the window, baseball glove in hand, waiting for his father to arrive.

"He said he'd be here," Charlie said quietly to his mother. "He promised."

"Your father has been busy," Mom said. What she wanted to say was that Charlie's father was unreliable and that he probably didn't even love his son. After all, he'd seen Charlie only once in the past six months. There was no excuse. Now she'd have to console Charlie one more time.

Charlie stood up and tossed his glove into the corner.

"Hey, I can play catch with you," Mom said. "I'm actually pretty good, you know."

Charlie didn't utter a word as he walked into his bedroom and closed the door.

After a divorce, many children expect that they will see each parent on a regular, predictable basis, only to realize that one parent (the noncustodial parent) has virtually abandoned them. While some of these parents walk out and never see their children again, typically the drifting apart occurs over time. These parents (usually the fathers since only 15 percent of divorced fathers live with their children) often stay involved the first year or so after a divorce and then slowly fade from their children's lives. Estimates are that less than half of divorced fathers see their children more than several times a year. One-third of fathers who remarry stop seeing their children altogether. The reasons are varied and often occur when the father and children live in different states. But sometimes the mothers—still bitter toward their ex-husbands—make the visitation a time to resume fighting, and the children suffer from the fallout.

Regardless, many children who were originally told that they were not to blame for the divorce begin wondering if they are truly worthwhile and lovable. What does a divorced mother say to a child whose father has consistently neglected him?

Things to Consider

➤ Look inward. Has unresolved anger toward your ex prompted you to hinder visitations or make them unnecessarily hostile? If so, your child is suffering. Make any changes you can.

➤ If you or your ex is considering a move that is more than two hours away from the other, please reconsider. Distance in miles is a natural barrier to parental involvement with children and sets the stage for what will inevitably be an emotional drifting. Within a few years the children will, at best, be the recipient of checks and gifts and phone calls but little else.

➤ Ridiculing your former spouse is never wise. However, if a parent truly has drifted from his children's lives, it is not your job to defend him. It is better to acknowledge the truth, but don't add fuel to the fire by taking potshots at your ex's character.

➤ It is vital to a child who has been virtually abandoned by a parent to have other adults who can serve as an appropriate and consistent role model. Your ex-spouse's parents may be wonderful grandparents and their relationship with your children need not be a casualty of the divorce.

➤ Younger children often put the absent parent on a pedestal. They fantasize about him as the good parent who simply cannot be there. Don't feel threatened. Your child will become disillusioned sooner or later.

How to Say It

Children need to hear three things: **EMPATHIZING** comments for their hurt feelings, a factual and fair **REPORTING** of your views about the abandonment, and **ENCOURAGING** words which reassure and indicate that they are loved, that you will not abandon them, and that their future can be happy.

- "It's your birthday, and you didn't get a card or phone call from Dad. Now you feel sad. I know it hurts when you don't hear from your father."

- "It looks as if your dad isn't going to show up again today. Even though you are trying not to show it, my guess is you feel pretty bad right now."
- "Now that your father has remarried and has a new family, he spends practically no time with you. That must feel awful."
- "I don't blame you for feeling angry."
- "Your father is wrong not to see you or talk to you much. You are my joy in life and your father is missing out by not being with you."
- "You are probably thinking that your dad doesn't love you. I don't know what is in his heart, but he certainly is not showing you love. There is no excuse for that."
- "You are lovable. Your mother does not know how to give love. I wish she did because you deserve much more of her time."
- "Some people don't know how to be a good parent. Your mother [father] is one of those people."
- "There is no way I would ever leave you. I will always be here for you. You are my wonderful child, and I'll love you forever."

How Not to Say It

- "What did you expect? Your father is a loser." Comments with a bitter edge can backfire. Children, especially as they enter adolescence, can resent such opinions.
- "Frankly, I'm glad you don't see her. She is not a good influence." You are missing the point. Chances are your child is hurting over the abandonment and doesn't really care about your opinion. Don't overlook the child's feelings.
- "I'm sure your father wanted to visit. He must be very busy." Don't pretend. If your ex-spouse wanted to visit, he would. Acknowledge the reality without attacking your mate and show understanding for your child's feelings.
- "Your father loves you." Don't say it unless you really believe it. Then be prepared to explain how it is he can love the child but not participate in the child's life. If you're unsure how your ex feels, say something like "The way he shows his love is not the way I show my love. He is making a mistake by not being involved in your life."

If you happen to be an absentee parent who cannot be as available as you would like, examine your reasons for being absent. Would you have to give up a better paying job in order to move closer to your children? Then give up the job. Why is the job more important? Is your new spouse object-ing to your involvement with your children? You have an obligation to your children. Don't expect your children to understand your reasons for not seeing them. They may not openly complain about your reasons, but deep down those reasons will ring hollow. In such a circumstance, do all you can to be in very frequent—almost daily—contact with them. Mail short notes every day, use e-mail, or call on the phone. Do whatever you can to show your children they mean the world to you.

21

Divorce and Feelings
About the New Stepparent

Carlos and Ana had a quiet moment alone with their father. They liked his new house and seemed to enjoy their weekend visits. Ana, the eight-year-old, particularly liked her stepmother, Maria. But her older brother was still standoffish.

"Want some more popcorn?" Dad asked.

"Carlos isn't eating his," Ana said. She pointed to an area behind the couch where much of Carlos's popcorn had somehow fallen.

"Carlos? What's that about?" Dad asked.

"Let Maria vacuum it up later," Carlos said. He tossed another piece on the floor.

"You pick those up right now," his father said. "You know better than that. Just because you have trouble getting along with Maria doesn't give you the right to make such a mess."

"Yeah, it does," Carlos said. He glared at his father, egging him on to make more of the issue.

His father just sighed and shook his head. "I wish you could see things the way your sister does."

Attitudes toward a parent's new companion are often a confusing jumble of emotions. On the plus side, children might like the stepparent and enjoy seeing Mom or Dad happy once again. But it is easy to resent the new grown-up in their life or be jealous of the parent's time with that person or to feel sad for the other parent who does not have a new companion. When feelings are mixed, a child can send confusing messages to the adults about those feelings. Imagine that Mom has remarried, but Dad is unhappy about it. What is likely to happen? If the child's mixed feelings are more positive than negative, she may learn not to praise the stepparent in front of Dad. If Dad doesn't hear good things, he may falsely conclude that the child does not like the stepparent. That same child might also learn not to reveal negative feelings about a stepparent when Mom is around. Mom, too, will get a distorted picture of what's really on the child's mind. In the case of Carlos and Ana, it *appeared* that Carlos disliked his stepmother, Maria, but that Ana liked her. The deeper truth might be that each child had mixed feelings, but Carlos displayed the negative side and Ana compensated by displaying the positive side. Ana may deny her own negative feelings because Carlos is negative enough for both of them. And Carlos may deny his positive feelings because Ana is acting positive enough for both of them.

Rule of Thumb: The more extreme and opposite your children's attitudes are from each other, the more likely neither child is displaying his truest feelings. It is best to assume that each child's feelings are more mixed than is apparent. Take time individually with each child and help them to sort through their positive and negative emotions. With patience and tolerance you may uncover your kid's genuine feelings. Then they can be addressed instead of overlooked.

Things to Consider

➤ The younger the child, the more likely she will adapt to the new stepparent.

➤ Whenever possible in a stepparent family, the birth parent should be the disciplinarian. Stepparents should have a say over rules but are better off taking a backseat when doling out punishments.

➤ Children often have mixed feelings toward their parents (loving and hating them at the same time). Stepparents are no exception.

➤ Your child is best served when he can learn to accept and get along with a stepparent. If you dislike your ex-spouse's new mate, don't automatically encourage your child's negative feelings. Your child may feel the way he does in large part because you feel the way you do.

➤ If you dislike your ex-spouse's mate and show it, your child has two choices: to resent the stepparent as a way to appease you or to feel guilty for liking the stepparent. Chronic resentment or guilt will harm your child.

➤ Look for clues to your children's feelings from the way they play or draw.

How to Say It

- Underneath anger is hurt or sadness. Getting at those deeper feelings will require an **EMPATHIC** response from you. However, if your child's behavior is truly disruptive—not just annoying—a clear statement about **DO'S & DON'TS** may first be required. "Pushing your stepmother like that will never be tolerated. I know it has been hard getting used to having a stepmother. You can feel angry but you cannot show it that way."

- "I'm glad we have this time alone together, I've missed that. Earlier today when I saw that you had thrown popcorn behind the couch, I knew it was still hard for you to accept that I've remarried. I'm wondering what the saddest part is for you."

- **TEACH** about mixed feelings. Many children might not know that it is okay to have opposite feelings existing at the same time. "Remember when you got mad at Shadow after he got his dirty paws on your school report? Remember how you also petted him a little while later? We all can feel different ways about something. We can change our minds every day. You can be mad at me for getting remarried and still love me."

- *"I hate my new stepfather!"* "Tell me about that . . ."

- *"She can't tell me what to do!"* "She is not your mother, but she is my wife. She can tell you what do. You don't always like it when I tell you to do things, and you may not like it when she tells you. But you still have to do it."

- "I know that the last time you were with your stepfather you didn't complain. You actually seemed to be enjoying yourself. You probably had some nice thoughts about him then. I wonder what they were."

- *"Daddy, I like my stepmother. But I feel bad for Mom."* "I'm sure you do. Maybe you feel guilty about liking my wife when you see Mom upset sometimes. That's normal. Mom and I talked, and we both want you to feel good about your stepmother. Mom understands your feelings."

How Not to Say It

- "You shouldn't feel that way. Ted [new boyfriend or spouse] is a wonderful guy." Don't dismiss your child's viewpoint. Be matter-of-fact and show a willingness to listen. "Oh? Tell me more about that."

- "I don't like your mother's new husband, either." Unless the new stepparent is harming your child, criticizing him in front of your child will only stir the pot. You could say instead, "I wish things hadn't turned out the way they did, but I hope we all make the best of the situation."

- "Why can't you learn to like her? After all, your brother likes her." Again, when siblings show opposite reactions, the truth about how each really feels may lie somewhere in the middle of the extremes. It is better to try to coax out a list of likes and dislikes from each child and thereby help them sort through their mixed emotions.

- "If you're going to act this way, you can stop coming over." Don't threaten rejection or abandonment.

- "If you don't like my new husband, then you and I will just spend our time alone together." You are giving your child too much power over the course of events. Besides, he has to learn to get along with (but not necessarily like) your new spouse. It is better to say, "I will try to have some time alone with you when you visit, but that won't always be possible. So we'll all have to do our best to get along as well as we can."

22

Drugs and Alcohol

Andy, age twelve, is a great kid. He is likable, smart, and has a variety of interests. He knows about the dangers of drug and alcohol use. He attended a D.A.R.E. (Drug Awareness and Resistance Education) program at school and has no obvious inclination to try drugs. Is he at risk?

Yes. Despite the fact that his parents are together and there is no drug use in the home, other factors place him at risk. One is simply his age. Now in middle school and preparing for high school, he will meet many new classmates, some of whom use drugs. (According to the American Medical Association, the average age that twelve- to seventeen-year-olds said they first tried alcohol was just under thirteen.) And as he approaches his teenage years, he increasingly needs to feel accepted by his peers. Unfortunately, he rarely sees many of his friends from grade-school, and he has to make new friends. Will they be the right ones? Also, while his parents have religious beliefs, they show little effort to go to church or discuss spiritual and religious issues—something that can reduce his vulnerability to later drug use.

Andy might survive adolescence without abusing drugs or alcohol. He certainly is at a lower risk than some other children. But a real risk is there. What can his parents do to help?

Things to Consider

➤ As children approach age thirteen, drugs, alcohol, and cigarettes become more readily available.

➤ Inhalants (glue, solvents, cleaning chemicals) are easily accessible. According to the American Academy of Pediatrics, about 25 percent of kids between the ages of ten and fourteen know someone who has used inhalants to get high. Children ages ten and eleven have no real knowledge about the dangers of inhalants (which can cause brain damage or even sudden death), yet they are exposed to them.

➤ Children who experiment with drugs before age fifteen are seven times more likely to use drugs regularly.

➤ Children who have been sexually abused, who do poorly in school, or who do not have enough parental influence are also at higher risk for substance abuse.

➤ Discussions about drugs and alcohol must be repeated and become more sophisticated as the children get older or attend different schools.

How to Say It

- Be the kind of parent that kids will feel free to talk to about any exposure they might have to drugs. Many children know that drugs are bad—so bad that they might be afraid to mention any exposure they have had to their parents. "I heard a story about a child who was afraid to tell his parents that some other kids tried to get him to use drugs. He was afraid his parents would get mad at him. Drugs are so harmful that I want you to know you can come to me anytime to talk about what you have seen at school or with your friends."

- "I want you to know a secret: When a parent gets mad because his child is caught with drugs, the parent is really very afraid. He is scared because he knows that his child is at great risk for harming or killing himself because of drugs."

- "Tell me what you have heard on the bus or at school or in the neighborhood about kids using drugs or alcohol."

- "If you wanted to get some marijuana or beer, do you know how you would get it?"

- **TEACH** appropriate ways that kids can say no to peer pressure. A child may believe that drug use is wrong but still be intimidated by peers. Rehearse assertive skills so your child has practice and more confidence in her ability to say no. "Here are some ways you can say no to kids who want you to use drugs:

    "'No way! You just want me to get in trouble!'

    "'You're crazy! I'm never going to use drugs!'

    "'Forget it!'

"'You're wasting your time. There is no way I'm going to try drugs or alcohol.'"

Remind your kids that they also need to walk away immediately. Getting into a discussion with a drug pusher may make it harder for them to resist.

- Praise your child for not trying drugs or alcohol or for resisting the temptation. "I'm sure that if you really wanted to, you could have tried some drugs or beer by now. I am so proud of you for doing the right thing. It isn't easy to say no when you see other kids trying it, but you showed that you can say no."

What to Say if Your Child Asks if You Ever Did Drugs

Most experts advise telling the truth. I generally agree, but exceptions are possible. The goal is to keep your children away from drugs or at least increase the time it takes before they start experimenting. If you used drugs when you were younger and you believe it was a mistake, will telling your child improve the odds he will resist drug use? The answer depends on how well you know your child. If you have a good relationship with your child and there is a good deal of parental supervision, your child may be able to handle the truth. You may feel ashamed and embarrassed, and you may not be the hero your kid thought you were but it can help. However, if your child tends to be impulsive or has been in trouble at school already, if there is little parental supervision between the hours of 4 and 6 P.M., if it is a single-parent family, or if your children's friends have been in trouble for using drugs or alcohol, think twice about telling the truth. You must also weigh the risk that your child will discover the truth from some other family member.

- "Yes, when I was in high school [or college], I did try marijuana, and I drank a lot of beer. I was stupid to have done that. I risked getting in a car accident and killing myself or someone else. I'm ashamed to tell you the truth, but I'm telling you so that I can convince you that using drugs or alcohol is dangerous and wrong."
- "I once told you I never used drugs, but you just overheard me talking to Uncle Pete about a time I did use drugs. I lied to you, and I probably shouldn't have. I did it because it scares me to think you might someday want to try drugs. I didn't want you to think that drug

use isn't risky because I managed to end up okay. Drug use is very risky. It can make you do poorly in school, it can get you arrested, and it can cause you to steal money or hurt yourself seriously."

Smart Talk

One consistent finding is that the more often the family eats dinner together during the week, the less likely the children will use drugs. Parents who insist on family mealtime tend to have more orderly lives, take an active interest in their children's well-being, and are more influential. Mealtime is often the only time parents and kids actually talk about their lives in a calm manner. How often does your family eat together? Think about the changes that would be necessary to increase the frequency of family mealtime. Chances are those changes need to be made anyway.

If your family is too busy to eat together, too many things are being given priority over family unity.

How Not to Say It

- "I know you may want to experiment someday, but be careful. Drug abuse begins by experimenting." Some parents believe that in order to get with the "real world" they must surrender to the idea that drug experimentation is inevitable and focus instead on how to resist continued drug use. Hogwash. Drug experimentation is not inevitable. The risk of experimentation does increase with age but is not a sure thing. Be firm that experimentation is wrong and risky.

- "You shouldn't be hanging around those other kids if you know they have used drugs or alcohol." If your child's friends use drugs or alcohol, then your child must not be able to see them. Period. But the above comment is phrased in a way that makes the parent sound weak instead of firm. The parent is using a **TEACHING** style but should be using a **DO'S & DON'TS** style. Saying "You shouldn't . . ." is not the same as saying "You can't . . ." or "I won't allow . . ." While you may not be able to enforce that rule when your child is at school, your child should never be in doubt about the firmness of your feelings.

- "If you ever drink beer, I want you to do it at home, not anywhere else. At least that way I know where you are." You are caving in. You are saying that beer drinking is acceptable. That is not a message a preteen or teen should hear.

Rule of Thumb: Children need rules and tools. TEACHING about drugs and alcohol and how to resist peer pressure without being clear about DO'S & DON'TS (tools but no rules) is evading your responsibility to make clear what is right and wrong. Stating DO'S & DON'TS without TEACHING about drugs and how to resist them (rules but no tools) is like sending your child into a danger zone unprepared.

23

Eat Your Vegetables!
Clean Your Room!

"Close your mouth while chewing! And wear a coat outside. It's freezing!"

Kids can trip up even the most adept parents over these issues. Parents can teach the intricacies of multiplication and assist with a science project where a volcano spouts lava; some parents even master the complexities of a video game. But many children still race outside without proper outerwear, and their bedrooms are filthy enough to grow the vegetables they will later refuse to eat.

I doubt there is a book or formula that will solve these issues once and for all even though they appear to be the simplest. Perhaps this is God's way of teaching parents humility. Still, if you are tired of yelling, there are things you can do to save your vocal cords from premature old age.

Things to Consider

➤ Assess just how important these issues are. Perhaps a child could tidy up his room every week or two instead of more frequently. You shouldn't have to be a short-order cook to please all members of your family, but giving kids a choice of vegetables from time to time may not be inconvenient. Besides, with most Americans on a diet and many allergic to certain foods, it is more common these days for family members to eat different foods at the same meal.

➤ Inconsistency is the main culprit. It is sometimes easier for busy parents to overlook a messy room or to make popcorn after dinner to compensate for lack of vegetables during dinner.

➤ Give kids an array of uncooked veggies as snacks. Topped with salad dressing, salsa, or peanut butter, these snacks can become favorites over time.

How to Say It

Sometimes parents shout demands not because they want vegetables finished or rooms cleaned, but because they feel underappreciated and overtired. It is better to focus on what needs to happen to feel more appreciated and talk about that—rather than barking out orders.

- "I'm beginning to feel overworked. Let's talk about ways I need you to help out more around here."

- Sometimes parents yell at kids because they are really angry at a spouse for a similar infraction. If you think your mate isn't helping enough with cleaning house, dinner preparation, or child care, don't holler at the kids just so he can overhear it. "I started to yell at the children to clean their rooms. But I guess what's bothering me is that I don't feel I get enough help from you, either. Can we talk about that?"

- If you want your children to eat their vegetables or clean their room, **REPORT** your expectation with firmness but without criticism. "From now on you must eat some vegetables. It is important to stay healthy. You can help me choose which ones, but even if you don't like them, you will have to eat them."

- "Your room does not have to be cleaned up every day, but when I start tripping over things, I know it's time for a cleaning. I'll tell you how I want you to do it, and I expect you to tidy up once a week. Which day is best for you?"

- **NEGOTIATE** if you have preferences. "Would you like to dust or use a vacuum? Do you want to clean up after breakfast or after lunch?"

- "Would you like me to make a cream sauce for these vegetables or do you want them plain?"

- **EMPATHIZE** when they give you a hard time, but don't back down. "I know you would prefer Jell-O instead of green beans, and I'm sure it annoys you. But I'm your father, and it's my job to make sure you have a healthy diet."

- "I know you'd rather play outside instead of clean your room. But we agreed you'd do it now, and it won't take long. Thanks."

How Not to Say It

- "For the last time, clean your room! . . . Eat your vegetables!" You are training your child to take you seriously only when you yell. You'll develop permanent laryngitis, and the veins in your neck may never retract. Ouch.

- "I'd really like it if you would eat your veggies tonight." You are polite but wimpy. Learn to be polite but firm.

- "How many times do I have to tell you . . ." If verbal persuasion doesn't work, there may need to be consequences. Not allowing a child to do something she wants until her room is cleaned makes sense. If she won't eat proper foods, don't allow her to eat junk food later because she is hungry.

- "You will sit at that table until you eat all your food." Be cautious. You may be in for a long night if your child has a stubborn streak. The better approach is to make sure he doesn't eat dessert, and then set up a time when the two of you can taste-test a whole bunch of vegetables in a manner he might consider fun. Vegetables don't taste horrible. Kids object because they want to get in a power struggle or because they've gotten away with it in the past. (Most children eat vegetables they might ordinarily push aside when dining at a friend's house.)

24

Embarrasses You in Public

Janet was divorced with two grade-school children. Engaged now to John, she was nervous about having him and his parents over for dinner. They had never met her before, and she was eager to make a good impression. The evening began with a bang, literally. Jason, age nine, was horsing around and bumped into an end table. He knocked over and broke his seven-year-old sister's handmade ceramic otter.

"Mommy!" little Kate cried as she ran into the kitchen where everyone was standing.

"It was an accident!" Jason said, running up behind her.

Kate shouted back. "You did it on purpose!"

"I did not!" Jason pushed his sister. "Besides, she farted in my face."

"Stop it, both of you. Can't you see we have guests?"

"But look what he did!" Kate showed her mother the broken ceramic pieces.

"It was a dumb thing anyway," Jason said. "It looked ugly."

Janet tried to keep her cool. "Jason, don't talk to your sister that way."

Right before the kids wrestled each other to the floor, Janet looked over her shoulder to see her fiancé and her in-laws-to-be staring slack-jawed at the scene. She pointed to the dinner table to distract their attention.

"Did I mention that those strawberries were freshly picked? Help yourselves while I take my kids into the other room."

The biggest mistake parents make when their children act up in public is being concerned about appearances. Fearing that others will view their kids as unruly or themselves as ineffective, some parents don't know how to act when their children need to be disciplined in public.

Things to Consider

➤ Children learn quickly that when guests are over, some rules may be easier to break. Some kids may purposely manipulate the situation, but they succeed only when the parents allow it.

➤ For particularly important public situations, plan ahead. Figure out how you will respond to some predictable fights, whininess, or rude remarks.

➤ Some public events such as group picnics or family reunions may get your kids wound up or make them bored and restless. Keep that in mind when disciplining them.

➤ You may have less patience for what might be considered "normal" but mildly annoying kid behavior (low frustration tolerance, crankiness, restlessness, etc.) when you are tense or the situation is important. Understand that when trying to get them to behave.

How to Say It

- An ounce of prevention . . . Whenever possible, discuss ahead of time how you want them to behave. Tell them what you will say or do if they act up. Once in a while you can **NEGOTIATE**. "The last time you went to a wedding, you started arguing in church. If you do that, I will remove one of you from your seat, and you will sit with Aunt Mary."

- "You may get bored tonight when we have a lot of guests and no kids to play with. If you guys act nice and don't fight, I'd like to do something special for you. Do you have any ideas?"

- **ENCOURAGE** (praise) good behavior frequently. "I'm very proud of you. It means a lot to me that you two are playing nice together while Mom and Dad entertain our guests."

- When disciplining the children in front of others, use a firm, stern voice that shows you are in charge but not intimidated. "You will stop fighting immediately." Don't hesitate to excuse yourself from your guests to discipline your kids in another room. There is no need for embarrassment; it is your job as a parent.

- "Come and sit down over here with me, and we'll talk about this for a minute." Sitting them down will actually improve the odds that they will calm down.

- When kids are being argumentative but not aggressive, acknowledge their feelings and then tell them what you expect. "You're angry at your sister. That happens sometimes. Right now I will talk to you about it, but I expect you to stop arguing."

- If you believe that your children are just trying to get attention, the best thing to do is give them attention—but on your terms, not theirs. "I wanted to stop talking to my guests and come in here to see how you were doing. Are you bored? What can I do that might make your night more interesting?"

How Not to Say It

Nonverbal signals to your kids (eye-rolling or raised eyebrows) done in place of verbal reprimands *may* work as a reminder to your kids, but often they signal that you are embarrassed and reluctant to discipline them. If your kids know you will not be afraid to correct them in public, they will be less likely to take advantage.

- "Remember what we talked about?" Your kids might take the hint, but if you have to say this more than once, it may be an insufficient response. The problem with a comment like this is that you are really trying to avoid a more public confrontation. If your kids know that you will not hesitate to correct them, they will more likely behave better.

- If you find yourself whispering harsh threats in your kids' ears ("Unless you stop fighting this instant, you can forget about your Halloween party next month"), take that as a cue that you are already at a disadvantage. Confident parenting does not require impulsive arbitrary threats. Once again, plan ahead of time how you will respond rather than have to think on your feet.

Rule of Thumb: The more anxious and nervous you are to appear calm and competent, the less likely you will be. Your kids should be nervous about misbehaving, not you.

Fostering Empathy
and Emotional Intelligence

Davey and Steve stood in the cafeteria line on their first day at a new school. Steve was a year ahead of Davey. Each had a tray filled with food, and each stood on the side, looking around for a place to sit. Since empty seats were few in number, they had to choose which group of kids they would sit next to. Steve plunked down next to a group of boys he recognized from his class. Everyone said hello, but the boys tended to ignore him. Steve spoke up once or twice and tried to get in the conversation, but it didn't help. By meal's end he was feeling alone and rejected. In contrast, Davey selected a group of boys and seemed to have no problem connecting with them. By the end of lunch he was feeling great. What did Davey do that Steve did not?

Of course, there could be many reasons that Steve didn't fit in. Maybe the boys he sat next to were not interested in making a new friend. Still, some children are more adept at reading others. They sense when to speak up and when not to. They may have a better skill at empathizing, which might also help them make friends easier.

Emotional intelligence is a new term that is not clearly defined. Daniel Goleman, the originator of the concept, describes it as "the capacity for recognizing our own feelings and those of others, for motivating ourselves, and for managing emotions well in ourselves and in our relationships." In sum, just as children need to learn about their bodies and their world, they need to learn about their emotional life. It can help them immeasurably as they navigate through relationships and life's ups and downs.

Things to Consider

➤ Emotional intelligence does not refer to being nice. It does not mean wearing your feelings on your sleeve. It means understanding your own emotions enough that you can use them in decision making, manage them better during stress, and be able to understand and relate to others better.

➤ Children with a capacity for empathy have better relationships and even perform better in school.

➤ While a great number of emotions exist, the most basic emotions are mad, sad, glad, fear, surprise, and disgust. Parents will often pay attention to some emotions of their children and ignore others. Consequently, children may learn to suppress some emotions and overuse others.

How to Say It

- Use moments when your child expresses emotion to **TEACH** about that emotion.

    "You're feeling frustrated right now because we are late for the game."

    "It surprised you to learn that Grandma was coming for a visit."

    "You were joyous when your team won the playoffs."

    "Last time you got so angry, you took longer to finish your assignment. This time you decided it wasn't worth it to get angry, and you finished your assignment more quickly. I bet that makes you feel good about yourself."

- Use moments with other children or animals to **TEACH** about their emotions. That way your child can practice empathizing.

    "The puppy cries whenever we leave it. What do you think she is feeling?"

    "The dog is wagging its tail when it sees its owner. What do you think the dog is feeling?"

    "That child over there just struck out with the bases loaded. Now he has his head down. What do you think he feels?"

    "You just said it seems as if your stomach has butterflies. What feeling is that?"

    "After studying hard, you complained of a stomachache. Sometimes stomachaches are a sign that someone is nervous. Are you?"

    "What could someone say that would make you feel angry? Sad? Happy? Disgusted? Worried? What sensations would you feel in your body if you felt any of those emotions?"

- **ENCOURAGE** and praise accurate identification of emotions and praise empathy. "You let her play with your doll because you saw that she was sad. That was very kind of you."

Smart Talk

Siblings teach one another how to read emotions in others. Research at the Institute of Psychiatry in London showed that siblings who fought less often were also more adept at reading other people's emotions. Evidently, children who fought less were improving their skills at empathy and using those skills in other contexts. Some siblings have very different temperaments. These kids tended to fight more often unless the older child's temperament was easygoing.

One positive consequence of the high divorce rate and the fact that family size is smaller and relatives often live far away is that siblings must learn to pull together and rely on each other for support.

How Not to Say It

- "Never give in to your emotions." Be careful. You are right that a child who feels angry should not hit someone, and so forth, but there are times when emotions are important cues that should not be dismissed. What if your child's friends wanted to steal another child's bike, and he felt guilty and did not want the owner of the bike to feel bad? You would want him to pay attention to those feelings.
- "Feelings are a weakness. You have to be tough to make it in life." Without empathy your child will have a hard time establishing close friendships.

26

Estrangement from Extended Family

Emma overheard her father talking on the phone to his brother.

"Don't expect us to show up at the party if you invite them, too," her dad said.

Emma knew what her dad meant. She had often overheard him complain bitterly about his sister and her husband. Emma couldn't remember the last time she had even seen her aunt. All she knew was that her father was angry at his sister.

Hard feelings among adult members of an extended family are not uncommon. Old hurts, misunderstandings, betrayals, and favoritism can sometimes add up to estrangement and divided loyalties. Little children may be unaware of these feelings, but usually not grade-school kids. Once they understand that the grown-ups don't get along, parents have an uneasy question to answer. Should they tell their children the reasons for the estrangement and make an uncle or aunt or grandparent look bad in their children's eyes? Or should they be discreet?

Things to Consider

➤ The more estranged you are from your family or origin, the more inner conflict you may have with intimacy. You may want it but also be afraid of it, thus making your primary relationship inconsistent in terms of the degree of closeness.

➤ If a close family member has betrayed you, you will be more sensitive to that issue and may overreact in your marriage.

➤ Examine how your family has hurt you. Did they affect your self-esteem? Your sense of fairness? Your sense of being lovable? These will be sore spots and will undoubtedly show up in your marriage at some point.

➤ History has a tendency to repeat itself. The more intense the estrangement with your family, the greater the odds there will be future estrangement among your children when they grow up.

How to Say It

- If the children ask pointed questions or if you believe they know about the estrangement, briefly **REPORT** your view of the situation. If you hope for a reconciliation, emphasize that point. "Your uncle Ed and I had a big argument about some money that he owes me. Right now I am mad at him. But he is my brother and I want us to be good friends again. I hope we will work it out."

- "Your grandmother and I just don't get along. It seems that every time we see each other, we argue. We've tried to solve our problems, but so far we haven't. I'll keep trying, but right now I don't want to talk to her."

- "Your aunt Mary doesn't want to talk to me. We have had problems getting along for quite some time. I wish we could talk and be friends, but she does not want to yet. I hope it changes."

- "My brother has a very big problem with drugs and alcohol. He won't get help, but he wants me to help him whenever he gets in trouble or runs out of money. I've stopped giving him money until he gets help. He is angry with me about that. Say some prayers for him."

- If your child seems distressed or even mildly concerned, **EMPATHIZE.** "You seem a little sad that I don't speak with my family. It is sad, isn't it?"

- "You look worried. Do you feel bad that I don't get along with Grandpa?"

- "It must have been scary when you overheard me argue with your uncle."

- **TEACH** your values about family togetherness. "One reason it is sad that I don't talk with my sister is that families should always stick together. I would rather that she and I got along."

How Not to Say It

- Don't demonize the estranged family member. "Your cousin is an awful person. I wish he had never been part of this family." Even if that cousin has done terrible things (sexual abuse of minors, for example), you don't need to voice contempt. You could say, "Your cousin committed a bad crime, and I do not trust him. He has hurt some children, so I cannot have him around here anymore. I wish that were not the case, but it is."

- "I'm not going to talk to my sister. She has to make the first move." Your anger may well be legitimate, but if you want to be a model for your children, you may have to put reconciliation ahead of pride.

- "I will never forgive!" What happened to you may seem quite unforgivable, and you are entitled to withhold forgiveness. If your children are observing all this, however, you may be teaching them things you hadn't intended, such as how to hold on to anger and bitterness. It is better to say things like "I can't forgive right now. I hope someday I can."

27

Family Meetings

Jane and Everett decided they wanted to expand their house. They had to decide on a downstairs addition or building a second story to their ranch house. The logistics became even more complicated as they imagined how the sleeping arrangements would change. They had four children. Would the kids mind switching bedrooms? Would the girls still want to share a room? If they had a new bathroom, should it be large or small? Jane and Ev decided to call a family meeting. It wouldn't be the one and only meeting, but it made sense to hear from all parties at the same time instead of trying to hash things out more haphazardly.

Things to Consider

➤ Family meetings are perfect when trying to understand everyone's opinion.

➤ Family meetings can be frequent. They are ways to touch base with everyone, especially when school and work schedules and extracurricular activities get hectic and overlapping.

➤ One or two generations ago, families were often together at night, watching a few select television programs together. Now kids have their own TV sets, they are more involved in after-school activities than ever before, and family mealtime has gone the way of the dinosaur. Even a fifteen-minute, twice-a-month family meeting, perhaps on a Sunday night, can help clarify everyone's schedules for the week. Upcoming events or concerns can be discussed, allowing problems to be managed before a crisis occurs.

➤ You might assign roles to each child. One could be the organizer responsible for calling everyone to the meeting. Another might take notes and summarize them at the meeting's end.

How to Say It

- "Mom and I decided that every Sunday night around seven o'clock we are going to hold a family meeting because . . ."
- Older kids, especially preteens and teens, might be less interested in attending. You can certainly force the issue, but these meetings are best if the kids want to participate. First, inquire as to why they are not interested. "You often have good reasons for feeling a certain way. What reasons do you have for not wanting to attend a family meeting?"
- **NEGOTIATE.** "I'd like you to attend the first two meetings. After that, we can see how you feel and discuss ways you might attend sometimes and not attend other times."
- "On days you don't attend we might have to make decisions that affect you. Do your best to let us know how you feel about an issue before the meeting; otherwise, you may have to go along with something you don't like."
- "Please complete these sentences: 'During this week, I wish Mom and Dad would . . .' and 'Things that happen during every week that I usually dislike are . . .'"

During the meetings, use the time to find out new information. Every kid has a school project or report or assignment that is coming due. Now is an opportunity to check on the status. Or discuss plans for an upcoming vacation. You might discover that some of the family has a different set of expectations than you do.

How Not to Say It

- "Everybody keep quiet and let me finish . . ." Decorum helps, but try to make the meetings enjoyable and interesting, not tedious or stressful.
- "Who wants to have a meeting tonight?" It is best if the meetings are regular and predictable. If you have them only occasionally, state that you intend to hold a meeting—not that it's just a possibility—and the family will take it more seriously.
- "If you have nothing to say, then just be quiet and listen." Again, kids will not always be eager to hold a meeting. You can state your expec-

tation without a nasty tone. Otherwise, you run the risk that the meetings will turn into forums for contention. "I know you'd rather not sit through this meeting. It's clear you are annoyed. But I want you to listen so you won't be in the dark about our plans."

Rule of Thumb: An uninterested child often becomes interested if he overhears the others laughing and enjoying the meeting. Also, if he overhears his name being mentioned, it will make him curious.

28

Explaining Family Obligations

"Do we have to go?" Alyssa said. "It's no fun. Aunt Celia's house is boring!"

"We don't visit that often," Dad said. "Besides, you get along with your cousin, don't you?"

"Oh, sure. If you don't mind playing with dolls. That's all she wants to do."

"It's just for a couple of hours."

"To you, maybe," Alyssa said. "To me it's a lifetime."

Sometimes children don't understand family obligations. Family get-togethers can be fun, but not always for the kids, especially as they get older. Or maybe Grandma has to move in with you. What begins as fun or exciting could corrode if Grandma's presence imposes too many restrictions on family life. Or perhaps you have to spend weeks or months visiting a sick relative, caring for him and cleaning his house while you are too tired to do much for your own family. The right words can soothe in these situations.

Things to Consider

➤ Do you mutter to yourself about family obligations within earshot of the kids? You may be setting them up to complain aloud for you.

➤ Do you and your spouse disagree about these obligations? Getting the children to honor them may be more difficult.

How to Say It

- **REPORT** the facts and expectations. **EMPATHIZE** if you know your children will be disappointed. If it isn't necessary that the kids attend, give them a chance to opt out. "Next weekend is Uncle Ned's surprise party. You'll miss your class car wash, but it can't be helped. I'm sure it bothers you, and I wish the party was a different day."

- "Grandpa's been living with us for several months now. Even though you like having him here, I know it has been inconvenient for you, especially when you can't have friends over as you used to."

- **TEACH** what a shy or resistant child might say to relatives. "Your mother's brother has a real funny story about when he was in summer camp. Be sure to ask him about it."

- **NEGOTIATE**. "Is there an upcoming family get-together that you'd rather not attend? This one you must attend, but maybe some of the others you can skip. What do you think?"

- Be clear on the **DO'S & DON'TS**. "You keep trying to get me to change my mind. You can try if you want to, but the answer will always be no. The wedding is too important for you to miss. I'm sorry. I know it isn't your idea of excitement."

- **ENCOURAGE** and praise cooperative behavior. "Even though you really were upset about going, you've been very pleasant in the car. I appreciate that."

- "I want you to know I appreciate that you tried to have a good time today. These family get-togethers mean a lot to me, and you made the day more enjoyable."

- If your child is being a stick-in-the-mud at the event, try to be unaffected. "I can tell you're miserable. If you can think of something I can do for you while we're here, just let me know."

How Not to Say It

- "Did you ever think that I do a lot of things for you that I'd rather not do? Huh? Do you ever see me complaining? No. So stop your whining." A very understandable sentiment, but it may not help as much as you think. (The same goes for expressions such as "Tough!" or "I don't care what you think!") If you really want your child to understand that everyone in a family must make sacrifices, it's best to say that in a way that does not sound critical. Otherwise, you are telling your child to understand your feelings without showing that you can understand her feelings. It is better to say, "It sounds as if you don't want to give up your Saturday for a boring old visit to your uncle's. Makes sense. Some days I feel exactly the same, such as when I helped Aunt Jess move furniture when I had a report to write. But making sacrifices is part of being a family. Please try to understand."

- "Now that we're on our way, you'd better not have a lousy attitude when we arrive." Don't overdo the threats. If your child is accompanying you despite his earlier protest, suggest that he will be able to cooperate rather than suggest he will have a poor attitude. "I know you'd rather not be doing this. Thanks for doing your best to make it an okay day."

- When the event is finished, don't rub it in. "See, I told you it wouldn't be so bad." It would be better to simply discuss what the child liked about the day and empathize when he speaks about things he didn't like.

29

Fears at Nighttime

"I'm sleeping on the couch tonight," eight-year-old Emily said. "That way I'm closer to you if anything happens."

"What could possibly happen?" her dad asked.

"I've had some scary dreams, and when I wake up, I don't like being in my room all alone."

"I see. Tell me about those dreams."

"They're too scary to talk about."

"They're just dreams, you know. They aren't real."

"I know that and you know that but my stomach doesn't know that."

Nightmares and fears of ghosts and such are common childhood concerns. They are different from fears of animals or bugs or heights in that they are purely in the mind of the child, whereas a child with a fear of dogs may actually have been bitten. It's easy to prove to a child that a daddy longlegs is harmless (though perhaps quite yucky). It's harder to convince a child that ghosts aren't real or that bad dreams won't return.

Things to Consider

➤ Fears of the dark or of monsters under the bed are more typical of preschoolers. If your child outgrew those fears but is suddenly complaining about them, it is good to be curious. The reasons may be simple (she watched a scary movie), or there may be deeper concerns (maybe a relative died recently, and the child is worried about ghosts).

➤ Repetitive nightmares, especially if they continue over a few weeks, are a sign of some distress. Look for obvious stresses such as a new school, a serious illness of a member of the family, marital fighting, etc. Discussing those concerns may get rid of the nightmares.

➤ Children over age seven with separation anxiety suffer nightmares more than kids without separation anxiety. (See chapter 31 on dealing with that issue.)

➤ Accommodating to your child's wish to sleep elsewhere may be okay for one night. Many children are fine by the next night. Beyond that, you need to try alternative means to help your child get over her fears.

How to Say It

- **EMPATHIZE, TEACH,** and reassure. "Most kids feel this way once in a while. And most kids discover that if they try to think of more fun thoughts, they eventually go back to sleep."

- "Nightmares can be very scary. Even though they are not real, they feel real. Everybody gets nightmares, and everybody eventually learns to go to sleep after having one."

- "You've been feeling scared a lot lately. I wonder if some things are bothering you . . ."

- **NEGOTIATE.** "You're worried about going to bed tonight. Last night you slept with us. Tonight you can go back to your bed. If you want, I'll stay outside your door for a few minutes. What do you want me to do?"

- "You just had a nightmare. They are scary but won't hurt you. I'll sit with you for a while, and you'll begin to notice that you are feeling better."

How Not to Say It

Common mistakes are made by parents when they feel frustrated that their child is not overcoming the fear.

- "It's the middle of the night. How many times do I have to tell you there are no such things as ghosts?"

- "You have to be brave."

Most children are helped when their parents teach them to cope on their own, but in small doses. For example, if a child is afraid of going to bed without a parent, the parent might lie with the child the first night. On the second night the parent can sit on the floor near the bed or stand out-side the door. The third night the parent may stand by the door for a minute, then leave for two minutes, return for a minute, etc. Using this pattern of small doses, a child soon learns she can handle her fears and anxieties.

Rule of Thumb: If the parents strongly disagree on how to help a child with his nighttime fears (one parent coddles the child, and the other advocates letting the child manage on his own), then a child's fears may persist. Parents need to agree on a plan that includes comforting, reassurance, and a willingness to let a child learn to manage some of his own fears.

30

Fears of Animals and Insects

Lizzie and Anna were playing outside when a strange insect landed on Lizzie's arm.

"Oh, get it off me," Lizzie cried.

"I'm not touching that thing," Anna said.

"Do something," Lizzie said. She started getting more scared.

Anna's little sister, Julia, heard the excitement and came over to investigate. "Cool," she said, looking at the strange bug.

"Get it off me," Lizzie cried. Julia flicked a finger at the creature, and it flew about them. Anna and Lizzie screamed. Julia just laughed.

Some children are more skittish around unfamiliar animals or insects. Having anxiety does not mean they have a phobia. A phobia is a strong fear reaction that interferes in a person's life. A child afraid of animals may qualify as phobic if she lives in the country and refuses to go outside because many dogs roam the roads. Her lifestyle is adversely affected. But she may not be technically phobic if she lives in a large city where all dogs are leashed and she feels comfortable walking around.

Things to Consider

➤ Phobias do not necessarily begin by having a bad real-life experience. Many people are terrified of snakes although they rarely encounter them and may never have been threatened by one. You can develop intense fears by observing others being afraid or by observing threatening situations on television or in books.

➤ Many common childhood fears are mild and easily changed. Kids might believe that certain insects are gross or disgusting but are not terrified of them.

➢ Avoiding a feared object (such as all dogs) or escaping from a situation (the presence of a spider) actually strengthens the fear. The child gets relief by avoiding or escaping a scary situation and believes that such relief can only occur in that way.

➢ A child overcomes strong fears by learning that certain situations are not as threatening as once believed (for example, dogs can be friendly) and by discovering he can cope with his uncertainty by staying in the situation long enough for his doubts and fears to diminish.

➢ Make sure you teach children appropriate caution. Never approach a strange dog with big movements, don't touch a snake you don't recognize, and so forth.

➢ If a phobia interferes with a child's life in a meaningful way (refusing to go to school, for example), professional help is required.

How to Say It

- Ask what the child's worst fear is and offer comfort and reassurance. "You're afraid the dog will bite you or knock you down. He is very friendly, but he can get excited and jump sometimes. Just because you feel scared doesn't mean there is really something to be afraid about."

- "When I was your age, I used to be afraid that a bat flying in the night would come at me. It never happened, and I learned not to be afraid. In fact, the bats ate a lot of the mosquitoes, and that was a good thing."

- **TEACH** coping by modeling it. "I'm going to pet the dog and let it lick my hand. Watch."

- "I'm letting the spider crawl on my hand. It tickles."

- "You can watch the dog and me from the window. That way you will feel safe. After a while you can watch me from the porch. Then you can watch me close up."

- "You did that very well. It isn't easy to do something that makes you nervous, but you did."

How Not to Say It

- "C'mon. No one else is afraid." You run the risk that the child will feel even worse if he doesn't succeed.

- "You did it yesterday. Why won't you do it today?" Most intense fears are not overcome by one successful experience. A person needs many successful exposures. It is better to remind him of past successes, but don't push. Try for a smaller achievable goal. For example, playing with a puppy or a newborn dog is far less frightening than a grown dog.

- "You're being a baby." Put-downs won't help. And if he does succeed, he won't appreciate your help. He'll resent your attitude.

- "It's all right to avoid dogs if you don't like them." But it isn't practical and will inadvertently intensify the fear over time.

Fears of Harm
or Injury

Tina sat looking out the window as her father prepared to leave for work. It was a cold, snowy morning, and the driveway was almost invisible.

"Don't go," Tina said. "What if you get in an accident?"

"I'll be fine, sweetheart. The snow will stop soon, and I'm always very careful."

"But I'm worried that this time you might die."

"I'll be fine. You should get ready for school."

"I'm not going to school today. I don't feel good. My stomach hurts, and I feel as if I might throw up."

Dad was concerned about Tina. She was in the third grade and never seemed to be this worried. She always enjoyed school, but she'd been complaining recently that she hated being away from home. There were no obvious reasons for her distress. Everybody in the family was healthy. Everybody got along. School was great. What was troubling her?

Tina had separation anxiety. It is not the same as the kind of anxiety a toddler might experience. Tina had been fine until recently, but she worried excessively about bad things happening and convinced herself they were likely to happen.

Older children may develop fears for the welfare of family members or their own safety. The reasons are unclear. They may have inherited a sensitivity so that they get anxious more easily. Sometimes the concerns are minor and temporary. Sometimes they blossom into intense fears and may result in a refusal to go to school.

Things to Consider

➤ Sleep may be disturbed in children with separation anxiety. They may fear sleeping as it is a form of separation from parents.

➤ Refusing to go to school should not be allowed. Once a child has remained home from school because of unrealistic fear, it gets harder to go back. Eventually, he may get behind in his schoolwork or disconnected from friends.

➤ Is one of the parents depressed? Some children feel a need to protect or look after a parent they think is unhappy. They need to learn that their parent can be safe and reasonably happy without their having to stay home from school.

➤ Sudden, unexpected, and intense fears of being harmed should be investigated. The child might have been abused.

➤ As if parents don't have enough to worry about, the National Institute of Mental Health has discovered that some anxiety or tic disorders in children might be triggered by strep throat infections. PANDAS (pediatric autoimmune neuropsychiatric disorders associated with strep infection) are not common but do occur. Strep can worsen a preexisting condition. Consult a physician if you notice an eruption of behavior problems following a strep infection.

How to Say It

- Offer **ENCOURAGEMENT**, but don't give in to the fears. "I understand you are worried, but I'm not going to stay home. I know that you will feel better in a little while." Children with separation anxiety need to learn to cope with their feelings without their parents giving in to the fears.

- "Today is Saturday, and I don't have to work. I will leave for a while but will return in half an hour. I want you to say to yourself, 'I'll be okay,' and then do something to keep yourself busy. I'll come home for a while and then go back out again, this time for a little longer."

- "On days you are not so worried, what do you say to yourself that keeps you from being scared?" Identify coping skills your child already may possess.

- "You will go to school today, but you can call me once at work."

- "You've called me at work for the past three days. Today we will skip the phone call. I think you can handle it."

- "Do you know how our dog sometimes barks at sounds because he thinks they are threatening? Well, the part of your body that causes you to worry is like that. It is barking to protect you from things that really are not problems. You have to train your mind not to be so overprotective."

- "You were worried about my safety today, but then you told yourself I would be fine. Good for you!"

How Not to Say It

- "If you kids don't clean up your mess, I just may not come home tonight." Don't ever threaten abandonment as a way of coercing kids to behave. It can make the more sensitive, worried child even more upset.

- "You're being silly." Don't dismiss the fears like that. You can reassure your child that the fears are unfounded without criticizing.

- "Actually, I'm glad you stayed home today. Your company always cheers me up." Don't reward your child's fears.

- "If you don't snap out of it, I'm going to call the doctor." A professional should be consulted if the problem persists, but don't make it sound like a punishment.

- "You have a stomachache? Okay, you can stay home with me." Children who experience separation anxiety will have vague physical complaints that come and go. Do not allow them to be an excuse for staying home from school.

32

Teaching Forgiveness

It was the third time that Joe missed his son's baseball game; today it was by fifteen minutes. What made it more difficult was that he had promised more than once he would be there. When he drove to the park, he saw that the field was empty, the game over. Cars were leaving, and he assumed his son rode home with one of the other parents as he had done twice before. To his amazement, Joe saw his son standing by a car with one of the coaches. Joe honked his horn and got their attention.

Once inside the car, Joe was full of apologies. "I tried, I really did, son. But traffic was heavier than usual—" His son interrupted. "That's okay, Dad, I understand. That's why I waited before leaving. I knew you'd get here eventually."

Joe was stunned. His son's eyes were red, but the boy managed a smile. He was hurt, obviously, yet seemed willing and able to forgive.

Joe put his arm around his son for the rest of the drive home. He thought of his own faults: how he had a tendency to hold grudges, to give others a hard time if they let him down in any way. Yet, here was his son, who had reason to be angry, still able to be understanding and forgiving.

"And a little child shall lead them."

Without forgiveness, relationships are at best superficial. More often they are unworkable. Forgiveness is a profound concept, easy to talk about but difficult to do when the hurts against us are huge. While your children may be unable to fully understand forgiveness, it is important that they be taught empathy, compassion, and a willingness to give some people second and third chances. Without parental guidance, kids will be at the mercy of television, music, and peers.

Things to Consider

➤ Esteemed researcher Robert Enright at the University of Wisconsin* has said that children have a different view of forgiveness compared with adults. School-age children seek justice, offering forgiveness only if a penalty has been paid. Adolescents may be willing to forgive but often do so more out of peer pressure or a need to belong than a genuine compassion for the wrongdoer.

➤ You should not compel a child to forgive. In fact, you cannot. Forgiveness is a form of love and cannot be forced. You can compel a child not to act out his anger, however.

➤ If someone genuinely hurts your child and you are quick to preach forgiveness, you may be forcing your own needs (to be liked or to be seen as good) on your child. Genuine forgiveness often takes time.

➤ Forgiving someone is not the same thing as continuing to have a relationship with that person (reconciling). Your child may have been hurt by a friend and, while able to eventually forgive, may be unwilling to remain friends with the offender. That may show good judgment on your child's part.

How to Say It

- When a friend has hurt your child, empathize and understand before preaching forgiveness. "You overheard your best friend making fun of you behind your back. Now you never want to be her friend again. You must feel very sad."

- After your child's feelings have been expressed and understood, inquire as to what forgiveness means to your child. "It's been three days since you've spoken to Margie. What would have to happen for you to forgive her?" (The minimal likely answer: "She has to apologize. . . . She has to be punished.")

- "You can tell her how she hurt you and that you want an apology. What would make it easier for you to do that?"

---

*Dr. Enright is the founder of the International Forgiveness Institute, which has been a forum for groundbreaking research and workshops on the topic of forgiveness. Their quarterly publication *The World of Forgiveness* is available by writing to International Forgiveness Institute, 6313 Landfall Drive, Madison, Wisconsin 53705.

- Remind your child of times she has forgiven others. "You forgave your brother after he teased you on the bus. Sometimes when we forgive someone it feels unfair. But if you get even, that is not forgiveness. That's revenge."

- "Imagine you decided to get revenge. What else might happen after you do that?"

- "Imagine you forgave your friend. What might happen after you did that?"

- Foster **EMPATHY.** "Put yourself in your friend's shoes. Why do you think she said those bad things about you?"

- **TEACH** simple definitions and plant seeds. "Forgiveness is a willingness to give someone another chance when they do not deserve it. What do you think about that?"

- "When you forgive people, you are not approving of what they did. You are saying that what they did was wrong and hurtful but you are willing to forgive them anyway."

- If your child tells you that she and a friend made up, use that as a springboard for future discussions. "You and Margie have been friends again for over a week. Are you glad you forgave her? Why?"

- "It has been two weeks since you've spoken to your friend who hurt you. Tell me what you wish would happen."

- **ENCOURAGE** and praise efforts to forgive. "It must not have been easy to forgive her, but you did it. I'm proud of you."

- Give permission for some anger to emerge later. Children may forgive quickly to please a parent or may not be in touch with the degree of hurt they have experienced. If so, some residual anger may show up later on. Don't criticize that but try to help your child understand. "It's normal after you forgive somebody to still feel sad or mad at times. Do you need to talk to your friend again?"

How Not to Say It

- "He only broke a toy. We can replace the toy. You shouldn't hold a grudge." Young children are often hurt by events adults consider very minor. But to the child they are not minor. Fighting over toys is a perfect scenario to help your child deal with frustration and problem-solving. Be **EMPATHIC** first. "I don't blame you for feeling sad when he broke your toy on purpose. It really bothers you."

- "If you forgive your friend, he'll only hurt you again later on." Some friends will take advantage, but many won't. If your child is mistreated again, he may choose not to be friends with the other child. That may be appropriate and a good lesson. But if he offers forgiveness and the friendship flourishes, that, too, is a good outcome. If you teach your child that friendship means "one strike and you're out," he will never have friends.

- "He apologized. What more do you want?" True forgiveness can be hard, and a genuine apology may not take away the sting completely. But if your child wants more than an apology, find out what. It might be that he wants justice; perhaps he wants something replaced that the friend broke or lost. Or it might simply be that he is still hurt. It is better to acknowledge that and praise the effort to forgive. "Your friend apologized, but you still feel mad and hurt. I'm glad you want to become friends again, but sometimes it can take a while for the bad feelings to go away completely."

Rule of Thumb: Your own capacity to forgive others will help or hinder your effort to educate your child on forgiveness. You run the risk of trying to make your child be forgiving so as to alleviate your own guilt about being unforgiving. Or you run the risk of teaching nonforgiveness as a way of life. Do what you can to resolve your own hurts.

33

God:
Common Questions

Lily and her brother, Brian, watched the television news with concern. The scene was of devastation caused by an earthquake in another country. Families were crying as workers searched the rubble for dead or injured relatives. Lily seemed particularly troubled. Her mother reassured her that the earthquake was far away and that they were in no danger. Still, Lily was not satisfied.

It was the next day on their way to church that Lily finally spoke up. "You always said God was good."

"Yes," her mother said. "He is."

"Then why did he let the earthquake happen?"

Perhaps not even the most learned theologian could answer that question definitively. Parents do not have to know the right answers to questions their children ask about God. But if parents want their children to believe in God and to one day be devoted to God, they must be willing to clearly state what they believe.

Things to Consider

➤ Polls show that 96 percent of adult Americans believe in God. Your children will hear about these ideas regardless of your personal beliefs, but your influence will be most important.

➤ It is a mistake not to give your children any particular religious instruction on the grounds that they will make their own choice when they grow up. Belief in God requires faith, a willingness to believe despite clear evidence. Without faith that is nurtured at an early age and throughout childhood, your children will more likely wander aimlessly through their spiritual life and not venture far with any real conviction.

➤ According to research discussed in my book *The 30 Secrets of Happily Married Couples,* the odds of having a successful marriage increase if you and your mate share the same faith. In measures of happiness, same-faith couples are slightly happier than interfaith couples, who are happier than couples where one or both partners have no religious faith.

➤ Marriages where partners are not of the same faith can become stressed when it is decided that the children must be taught religion. Parents who agree ahead of time on the kind of religious instructions their children will have, and who show respect for any religious differences, fare the best.

➤ In their fine book *Where Does God Live?* Rabbi Marc Gellman and Monsignor Thomas Hartman state that answering questions is less important than living your religion. If you tell your child that God exists but do not connect any of your actions to God, you miss out on the most important way to teach.

How to Say It

Obviously, answers to questions about God reflect belief and opinion, not objective truth. While the content of your answers may differ from someone who possesses a different set of beliefs, the tone behind the words should show interest in the topic, reverence for God, and a sense that the mystical aspects of God cannot always be understood.

- *"What is God like?"* "I have never seen God, but I believe he is all loving and all powerful, and that he knows everything. He even knows that we are talking about him right now."

- *"What is heaven like?"* "Nobody knows for sure. We believe it is a place where we can be with God and with people we love and be very, very happy forever. I don't know if there are trees or flowers or lakes or mountains in heaven. What would you hope to see in heaven?"

- *"When our dog dies, will he go to heaven?"* "I'd like to think so. I think God wants us to be as happy as we can be, and he wants us to be with people and pets that we loved."

- *"What is a soul?"* "Our soul is the part of us we cannot see that is most like God. It is our spirit. It will never die. When our body dies, our soul continues to live forever."

- *"If God loves us so much, how come he lets bad things happen?"* "So many people get confused about that. One answer is that he gave people freedom to make good choices and bad choices, and some people make bad choices. When bad things like earthquakes or serious illnesses happen, God wants us to help people who are hurt or very sick. When we show love to other people, we are doing what God wants.

  "What God wants most of all is for all of his children to be with him in heaven. Sometimes when bad things happen, people talk to God and feel closer to him. Maybe some bad things happen so that people will turn to God."

- *"Does God punish me if I am bad?"* "He doesn't have to. If we do bad things, we usually pay for it at some point. If we treat other people in a mean way, they don't want to be around us. If we steal things, we might get caught or people will learn not to trust us. God wants us to be good and to try to love him."

- *"How can I love God if I've never met him?"* "There are at least two good ways. First, since God is part of people's soul, every time you do nice things for others you are doing good things for God. Second, he wants you to pray to him. You won't hear him answer the way I answer you, but talk to him all about your day and what is making you happy and sad. Pretty soon you will feel as though you know him."

- *"Are people who don't believe in God bad?"* "No. And some people who do believe in God do bad things. People who don't believe in God believe that once you die, that is it. There is no heaven and you won't see people you love. I don't believe that way. I know that even though I miss Grandma, she is with God and someday a long time from now I will be in heaven with her."

- *"Are angels real? Do I have a guardian angel?"* "If you believe in the Bible, then, yes, angels are real. Angels are good spirits whom God sends to help us. Angels want us to be good people and to love God. You can pray to your angel. You can even give him or her a name."

Rule of Thumb: Excessive devotion to the material things of this world will cause you to lose sight of the spiritual needs of your children.

How Not to Say It

- "Ask Grandma . . ." It is fine to say you do not know an answer and that your child can find out from someone else. Just don't give the impression that you are not interested.

- "You can believe whatever you want to believe." Technically, you are right. But it is better to teach them first what you believe and let them know that eventually they must choose to believe in God or not. Give guidance, state your beliefs, and try to live your beliefs. Tell your kids you are *choosing* to believe in God and love him. They will learn that they, too, have that choice.

- "If you don't obey me, God will punish you." The idea that God is a policeman or court judge is a very limiting idea. Besides, *you* should provide consequences to your children if they don't behave. That is why God made you the parent.

- "If you don't obey me, God won't love you." God should not be used as a threat. You want your child to approach God with warmth and respect, not fear.

- "Bad things happen to people who are bad." That simply isn't always true.

God: Prayer

Six-year-old Patty listened as her father said grace before their Sunday dinner. When he finished, Patty finally asked him the question that had perplexed her for some weeks.

"Dad," she said. "Why does God use paper towels?"

Now her father was perplexed. "Paper towels?"

"Yes. Why does he use them? Is it to wrap the food?"

Her father glanced at his wife, and they both looked at their daughter. "I have no idea what you are talking about, Patty," he said.

Patty tried to explain. "You said it in the prayer. You said, 'Bless us, Lord, and these gifts from your bounty.' Why does God use Bounty paper towels?"

For many children, saying prayers is the same as singing the national anthem or reciting the Pledge of Allegiance. Some of the words take on meanings the authors never intended. Ready-to-wear prayers are certainly not harmful and may give a child some comfort, especially if recited with a parent or just before sleep. But they can be limiting to a child who does not understand the words.

Since 90 percent of Americans admit to praying, it is logical to assume that parents would like their children to pray. But teaching prayer can get cumbersome. Many children do not comprehend its value or quickly lose interest. In an era of the internet and instant access, where kids can press control buttons and immediately affect the image on a video game screen, praying lacks both instant gratification and pizzazz. What's a parent to do?

Things to Consider

➤ The meaningfulness of prayer to a child will rise or fall depending on the meaningfulness of prayer to a parent.

➤ Don't be discouraged if your older children seem uninterested in prayer and require frequent reminders. They may not truly understand the value of prayer until they become parents themselves.

➤ Teaching children to pray for others—not just themselves—is important in the development of empathy and compassion.

➤ Discourage prayers where your child is only making requests for items, as if God were Santa Claus.

How to Say It

- **TEACH**. "Prayer is simply a conversation with God. Talk to him the same as you would talk to me. Tell him what's on your mind."

- "Prayers can be very short. Saying 'Good morning, God. Thanks for the day!' is a great prayer."

- "If you don't know what to pray about, think of things you are thankful for. God gave you to me, so I thank him that I have you."

- "You didn't realize it because I was silent, but I just said a quick prayer while we were walking. You can pray anytime, anywhere."

Your child may have other questions, such as:

- *"Does God answer my prayers?"* "God hears your prayers. But he knows what is best for you and sometimes says no and sometimes says yes, and sometimes he says, 'Not right now.'"

- *"If God knows everything, why do I have to pray to him when he knows what I want before I ask?"* "He wants you to talk to him. He wants you to think about him and realize how much he loves you. He doesn't want to be ignored."

- *"If I want something, should I ask God once, or should I keep bothering him about it?"* "You never bother God by talking to him. It is better to pray often because you may want to talk to God about many things other than what you want. He wants you to love him, and he knows you will learn to love him if you pray more often."

- *"What is the best prayer?"* "The best prayer is any prayer that is deeply felt by you, that you say from your heart. It shows that you believe God hears you and can answer your prayers if he thinks it is best."

- *"What if I don't get what I want?"* "When you pray for something, tell God that you will try to understand if he chooses not to give you what you ask for. That shows you trust God's judgment. You trust that he knows what is truly best for you in the long run."

- "Here is a fantastic secret that will help you for the rest of your life: Whenever you are really angry at somebody, say a prayer for that person. You will feel better, and God will smile."

- "Pray for people who don't pray."

How Not to Say It

- "After what you just did, you should tell God you are sorry for being so bad." Your intent is good and important. Showing remorse to God is healthy and builds character. But don't make it sound like a punishment. It is better to bring up the idea when feelings are calm and suggest to your child that he talk to God about what happened earlier in the day.

- "You don't need to pray. Just try to be a good person." If you believe in God, why would you discourage personal conversation with God? Besides, being a good person may be more easily accomplished if one already has an active prayer life.

- "Say your prayers before you go to sleep." This is fine as long as you are not teaching a child that the only time to pray is before bed. **ENCOURAGE** praying often during the day.

God:
"I Don't Want to Go to Church"

Phil and Donna wondered if it was really worth it. Most of the time their kids cooperated when it was time to get in the car and go to church. But some days—like today—were torture. The kids had been playing with their friends and didn't want to be interrupted. Their minor protests about going to church turned into more intense pleading and ended in a heated exchange. As the family car pulled into the church parking lot, the kids were angry and sulking. The tension was high.

"We're supposed to be going to church to worship God," Donna said to her sullen children. "Would you guys take those nasty looks off your faces and try to get in the right mood?"

"I'm staying in the car," one of the kids said.

"Me, too," said another.

"Get out of this car *now!*" Phil yelled into the vehicle.

The kids obeyed. But church services were not serene and meditative as Phil and Donna had anticipated just an hour earlier.

Church is a challenge when children act like chumps.

Things to Consider

➤ Ideally, the time before going to church or synagogue should not be rushed or chaotic. You increase the odds that churchgoing will be a chore.

➤ If you don't attend religious services regularly, your kids might challenge your decision to go on any given day. If it becomes part of the routine, they are more likely to cooperate.

➤ If only one parent attends regular services, the kids will question the fairness of being forced to attend.

➤ According to a groundbreaking Gallup survey, how often a couple prays together is a better prediction of happiness in marriage than how often they make love. Couples who pray together (compared with couples who don't) report having more respect for their spouse (83 percent versus 62 percent) and are more likely to agree on how to raise children (73 percent versus 59 percent).

How to Say It

For it to be meaningful, churchgoing should be a family ritual, not a once-in-a-while pastime. If your children give you a hard time about attending church, the first factor to examine is the frequency of churchgoing. If you decide you want the family to attend church more regularly, explain your reasons.

- "I understand that you might want to stay home. After all, that is what we have done most Sundays. But we have decided it was a poor idea to stay away from church, and we plan to go as often as possible."
- **EMPATHIZE** if your kids were in the middle of some game or project when it was time to leave for services. But be clear that worshiping God is a **DO**, not a **DON'T**. "I know it can be annoying to interrupt your game, but you know it is time for synagogue. You have five minutes to get ready. Thanks."
- Give them plenty of advance notice and one or two additional reminders before it is time to leave. You may head off major hassles if they register complaints early—before you are feeling rushed. "We're leaving for church in half an hour. You should be dressed and ready in fifteen minutes."
- "You don't have to like going to church, but you do have to go."
- "Just as you have to go to school on days you don't want to, you have to go to services. Mom and Dad believe it is important."
- "When you go to synagogue [or church], you have two choices. You can think about other things, or you can try to spend time talking to God and thanking him."
- **ENCOURAGE** and praise. "Thank you for being ready on time. I like it when we all go to church together and everyone is in a good mood and not rushed."

- **NEGOTIATE.** "If everyone is in a good mood this morning, we will all go out for breakfast after services. Or would you rather go out for lunch later on?"
- **REPORT** your feelings. "This is the part of the service I like the best . . ."
- **REPORT** during the week how important going to church or synagogue is to you. "I stopped off at church just to pray for a few minutes on my way home today. Sometimes I like doing that."

How Not to Say It

- "You should want to go." It is better to try to teach them the important and beautiful aspects of the service and pray that their desire to attend will increase.
- "I don't care what you think. You're going to church, and that's that." It is good that going to church becomes a routine and not a choice for the children. However, it is also a good idea to try to empathize with their complaints ("But, Mom, I get bored . . ." "I have homework to do . . ." "I want to go out and play . . ."), but don't give in to their pleading. Instead of saying you don't care what they think or feel, say, "I know how you feel. Some days I'd rather stay home, too. But it is important for us to go and give thanks to God and to pray for our family and people in the world."
- "I didn't see you praying at church. How do you expect to get anything out of the service if you don't put anything into it?" Many adults don't put much into it, either. Contemplating scripture requires a concentrated effort. It is better to discuss aspects of the readings later on and **TEACH** what was important to you.
- "If you act nice and don't cause trouble, we can skip church next week."
- "What will the priest [minister, rabbi] say if we don't show up for services this week?" What people think of you should not be a reason to go.

36

Gratitude

"What do you say, Natalie?" Mom said as Natalie grabbed the gift from her aunt.

"Thank you," Natalie said. She thrust her hand inside the package and pulled out a pair of decorative socks. It was not what she was hoping for.

"Aren't they pretty?" Mom said.

Natalie nodded. "They will look nice with my new dress," she said.

Natalie found a way to say thanks even though socks were not on her A-list.

She had learned how to be polite. Politeness is certainly a missing element for many children, but politeness is not gratitude. Gratitude goes deeper. It is a more heartfelt appreciation for what has been given you. It implies an awareness of what others must have sacrificed or went through in order to provide for you. Instilling a sense of gratitude in our children is critical for their well-being. Without it, they will possess a sense of entitlement whereby very little is appreciated and most things are taken for granted.

Things to Consider

➤ You must show gratitude if your children are to learn how to be grateful.

➤ Without appreciation for the small things, the big things will never truly satisfy.

➤ Gratitude at its fullest is other-focused. It rests upon empathy and joy. Without empathy, gratitude is superficial and even condescending. Without joy, gratitude is fleeting and hollow.

➤ If we spoil our children, we will take away their ability to feel truly grateful.

➤ What children will remember with fondness and gratitude is our time spent with them, not the time spent with toys. The more time you give your children, the fewer material things they will crave and the better able they will be to show gratitude.

➤ Saying grace before meals can instill a sense of gratitude for things most Americans take for granted.

How to Say It

- **TEACH** gratitude by explaining more in depth the time and thought that went into gifts. "Your grandma drove to the store thinking about what to get you. She went from shop to shop until she found something she hoped you would like. Then she paid for it with her money. All because she wanted you to smile and be happy."

- "When you make me things at school, I am very grateful because I know how much time you spent making it. That makes it special."

- "Imagine that you took the time to get me a special gift, and I wasn't grateful. How would that make you feel?"

- "Let's think of things we should be grateful for that we usually take for granted."

- "Everything on earth—the flowers, the water, the animals, the air, all the people, your family—are gifts from God. That is one reason we pray: to give thanks to God."

How Not to Say It

- "Tell Aunty Chris it was the best present you ever received and you'll love it as your favorite toy." Don't exaggerate. If the gift itself falls short, it's better to have your child appreciate all that went into making or purchasing it. Then she can express a more sincere form of gratitude that will mean more than inflated appreciation.

- "Saying thank-you is enough. You don't have to send a note." Going that extra step can help your children appreciate gifts they receive.

- Don't overlook day-to-day thoughtful gestures. "You found my sunglasses for me? I wondered where they were." Where is the gratitude? Use this as an opportunity to teach why the action (finding something you lost) meant a lot.

37

Hitting

"Bobby! Stop hitting your sister!"

"She hit me first!"

"No, I didn't," Karla cried. "He got mad at me because I won the card game."

"I did not!" Bobby screamed.

Mom was exasperated. "I don't care what the reason is. You know you're not supposed to hit your sister. Go to your room and come out when I tell you."

Every child will hit a sibling. Kids misbehave that way for a variety of reasons. The most common include getting even, to gain attention, to get one's way, being overtired, hungry, or ill. Parents must try to determine the reasons so they can respond appropriately.

Things to Consider

➢ If there is violence between the parents, a child is more likely to act violently.

➢ If parents disagree on how best to discipline a child who hits, the hitting behavior will probably not go away.

➢ No approach is perfect. When you try a new approach, stick with it for a while before you decide it is not effective.

➢ A helpful tool for reducing negative behaviors is to give a child a certain amount of "points" at the beginning of the week. Points are deducted for each wrong behavior. A child can trade in the points for certain pre-agreed items.

➤ Normal aggression must be distinguished from what is called conduct disorder. Conduct disorder is a persistent problem that does not seem to be affected by ordinary interventions. Children with conduct disorder are more defiant; often destroy property; are dishonest, impatient, and willing to take big risks; and often show a lack of empathy for others. Professional help is usually required, and teachers must often be involved in the process so that interventions are consistent.

➤ In recent years, violence in schools has been the focus of national attention. Children who commit more violent acts may give warning signs. These are the most common signs:

Feeling rejected and frequently picked on by peers

Decline in academic performance

Previous aggressive behavior

Drug or alcohol use

Easily angered over small things/loss of temper almost daily

Enjoying the hurting of animals

Writings or drawings that depict extreme violence

How to Say It

Proper discipline usually requires more than a verbal response from the parent. What a parent says is necessary but often insufficient if the goal is to help a child hit less often. However, saying the wrong words can aggravate the situation. Children ages ten to twelve especially may resent words they view as harsh or unfair. Then a parent has unwittingly added to the problem.

- **REPORT** your expectations as clearly as you can ahead of time. "When you two are playing together in the other room, I expect you to come to me if you have a problem or for the two of you to talk it out. Hitting is not allowed."

- **DO'S & DON'TS.** "Hitting when you get mad is wrong."

- **ENCOURAGE** and praise cooperative behavior whenever you can. If you are trying to reduce hitting behavior by a child, frequent praise will also serve as a positive reminder how to act. "You guys played so nicely together. Even when you argued about something, you didn't hit. That makes me very happy."

- After you correct a child for hitting, allow a minute of silence. Then listen to your child's reasons for his hitting behavior. Obviously, you don't agree that hitting was a solution, but you will fare better if you try to listen and, when possible, show **EMPATHY**. Don't try this until you have calmed down. If you are still angry at your child for hitting, you will dismiss his reasons too quickly. "Okay. Now I want to sit and listen for a minute. Please tell me why you chose to hit your sister. . . . Oh, I see. When she made a face at you after winning the game, you didn't like that. I'm sure it bothered you when she teased you like that."

- After you have shown some empathy, **TEACH**. Don't lecture. Instead, try to help your child figure out what he could have done differently. "When your sister teases you and you feel like hitting her, what other things could you do that would help the situation and not get you into trouble? . . . Good idea. Let's rehearse it now; it might be fun."

- Recurrent hitting should be punished. Ideally, explain ahead of time what the consequences will be. "If I see you hitting your little brother, you will have to stop playing for a half hour."

How Not to Say It

- *"Mom, she stuck her tongue out at me."* "Oh, just ignore her." If your child might ordinarily hit his sister but instead complains to you (which is what you asked), don't easily dismiss him. If he thinks you will not do anything, he will conclude that he must take matters into his own hands and probably end up hitting his sister again.

- "If you hit her once more, you will be punished." The first time he hits her should result in consequences. Telling him not to hit again does not teach him what he could do instead. Say instead, "I want you two to talk to each other about what's bothering you without hitting."

Smart Talk

A recent study at the University of Illinois examined three ways that parents might act when kids fight: ignore the conflict; teach children strategies such as negotiation, compromise, and problem solving; or punish the children. While both moms and dads believed that ignoring the problem was the least useful, parents used that approach three times as often as the other two approaches. When fathers used control strategies such as punishment, they did so because they lacked confidence in their skill at teaching children effective ways to negotiate or problem-solve, not because they felt it was the best approach overall. The upshot? Parents need confidence in helping their children learn to problem-solve. That takes a little time and practice, but the reward will be worth it.

38

HIV/AIDS

Phil mentioned to his family when he arrived home from work that he had donated blood earlier that day. Nine-year-old Sarah looked at him with fear. "Can't you get AIDS?"

Phil was surprised. How did Sarah hear about AIDS?

He shouldn't have been so shocked. Children hear about AIDS from television, older kids, discussions at school, and playmates. Some parents are understandably reluctant to discuss the subject with their grade-school children. It is yet another scary topic that seems to whittle away at a parent's fantasy that children can be spared from the harsher realities of life.

But a parent's wishes won't change the fact that children will hear about AIDS. It is better to inform them in a straightforward manner what AIDS is rather than allow them to be misinformed and unnecessarily afraid.

Things to Consider

➤ Know the facts. Many adults are misinformed and believe falsehoods that AIDS can be contracted from an infected person sneezing or by drinking from a shared cup—or that transfusions pose a high risk. According to the Centers for Disease Control, donated blood is tested not once but twice. While some risk always exists, the CDC said that at most, blood tainted with HIV may go unnoticed in one out of four hundred thousand pints, with the actual risk probably much lower than that.

➤ Unless your child is educated about human sexuality, there is no need to discuss the specific ways that AIDS is transmitted sexually. You know your child best and can determine what he is able to really understand at his age.

➤ Don't be stiff and formal or prepare a lecture. Simply have a brief conversation in which you give facts and answer your child's questions.

➤ Be prepared to discuss the topic again (and again) as your child matures and more advanced knowledge is necessary.

➤ The topic will come up unexpectedly—your child may overhear a commercial or news report, for example—so plan ahead.

➤ Research shows that parents who discuss AIDS with their kids overemphasize the medical end and ignore their children's emotional issues (fears of getting AIDS). Studies show that only one in five parents believes that kids worry about AIDS when in fact almost 60 percent of sixth to eighth graders are concerned.

How to Say It

Mostly you will be **TEACHING** facts and reassuring your child that he won't get AIDS from his normal activities.

- "I'm wondering if you have ever heard of AIDS and what questions you might have."

- "AIDS is caused by a virus called HIV. Some diseases such as a cold or flu are easy to get. AIDS is very, very difficult to get. You would have to mix your blood with the blood of someone who had the HIV virus."

- If your child asks if children get AIDS, say, "Yes, some children have been infected with HIV. Some were infected when they were born because their mother had the virus. Some children who needed extra blood when they were in the hospital got the virus from the blood. But all blood that is donated is tested for HIV, and blood that has the virus won't be used in hospitals."

- "You look worried as we talk about AIDS. Tell me what your concerns are."

- "Many people have died from AIDS but the medicines they use today help more than they used to. It is hoped there will be a cure someday."

- If your child worries that someone he plays with might have AIDS, more reassurance and facts are called for. "Since it is so hard to get AIDS, especially if you are a child, I believe that none of your friends has it. Did you know that if a person with AIDS has a bleeding cut, the virus is even more difficult to get because once it hits the air the virus gets very weak."

How Not to Say It

- "You get AIDS if you do drugs or try to have sex before you are married." Trying to scare your child to avoid drugs or sex won't work if you give them the wrong information. Once they learn the truth from books, teachers, or friends, you risk having them view you as ignorant or untrustworthy.

- "People who get AIDS have only themselves to blame." Many people have acquired AIDS through no fault of their own. Besides, talking about people who have AIDS is an opportunity to foster a sense of compassion in your child. Having HIV or dying of AIDS is a very sad thing that affects not only the AIDS patient but his or her family and friends. A better choice is suggesting that your child say a prayer for people with AIDS and their families.

- "AIDS is a disease that other people get. You don't have to worry about it." The tone is dismissive. What you are really communicating is "Let's drop the subject." Are you sure your child has no concerns? If your child is between five and eight, telling him AIDS is a disease is accurate and may be all that's required. But it is better to inquire if he has any questions and to leave him with the belief that you are available to talk about the subject at any time.

Smart Talk

When you speak to your child, keep in mind that you are communicating two things: verbal information and nonverbal information (body language). A child from age five to twelve becomes more adept at picking up on your body language. If she senses that you are uncomfortable with a topic, even though you are trying to act as if you are comfortable, she might choose to ignore that issue in the future. Either loosen up or let your child know that while the topic is not an easy one for you, it is important for you to discuss it. That way your child doesn't have to read between the lines and misread your intent.

39

Home Alone/Latchkey Kids

Gabriel said she didn't mind being home alone after school. During the two hours she waited for her father to arrive home from work, the twelve-year-old usually did her homework or watched television. She was good at monitoring the answering machine and not opening the door to just anybody who happened to knock. She liked the sense of being trustworthy and the feeling of independence that came with being home alone.

Her best friend, Cindy, didn't like being home alone after school. She understood the necessity of it, but she often felt afraid. On winter days when it was dark outside by 4 P.M., she grew more frightened.

With two out of three mothers of school-age kids in the workforce, latchkey kids are growing in numbers and total about seven million at last count. Helping them adapt depends on several factors.

Things to Consider

➢ While some kids may do fine being home alone, no study of "self-care" has shown it to have positive outcomes. The most optimistic reports conclude it has no negative outcomes.

➢ Children who are on their own for at least eleven hours a week are twice as likely to use alcohol, cigarettes, or drugs.

➢ Kids (fifth to seventh graders) home alone more than two days a week were four times as likely to report getting drunk in the past month.

➢ Self-care is more risky in urban environments than in suburban.

➢ Some kids stay with friends under adult supervision. Others use their free time after school to "hang out" with peers. The latter group is at higher risk for trouble than the former.

➤ Girls without supervision tend to be more at risk for problems than boys of the same age. That is probably due to the fact that girls develop physically at an earlier age and are more apt to hang out with older teens.

➤ A study that compared college students who were former latchkey kids with nonlatchkey kids showed no difference between the groups in personality or academics.

➤ A survey of 18 pediatricians, 96 police officers, and 209 parents asked at what ages kids can be left alone without supervision. For fifteen minutes or less, the average age given was nine. For an hour or more, the age was twelve. For babysitting, the age was fourteen.

➤ When more than one child is left alone, the children are likely to behave somewhat more disruptively or ignore each other than when a parent is present.

➤ Authoritarian parents (attentive, warm, but firm about discipline) are a buffer against a child conforming with antisocial peers (during and after school) compared with inattentive or more permissive parents. Tough but loving parents, take heart: You have the right idea.

How to Say It

Most kids are inadequately prepared to avoid injuries (burns, cuts, etc.), deal with emergencies, handle phone calls or visitors at the door, or cope with kidnapping or molestation possibilities. **TEACH** them what to say or do and rehearse with them.

- "Listen to the answering machine and don't pick up the phone unless it is someone you know well. Always say, 'Mom is busy at the moment,' and take a message."
- "Call 911 if you have any doubt about what to do. Here are the phone numbers for the neighbors who will be home."
- "The first-aid kit is always in the bathroom. Let's review how to use some of those items."
- Discuss ahead of time what your child plans to do when he arrives home. You should always know your child's home schedule. "Your plan is to make a sandwich, do your homework, and maybe play a video game. I'll call you and check in."

- "Don't go outside until I'm home." This is especially important in urban areas. Children in large cities are more likely to get into trouble when left to roam outside than are children in the suburbs.
- "You can't have any friends over until I get home."
- If your child expresses fear or dislike for the latchkey situation, take the concerns seriously. Find a way to provide supervision. "I feel bad for you. I can understand why you don't like being home by yourself. Let's figure out what can be done differently."
- "I know you'd like to have your friends over after school but there needs to be supervision. I'm sorry. I know it isn't fun."

How Not to Say It

- "Just keep the doors locked, don't answer the phone, and you'll be fine." Much more preparation is needed. Review as many scenarios as possible. Give them pop quizzes on occasion. "So what would you do if your brother cut himself badly?"
- "If you go out, be sure to leave me a note." Not advisable. With grade-school children you should know ahead of time where they plan to go, for how long, and how they plan to get there.
- "There really isn't anything to be afraid of. You'll get used to being home alone, and you'll probably like it." Your child may go along with it but may never learn to like it. Knowing that a parent is not in the next room can create much anxiety in some children even if they seem old enough. If your child remains anxious, you will have to do all you can to modify your schedule so you can be available to him. Perhaps in a year or two he'll be old enough.
- "You're such a big girl, being able to stay alone by yourself for an hour." If being home alone is infrequent, such praise is nice. But if a child must be home alone frequently, you may be making it harder for her to voice any objections. A better way to say it: "You certainly are taking on more responsibilities by being home alone. But it isn't always easy, and many kids don't like it. If you have any problem with it, let me know."

Rule of Thumb: Always phone your children when they are left alone. Get periodic updates on their attitude about staying home alone.

40

Homesickness

Tommy placed his backpack on the floor of his cousin's bedroom, the place that he'd call home for the next two weeks.

"It looks as if we got everything from the car," his dad said after their long drive. "We'll be going now, Tommy. Have lots of fun!"

Tommy's mother hugged him hard. "We'll miss you," she said. "But we want you to enjoy yourself. You always enjoy playing with your cousins."

Tommy's parents waved good-bye to their son and left. When they arrived home two hours later, the phone was ringing. "Mom!" Tommy said when she answered it. "I changed my mind. I don't want to stay. I want to come home."

Homesickness is not unusual, but parents can make the problem worse if they mishandle it.

Things to Consider

➤ While many children experience homesickness, most feel much better within a day or two. If you can handle their temporary discomfort, they will probably be able to handle it, too.

➤ Homesickness may be more pronounced if the family went through a recent loss or stressful period such as a death of a relative or marital separation.

➤ Homesickness, while uncomfortable, can make a child feel competent when he learns he can overcome it.

How to Say It

There are three phases: preparation, the actual leaving of the child, and postseparation. What you say at each phase can mean the difference between homesickness or away-from-home wellness.

- In the preparation phase, listen to your child's concerns and questions, and explain what he can expect while away. "Here is the brochure for camp. As you can see, every day you will take part in activities such as swimming and boating, plus you can pick certain things to do that are special such as archery."

- **TEACH** about homesickness if you think it is likely your child will feel lonesome. Don't belabor the point. "When you feel homesick, you may feel kind of sad in your stomach. It just means you miss us. But the feeling goes away after a day or so. It's just a feeling, and it won't hurt you."

- If your child asks what will happen if he misses you when away from home, **EMPATHIZE** and **TEACH** ways he can cope. "Most kids do feel a little lonesome. That's normal. When you feel that way, the best thing to do is some fun activity. Then later that night you can call me and tell me all about your day."

- If your child protests your leaving, try to find out if he has any legitimate concerns. Maybe he needs to be introduced to another child or the camp counselor to feel more at ease. "Tell me what your worst fear is right now. . . . What would have to happen for you to begin to feel better?"

- If your child calls you later on, be optimistic and upbeat. Reassure him that any concerns are normal and give suggestions where appropriate. Chances are your child will feel better soon. Hang in there. "I bet you did interesting things today. Tell me what you did."

- Find out what your child did that made him feel better and praise him. "So when you were feeling lonesome, you went swimming with the other kids. What a great idea."

- If your child is absolutely miserable and cannot be consoled, he simply may not be ready to be away from home for too long. "It's okay that you came home early. Maybe you have to be a little older to enjoy yourself away from your family."

How Not to Say It

- "No one else is feeling this way. You should be excited." That is not reassuring and can make him feel worse. It is better to let him know that it is normal to feel a little sad or scared.

- "Well, that was a waste of money. Next time you want to go away to camp, don't ask." You're not teaching him anything useful. He'll just feel bad about himself or bad about you. What good does that do?

- "We'll all miss you so much while you're gone. It won't be the same here without you." Don't make him feel guilty about leaving. Mastering separation from one's family is an important developmental task.

- "Remember, if you want to come home, just call us and we'll come right away. Call at any hour, day or night." Don't go overboard on the reassurance. You are actually planting the suggestion that he will have a hard time coping. Besides, since many children feel a little homesick, rushing in to rescue them never gives them the opportunity to see that the feeling can go away.

- "You're too old to get homesick." No, he's not, and he might be feeling that way for good reason. A seventh grader had to return home from a friend's house because he witnessed his friend's parents arguing and it scared him. Whatever the reason for homesickness, your child is experiencing it. Try to figure out the reasons.

Rule of Thumb: If you were very homesick as a child (or not at all homesick), you run the risk of overidentifying with your child. Your child may have feelings different from yours. Be open to that possibility.

41

Internet Concerns

Elliot typed in his favorite sport in the search engine of his internet site. He got more than he bargained for. Listed among the various sites he located were those that dealt with pornography.

Camille's friend showed her how to get into a chat room. Up until then the only communicating she'd done on the computer was to e-mail her friends. Now a whole new world was opened up. Fortunately, she told her friend she didn't like the chat room. Some other child, however, might have found it tantalizing talking to strangers.

The internet is like nothing the world has seen. Many parents are not computer literate, let alone internet savvy. Parents who would never let their children attend a PG-13 movie would be shocked at what is available to any knowledgeable user on the web.

And most kids are very knowledgeable when it comes to computers.

Things to Consider

➢ Place restrictive filters on the computer that don't allow access to certain websites. (This is a must if your child is used to spending time alone and unsupervised.) With powerful ads, lots of colors and games, and freebies to entice the audience, children are at risk for surfing areas they shouldn't.

➢ Place the computer in a family room or place where people gather. Kids who have computers in their room are likely to receive less supervision than is wise.

➢ Spend a few hours and get acquainted with the technology. The more you know about the internet, the better choices you can make for your children.

➤ Never allow your children to chat with strangers. Never allow your children to give their name or address (or your credit card number) to anybody on the internet.

How to Say It

- **DO'S & DON'TS.** Set very clear rules about using the internet. Enforce them and don't get lax in your supervision. "It's fine to use the internet to look up information for your school report, but I don't want you surfing around or downloading anything without my permission."

- "Sending e-mails to friends is fine if you limit the time to . . ."

- "Never use the internet unless I am here helping you."

- "Chat rooms are not allowed. They can be dangerous to young children like you. Some people chat who only want to take advantage of children."

- **TEACH** about risks and dangers. "Some people have been hurt by people they met in chat rooms."

- **ENCOURAGE** proper use. "You used the internet for your school report, and that was all. It is wonderful knowing I can trust you and that you are smart enough to avoid unnecessary risks."

- If your child gets annoyed with your cautiousness and insists that he can play it safe on the web, **TEACH** more about the dangers. "If somebody knocked on our door and wanted to teach you things about Satanism or wanted to show you dirty pictures, would I let him in? Of course not. People on the web care nothing about you personally. They only want to make money off you or lure you into trusting them."

How Not to Say It

- "I don't want you going online. It's dangerous." So many things are dangerous if misused. The internet can also be a marvelous source of important information. Besides, it will be necessary for your child to be computer and internet literate as he gets older. Teach the dangers and supervise when necessary, but let your child have access to the web.

- "Honey, come out of your room. You've been on that computer for hours." And it has been unsupervised. You may as well be allowing people who only want to take advantage of your child into her bedroom.

- "Isn't two hours long enough to be on the web?" You are too lax in supervision. Even if your child is not exploring inappropriate sites, computers can be addictive. Time spent doodling on a computer is time wasted.

42

Jealousy

"Why does she always get what she wants, and I never do?"

"How come they get to go to the beach, and we have to go to a dumb barbecue?"

"Why do I have to wait until I'm thirteen to get my ears pierced?"

"How come I have to wait for my birthday to get a new bike when all the other kids on the block have new bikes?"

"How come he always takes the bigger piece?"

"It's not fair!"

Kids get jealous. Just as an art expert might detect subtle shadings in a painting, grade-schoolers detect the subtlest variations in fairness. They keenly feel when they are getting the short end of things and demand justice. When it doesn't happen according to their sense of fair play, they get jealous.

Things to Consider

➤ Jealousy stems from a perception of loss. Jealous children may feel a loss of their lovableness, such as when they believe a parent or grandparent favors another child over them. It may stem from loss of esteem, as when a child is jealous of another child's skill. Or it may stem from loss of control (or the sense that matters are unfair) when something happens they can do nothing about such as a divorce (jealous of kids whose parents are together).

➤ Petty jealousies may come and go. If the jealousy persists, it is important to determine what the underlying loss might be.

➤ Parents who do not get along may unwittingly be more critical of a child who reminds them of their spouse. Unhealthy alliances may form (Mom and son on one side; Dad and daughter on the other) that can foster jealousy.

➤ Parents unhappy with their lot in life may reveal their jealousy of others and thereby encourage jealous thinking in their children.

➤ If a parent has a serious problem such as alcoholism or severe physical illness, one of the kids may have taken on adult responsibilities and become jealous of siblings who are more nurtured.

How to Say It

- **EMPATHIZE** and probe for the underlying loss. Don't rush in to make your child feel better; you may never understand what's really bothering him. "You seem hurt that Grandma gives a lot of attention to your little brother. Do you wonder if Grandma loves you as much as she loves him?"

- "Many of the kids in your class wanted to sign your friend's yearbook, but fewer wanted to sign yours. That hurts your feelings, and you feel a little jealous."

- "You're right. You've been doing so much extra housework because Mom and Dad have had to work longer hours, while your little sister hasn't had to do much at all. We haven't let you know just how grateful we are and what a good job you've been doing."

- **ENCOURAGE** your child by reminding her of past successes. "Yes, Kelley won the tournament and got her name in the paper. You won an award two years ago."

- **TEACH** your child to cope. "I understand that right now you're not feeling lovable [or competent or that life is fair]. But could you take a minute and think of the many ways you know that you are loved?"

- "Last week you felt jealous of your friend. You seem to be doing better today. What happened that helped you think differently?"

- "I know you're jealous of Tim. Have you ever wondered if he felt jealous of you?" (This can appeal to a child's sense of fairness. If jealousy goes both ways, it may not feel so bad.)

How Not to Say It

- "It's a sin to feel jealous." Yes, the Ten Commandments do prohibit envying thy neighbor. But stating such a rule won't help your child feel differently. He may simply learn that you cannot help him deal with difficult feelings. If you wish to use a biblical approach, say something like "God made all of us different. Nobody is the best at everything. Instead of being jealous, God wants you to focus on the things that you are thankful for. You can focus on what you don't have and be unhappy, or you can focus on what you do have and try to be thankful."

- "That's life. Who said it was supposed to be fair?" Trying to teach before showing empathy may close off communication and just frustrate your child more.

- "You're overreacting. You know Grandma loves you as much as she loves your brother." It is better to ask for specific examples of why your child feels jealous and challenge them. "Yes, you're right. Grandma did spend more time with him this weekend. But that was because she had to baby-sit, and your brother needed more of her attention. Whenever we are here to watch over your brother, Grandma spends more time with you."

- "Don't worry. I'll cut the cake so everybody gets exactly the same size piece." Don't worry about being so precise. It's okay for your kids to get used to the idea that life isn't always fair.

Rule of Thumb: Older children who receive less parental attention because they have a sibling who is very ill or disabled seem better able to accept the unequal treatment. Still, extra attention for those children can go a long way in helping them continue to cope well.

43

Little White Lies: "Why Did You Lie About Santa Claus?"

When seven-year-old Moiré learned the awful truth about Santa Claus from her highly-impressed-with-himself older brother, Sean, she had three immediate concerns.

1. Will Christmas ever be the same?
2. Why did her parents lie?
3. What else have they lied about?

Children vary in their reaction to learning the truth about Santa, the tooth fairy, and the Easter bunny. Some feel proud for having figured it out, but many find out the hard way: from friends or siblings who have no interest in letting them down easily. It need not be a traumatic event and is sometimes harder for the parents when they realize that more of their child's innocence has faded. Rarely do parents overreact to this issue, but often they underreact. Children, especially in the five- to eight-year-old range, may be confused or feel betrayed. They know how to think only in concrete, literal ways. They do not understand Santa Claus as an abstraction meant to signify love and sharing. They may therefore have specific concerns about what will happen differently next Christmas.

Things to Consider

➤ If your child seems particularly sad, moody, or withdrawn (or, conversely, is more disobedient), it is possible that the news about Santa is touching on some past loss. Has a grandmother died recently? Or a pet? Has the family relocated so the child moved away from old friends? Are you and your spouse arguing a lot? Have you separated or divorced? If so, you will have to take time to discuss those issues further.

➤ Some children still *want* to believe in Santa, and they are young enough (usually nine years or less) to be reconvinced Santa exists, at least for one more holiday. This is an option, especially if you want them to continue believing a while longer.

➤ The younger children may not fully grasp the concept of a *white lie*. Lying is lying is lying. Don't expect that any fancy reasoning on your part will help them fully understand. They simply must grow older.

➤ Once a child knows and believes the truth, don't automatically change your gift-buying strategies. Children may want to ease into their new understanding. They still may want to hear you mention Santa Claus and certainly be surprised on Christmas morning. A father of four children whose oldest son just found out the truth about Santa mistakenly saw it as an opportunity for his ten-year-old to help buy presents for his younger siblings. The child did help out, but with a distinct lack of enthusiasm. After many attempts to get the child to talk, the father finally realized that his son still wanted to *pretend* that Santa existed. Helping to purchase presents made it impossible for him to pretend.

Smart Talk

Sometimes parents can overidentify with their children, especially their same-sex children. How did you react when you learned the truth about Santa? Are you automatically assuming that your child will handle it the same way? Use your past for possible insights but consider that your child may react differently from the way you did.

How to Say It

The best way to begin is by using **EMPATHY**. Even if your child asks you a direct question such as "Is there really a Santa Claus?" or "Why did you lie to me?" you may be better off (and be able to delay the inevitable moment of truth) by saying such things as:

- "You sound really hurt [or worried]. Are you?"
- "This bothers you enough that you want to talk about it, right?"

- "You might be wondering what else isn't true that you once believed was true."
- "It made you upset when the older kids on the school bus told you about Santa."
- "Perhaps you are worried that Christmas won't be the same anymore."
- "I'm wondering if you feel I've let you down. You sure sound disappointed."

If your child is worried that next Christmas (or the next time she loses a tooth) it will all be different, reassure her:

- "No, next Christmas will be exactly like last Christmas. You'll still get toys, we'll still put up a Christmas tree, and you'll have a lot of fun with many surprises."
- "What would you like to see happen next Christmas that would still make it a special time, even if Santa is really Mommy and Daddy?"

If your child is troubled that you lied about Santa, using examples that he or she can understand might help:

- "Remember on Daddy's last birthday we told him we would be out shopping when he came home from work, but instead we surprised him at home with his present? It is true we lied to him, but we did it because we wanted him to be surprised. We wanted to make him happy."
- "Remember how excited you get when you get dressed up like a fire fighter? [or a cowboy or Superwoman or a ghost] on Halloween? You know you are only pretending, but you act as if it's true because it's fun to pretend and make believe. Mommy and Daddy have a lot of fun pretending about Santa Claus."
- "Remember how excited you were going back to the lake for vacation even though you hadn't been back there for a few years? At Christmas I remember how much fun it was for me when I was a kid, and I told you Santa was real so that you could have the same kind of fun I had."

If you think your child might want to be reconvinced that Santa exists, say:

- "Isn't it interesting that the weather reporters like to talk about Santa's whereabouts on Christmas Eve?"

- "Why do you think we have so many songs about Santa Claus?"
- "I just saw a shadow in the window. It looked an awful lot like an elf to me. Did you see it, too?"
- "I know some of the kids in school are saying Santa doesn't exist. I don't know about you, but I love to pretend that he does exist."

The above won't convince some children, but a child who still wants to believe may allow him- or herself to be convinced.

How Not to Say It

Anything that discounts your child's feelings or makes her wrong for feeling disappointed is a poor move, such as:

- "It's about time you learned the truth."
- "You're old enough to know. Many children find out when they are younger than you."
- "That's life. You'll learn many things are not what you think they are."
- "I've heard enough from you about this Santa Claus thing. Get over it."
- "You're making a big deal about nothing."

Finally, don't drag out the old newspaper clipping of "Yes, Virginia, There Is a Santa Claus." That sentimental favorite may touch the heart of adults, but children are unable to grasp Santa as a metaphor. Saying that Santa exists just as surely as love and joy and faith exist may only get you the following response: "That's nice, Dad, but is there *really* a Santa Claus?"

44

Lying

Julia, age nine, didn't mind making her tuna fish sandwich all by herself. She opened the can, dumped the tuna in a bowl, stirred in the mayonnaise, and slapped it all on bread. Her mom walked over to inspect the finished product.

"Looks delicious. Hey, how did this mayonnaise get smeared all over the counter?"

"I didn't do it," Julia said.

"Nobody else was in the kitchen except you, and you used the mayonnaise."

"But I didn't get any on the counter."

"Then who did?"

"I don't know but it wasn't me!"

Julia lied—or did she? She was genuinely surprised at the extent of the mess. She had no memory of doing it, so in her mind she was not guilty.

At other times kids lie and they know it. They do it to get out of trouble or to attract attention. Then it's a parent's job to do something.

Things to Consider

➤ Since every child will lie, a firm but low-key approach is best most of the time.

➤ Lying is much more serious when it is accompanied by violent behavior or stealing.

➤ Children who lie a lot probably have friends who do the same.

➤ While a child who lies may have honest parents, parents who lie or break rules are more likely to have children who do the same.

➤ Adults admit to lying about thirteen times a week (did they lie in the survey?). Many adults lie to make social interactions more acceptable (saying someone's new haircut looks great when thinking it looks awful).

How to Say It

- If the lie is over small matters ("I didn't mess up the counter, Mom"), don't debate it. "Well, however it happened, the counter needs cleaning. Grab a towel and start wiping, please."

- Don't debate when the evidence is clear that your child is lying. "You can say you didn't do it if you want, but I saw you throw the apple core behind the couch. Pick it up and throw it in the trash."

- Always correct a lie. "No, that's not the truth. The truth is . . ."

- Authors Jerry Wyckoff and Barbara Unell, in the book *How to Discipline Your Six- to Twelve-Year-Old,* recommend rehearsing telling the truth. "Millie, just please say, 'Dad, I was the one who accidentally erased the messages on the answering machine.'"

- If lying becomes more frequent or more serious, you will have to make lying an issue. "You're getting older, and I need to be able to trust you. If I think you are lying to me, then I will not be able to allow you to do things that require trust, such as spending a night at a friend's or carrying extra money."

- Recognize that children may lie to avoid disapproval, to make themselves appear better than others, or to deal with frustrations—in other words, as a way of coping with a flagging self-esteem. If you suspect any of the above, focus on the underlying concern the child might have. "I notice you tell stories about how strong you are. I wonder if some days you worry that other kids might not like you, and you want to impress them."

- "I think you lied to avoid getting into trouble. Actually, I'd be more proud of you for telling the truth even if I didn't like what you did."

- Praise truth telling, especially when your child could have lied. "Thank you for coming to me to say you broke the window. It means a lot when you tell the truth, especially when you think you might get into trouble for it."

- "Even though you lied today, I know you are someone who will try to tell the truth." Show that you have faith in him.

- **TEACH** by example. "When I came to pick you up at school today, I found a twenty-dollar bill in the parking lot. I turned it in to the office in case someone lost it."

- **TEACH** about white lies. Older children will understand that sometimes you might lie to protect someone's feelings. "Remember when Grandma gave me that sweater for my birthday and I told her I loved the color? Well, I didn't really love it, but I knew she had spent a long time looking for the right gift for me. I didn't want to hurt her feelings. What other examples of white lies can you think of?"

How Not to Say It

- "You're a liar." Don't label your child that way. Distinguish between the act and the person.

- If you already know the truth, don't ask, "Who broke the lamp? Did you?" That may set up your child to lie. Don't give him the opportunity to practice.

- "You did *what!*" Be careful not to punish truth telling. Yes, some wrong acts deserve punishment or corrective consequences, but make sure you praise telling the truth.

- "Are you sure you're telling me the truth? Kids lie, you know." You should convey to your child that you expect the truth, not that you expect lies.

- "You lie just like your father did." Deal with your children as they are, not as a projection of somebody else.

45

Manipulative Behavior ("But Mom Said I Could!")

"What are you doing, sweetheart?" Dad said to ten-year-old Vickie. She was thumbing through a jewelry catalog.

"I'm trying to decide which earrings to buy when I get my ears pierced," she said.

"You mean when you turn thirteen? That's a few years away."

"Thirteen? Mom said I could get them pierced this weekend!"

"She did?"

"Yes! Dad, all the girls in my class have their ears pierced. I'm the only one who doesn't."

"Well, I thought—"

"Dad, if Mom says I can get them pierced you have to let me. You just have to!"

Mom heard the ruckus and came in to investigate.

"Hon, did you tell Vickie she could get her ears pierced?"

Mom looked astonished. "Absolutely not. I told her that if you thought she was old enough, I *might* reconsider, but that's not the same as telling her it was okay."

Sometimes kids really do misinterpret what a parent says because they hear what they want to hear. Other times kids will try to divide and conquer.

Things to Consider

➤ This kind of behavior is normal and a sign of more sophisticated development. For some kids it can get out of hand, however.

➤ If parents disagree on child-rearing, kids will easily find a wedge and take advantage of it.

➤ If parents are overtired or overworked, they are vulnerable to the divide-and-conquer approach.

➤ While giving in to children's manipulations is bad strategy, so is being rigid and inflexible. In fact, the more rigid you are, the more likely your children will be manipulative to get what they want sometimes.

➤ Sometimes siblings pull together and gang up on a parent. Manipulative? Perhaps. But kids do not have much authority and may need to rely on such tactics. Hear them out; they may have a good point to make.

How to Say It

- **DO'S & DON'TS.** "This is the first I heard of this. Until I speak to your Mom [or Dad] I'll have to say no." This is especially important if your child frequently rushes you and insists you must make a decision immediately.

- "If you remember, the rule is that I don't agree to something I'm unsure about until your father and I have a chance to discuss it."

- "Let me talk to your mother now." This shows him he can't get away with manipulating, but neither are you rejecting his request out of hand.

- **REPORT** what troubles you. "Your friend called and invited you to sleep over. I said okay, and I assumed your friend's mom already said it was okay. Then I found out she had no idea what you kids were planning. That is not the way you go about asking for permission."

- "I need to think about it first" or "I need to speak to your friend's parents first."

- **ENCOURAGE** honest, straightforward requests with praise. "You asked me to think about your request and to talk it over with Dad. I really like that way of asking."

Smart Talk

In a study of 137 families with kids ranging in age from three to thirteen, parents were asked to judge whether or not children engaged in specific behaviors that were listed. Parents disagreed with each other twice as often as they agreed. Mothers tended to report more negative behaviors than did fathers. What does this signify? Don't presume you and your mate are on the same wavelength. Check out your presumptions early and often. Otherwise, your kids will have a field day trying to manipulate you.

How Not to Say It

- "You are being tricky and dishonest. I won't stand for it." This comes perilously close to calling your kid a petty criminal. Many good kids act in a manipulative way for one of three reasons: because in the past it was rewarded ("Daddy, *pleeeeease!"*), because parents don't agree on rules, or because a parent has been inflexible about rules that could be modified. If the behavior happens once in a while, it will likely diminish if it is not reinforced. If it happens frequently, the possibility is strong that other family or marital problems are lurking that need to be fixed.

- "It's fine with me if it's okay with your mom." Used sparingly and about noncontroversial issues, this statement is okay to make. It shows flexibility. It becomes problematic when parents say it out of laziness. Then the children learn that if they can soften up the parents one at a time, they will get what they want. Whenever possible, talk to your spouse directly about your child's request. Don't let the child be the go-between; messages can get misunderstood.

- "I wish you wouldn't ask me these things at the last minute." This is rather wimpy. If you don't want hurried, last-minute requests, don't reward them. Much of the time children can plan ahead and give you plenty of time to think about what you want to do.

46

Medical:
Shots, Blood Tests,
and Dental Procedures

Eight-year-old Debby clenched her jaw as the shot was being administered.

"Ugh, I'm glad that's over," she said. Then she watched the lab technician prepare a new syringe—a much bigger syringe.

"Another shot!" Debby cried.

"Oh, no, no," said her Mom. "This is a blood test. It's like a shot except they take blood from you. It feels the same as—"

"Noooo! You told me all I needed was a shot! You never said anything about blood!"

Debby had a point. Being surprised will only increase her apprehension the next time she visits the pediatrician. But her mom's reluctance to warn her about the blood test was understandable. She didn't want to hear the protests while driving to the doctor's office.

If you want to make doctor and dentist visits a little easier, try these suggestions:

Things to Consider

➤ Severely phobic children may need professional help. Fear and apprehension and saying "I hate shots" don't qualify as a phobia. A truly phobic child may feel and act terrified, may cry uncontrollably, or may physically resist the medical procedure.

➤ Almost all children are nervous about shots and dental work.

➤ Unlike other situations that might cause fear, the infrequency of shots and dental drilling make adapting to the situation harder.

➤ Most apprehensive school-age children will comply with getting shots, but they may try hard to get you to postpone it. Don't give in.

How to Say It

- Use words that are accurate but less painful sounding. "The shot of novocaine feels like a mosquito bite" or "It feels like a little bug bite, and then you'll feel some pressure."

- "It takes about three seconds for a shot [about one second to poke your finger *or* about thirty seconds to draw blood from your arm, which is about as long as singing Happy Birthday four times]."

- Tell the truth. If your child's experience is worse than you said it would be, he won't trust what else you say. "Shots can hurt like a little pinch hurts. Most kids don't like it much and are glad to get it over with."

- "The dentist drill sounds scary and you can feel it rumble on your tooth, but the most it should hurt is like a few mosquito bites."

- "Do you see how the third shot of novocaine didn't hurt at all? That's because the first two shots made your mouth numb so you won't feel pain."

- "When the nurse is taking blood from you, the only part that hurts a little is when they poke you with the needle. That takes a second. It doesn't hurt at all when the blood goes from your arm and into the tube."

- **TEACH** why the shot or the drilling or the blood test is necessary. "If your infection gets worse, it could become very painful. The shot will help you get rid of your infection."

- "The blood test will tell us what kind of treatment to give you. Without a blood test, the doctors might waste time giving you medicines you don't need."

- **TEACH** by rehearsing when possible. For example, to rehearse getting a shot, wipe an area of your child's arm with rubbing alcohol, gently pinch a fold of skin, and carefully squeeze a piece of skin between your fingernails. (Approximating the discomfort of a shot. Practice on yourself first.) "This is what will happen, and this is what it will feel like. I bet that feels like something you can handle. Doesn't it feel like a mosquito bite?"

- **EMPATHIZE**. "I know you feel scared and will be glad when it's done."

- "Your stomach may feel nervous. That's normal."

- Praise is also very important during the procedures. "You're doing great. It's almost over. The part that pinches is the hardest part, and that part is over." A reward after the procedure isn't a bad idea. Bribery (offering some reward ahead of time out of desperation) is not advisable, but since shots or blood tests are infrequent, a special treat afterward is fine.

How Not to Say It

- "This will sting" or "It feels like a little stabbing." Those words are too strong and scary. Even the words *hurt* and *pain* are vague. What will your child imagine when he hears those words?
- "You won't feel anything." Tell the truth.
- "You're older than your sister, and she didn't cry." It may not help, and it can make him feel worse. It is better to empathize with the anxiety and discomfort, and praise him for his achievement afterward.
- "Don't be a baby." You may get cooperation (or you may not), but you will definitely teach your child not to bother talking to you about upsetting feelings. You are adding insult to injury.
- "The doctor will get mad at you if you don't get the shot [if you don't get your teeth cleaned]." Your child may not care what the doctor thinks. Besides, teaching children to cooperate so they will be liked is potentially dangerous. Peers or adults who may want to take advantage of your child will often use that strategy.
- "Stop complaining. Look, if you promise to be really, really good, I'll buy you a toy later." This is dangerously close to emotional blackmail. The next time your child has a doctor's appointment, he may act up again, knowing he'll get a reward. Or your child may not care if he gets a present. If you want to reward your child, say this: "I thought it might be fun for us to get you a little present after your doctor's visit. That way we have something to look forward to." Try discussing that present during the medical procedure as a distraction.

Medical: Hospitalization

When nine-year-old Christina ran through the family room and turned a corner, she tripped and hit her head on the television set. Her mom, Donna, knew that the cut was deep and immediately drove Christina to the emergency room. The girl was scared. It was her first time in a hospital, and she overheard the doctor say that stitches were required. Mom was nervous, too, but she also had an idea. Crouching next to her daughter's bed, she pulled the sheet over their heads, leaving only the head wound exposed, and together they sang Christina's favorite songs while the doctor stitched her up.

Some hospital stays are short. Some are longer. Some are unexpected. But parents can say things that can make a child's time in the hospital less scary.

Things to Consider

➤ School-age children are primarily concerned about suffering any pain from surgeries or medical tests. They may also worry about being separated from their parents.

➤ Most hospitals allow a parent to sleep in a child's room if necessary.

➤ A parent's attitude will have a large impact on the child's attitude.

➤ If a hospital stay is elective, let your child tour the facility ahead of time. Introduce her to a nurse or doctor whom she'll recognize later.

How to Say It

• **TEACH**. Inform your child what he can expect: the sign-in, any blood tests or X-rays, the surgery and postoperative experience. Be calm, matter-of-fact, and enthusiastic where appropriate. "Part of the fun is that you get to order the kind of food you want for supper, and you get to eat in bed. What's really neat is you are given a special medicine that makes you sleep, and you don't feel a thing during surgery. When you wake up, I'll be there waiting for you."

- Explain that it is okay to call a nurse (some children may be reluctant or may assume the adults will take care of everything). "If you need anything or have a question, all you have to do is press this button, and a nurse will come to you as soon as she is able."

- **NEGOTIATE.** It is not appropriate to plead with your child to cooperate with medical procedures and bribe her with goodies. However, since hospital stays are usually infrequent and stressful, you can discuss how you might celebrate when she returns home and is well again. "Would you like a little party with your friends? We could have it at a restaurant or at the house. Or would you prefer going to the amusement park?" The reward is not an enticement to cooperate but something to look forward to.

- **EMPATHIZE.** Resist the urge to reassure your child before you make empathic comments. Otherwise, you might cut off your child's concerns before she has fully expressed them. For example, if offering only reassurance, you might say, "No, it won't hurt." But an empathic comment might be: "You keep asking if the surgery will hurt. You're still worried that you will feel some pain during the surgery." That allows your child to express herself more fully and perhaps get to an underlying concern that has yet to be expressed. Other **EMPATHIC** comments include these:

    "You get worried when your friends tell you that going to a hospital is scary."

    "It can be a little exciting doing something you haven't done before."

    "You're upset that you might miss something fun at home while you are in the hospital."

- Reassure your child only after you believe you know his concerns. Be honest. "You won't feel a thing during surgery. You'll be asleep and won't even know you are having surgery. After you are awake, you might have a sore throat, but medications will help that, too."

Rule of Thumb: A hospitalization can cause some regression even in older children. Extra handholding is fine and helpful. Don't criticize your child if he acts younger than his age.

How Not to Say It

- "Most kids enjoy being in a hospital. It will be a lot of fun." Be honest. There can be enjoyable moments in a hospital, but most kids are glad to go home. The stay can be pleasant and interesting, however, so say that instead.

- "If you get upset, you'll have to stay longer [or they'll have to give you a shot]." Don't make the hospital a threatening place. Be sympathetic, not harsh.

- "You can go home if you want." If it isn't true, don't say it. Otherwise, your child will question the truthfulness of everything else you've said.

- "I'll feel so much better when you get back home." Tone down your own anxiety. It is better to say, "I'm glad the doctors are helping you, and I'm looking forward to Friday when you come home."

Smart Talk

If you are worried about your child's ability to cope with cancer, here's some good news. A 1997 study compared over three hundred cancer-surviving children with healthy children. The parents of these children were also evaluated for stress. Not only did children have fewer signs of stress than the parents did, but the cancer survivors were no different from their healthy counterparts in measures of stress. However, the parents of the sick children showed significant signs of post-traumatic stress disorder. Why? Those children were provided with tremendous social support, and they did not view the cancer as life threatening as had their parents. The bottom line: Parents of children with cancer need more support, and they need to remind themselves of the rise in the successful treatment of childhood cancers.

Medical:
When a Child Has
a Chronic Illness

Annie is one of five million children in the United States who suffers from asthma. According to the latest statistics, over 160,000 children will be hospitalized for asthma this year, and the number of new asthma cases has doubled in the last twenty years.

Arty is the unlucky one in a thousand children who suffer from juvenile arthritis. Sometimes for months at a time his knee swells up, and he has a hard time walking.

Severe food allergies, irritable bowel, migraine headaches, epilepsy, and diabetes are also among the chronic illnesses children face. Then there are the more debilitating diseases such as muscular dystrophy or diseases such as cancer that can sometimes be cured but that may require lengthy treatments. Kids who must deal with an acute medical problem know that they will soon feel better. But when a medical problem is chronic, children must learn to adapt to a more restrictive lifestyle.

Things to Consider

➤ You are not responsible for your child's chronic illness. Your responsibility is to see to it that your child receives appropriate care and treatment.

➤ Be on the alert for catastrophic thoughts ("She'll never have a normal childhood"). When treated properly, most chronic illnesses are not life threatening and are not usually too restrictive.

➤ Resist being overprotective. Research is clear that overprotective parents can unwittingly reinforce certain symptoms in children (such as pain and vague stomach or muscular aches). Similarly, don't grant your chronically ill child special privileges.

➤ Become an expert so you can teach your child how to manage his condition and how to detect warning signs.

How to Say It

- **TEACH** what the disease is in a matter-of-fact way. Don't be so serious or formal that your child worries unnecessarily. "You have asthma. That is an illness where once in a while you will have to work harder to breathe. It feels very uncomfortable, but the medicines we have will help a lot."

- "Many kids have allergies. Some children cannot drink milk or eat ice cream. Some kids can't eat corn or bread. Other kids can eat what they want, but they sneeze if they get near dogs or cats or certain flowers."

- "You are not an epileptic [an asthmatic, a diabetic, etc.]. You are a person with epilepsy."

- Offer **ENCOURAGEMENT**. "Many children have this problem. You are definitely not alone."

- As your child gets older, he needs to assume greater responsibility for taking proper medications, staying away from triggers that cause flare-ups, and recognizing the warning signs of a flare-up. "You remembered to use your ventilator before gym" [or "You remembered to tell Mrs. Jones you could not eat peanuts" or "You stayed away from the neighbor's new cat"]. Good for you!"

- "If you take your medicines properly and eat the right kinds of foods, you will feel good most of the time."

- Let your child down easily when restrictions are necessary. Suggest alternatives whenever possible. "No, you can't sleep over at Mary's because you are allergic to dog hair and it makes your asthma worse. I'm sorry. I wish you could go. Maybe I can talk to Mary's mom and see if you two could camp out in their backyard instead."

- **EMPATHIZE**. Chronic illnesses are by definition long-term. Your child will adapt but still be frustrated from time to time. "I know you felt disappointed when your class had a pizza party and you couldn't eat the pizza. What else did you feel?"

- "Some days taking your insulin shots makes you feel different from the other kids, and you wish you didn't have diabetes."

- "I know it can make you feel sad that you can't eat most of the Halloween candy. I'm glad you still got dressed in your costume and went out with your friends."

- If your child suffers a flare-up or goes through a difficult episode with her illness, speak as calmly and reassuringly as possible. "You are taking your medicine and know what to do. This flare-up is temporary. I know it feels a little scary and uncomfortable, but you've handled it before."

- Rehearse with your child some positive coping statements. "Next time you are upset that you walk with a limp and can't run as fast as the other kids, tell yourself 'I don't have to like this, but I can get used to it. I'm like every other kid: I'm better at some things and not as good in other things.'"

How Not to Say It

- "Your asthma is acting up? Let's get right home. We can go to the movies some other night." In their book *Natural Relief for Your Child's Asthma,* Drs. Steven and Ken Bock suggest you think twice about postponing enjoyable activities when the condition can be managed. Otherwise, children may not alert a parent when they are experiencing symptoms because they fear they will be forced to miss some activity.

- "You're feeling light-headed? Maybe it's your diabetes. Go lie down, and your brother can put away the dishes for you." When "illness behavior" is followed by some reward, the behavior can be reinforced. Don't let children out of their chores unless it is clearly necessary.

- "You've had diabetes for three years. You know you shouldn't be eating that!" You are right, of course, but you may be missing the point. A child who goes against medical advice (haven't you ever cheated on a diet?) is frustrated, not ignorant of the rules. It is better to empathize with her frustration than criticize her.

- "Be nicer to your sister. She has asthma." Your other children do need to be educated about their sibling's illness, but don't foster jealousy or resentment. If you ever overhear one of your other kids say "I wish *I* had diabetes," then you've overreacted.

- "Do you feel dizzy? Are you in any pain? Can you breathe okay? Are you sure you want to stay and play?" Overdone, your child may pay too much attention to his body and give in to the illness when he otherwise could get along fine despite having symptoms.

Smart Talk

In a study of seven- and eight-year-olds with migraines, treatment consisted of either biofeedback to reduce pain or biofeedback plus parental training in pain management. Both groups experienced less pain, but the second group did even better. What were parents trained to do? They encouraged normal activity for their children and encouraged the kids to try to manage the pain as much as possible by themselves. They did not ask children how much pain they were feeling and did not go overboard responding to their pain, and they asked the schoolteachers to follow the same guidelines.

In a different study of children with asthma, the father's role seemed influential in predicting school absences or asthma-related medical visits. Specifically, when fathers expressed a lot of criticism, the child was absent from school more often. The more time that fathers spent with their children on weekends, the fewer the medical visits for asthma needed by the child. This suggests either that fathers don't like spending time with asthmatic children or that asthma flare-ups can sometimes be triggered by emotions.

Medical:
Talking to Siblings of
Children with Chronic Illness

Ten-year-old Bruce did not hesitate to hold his younger brother's hand in the mall. His brother Tommy has Down's syndrome and looks up to Bruce.

"We're almost at the food court," Bruce said. "We can find a table while Mom buys our lunch."

Often, a heartwarming side effect of having a child with a disability or chronic illness is that siblings learn more about compassion and tolerance than they otherwise would. In fact, many of today's health care providers got their start by helping out at home with a family member who needed extra care or attention.

But there can be a downside. Siblings of kids with chronic conditions might receive less attention. They frequently take on added responsibilities or at least *feel* responsible for ensuring the safety of their brother or sister. In moderation that is not a problem. But if the illness is debilitating or if the parents are overwhelmed or overprotective, siblings may be saddled with too much stress.

Things to Consider

➤ Research evidence suggests that siblings understand and tolerate unequal treatment if there is a good explanation for it.

➤ Siblings can worry about their ill sister or brother, or may worry that they may become ill. They need to be educated and reassured.

➤ Were you a caretaker for a sibling (or even for a parent) when growing up? That background can make you either overly sensitive to your healthy children's needs or less sensitive. Try to adjust your reactions accordingly.

➤ Single parents or dual-career couples may expect more help from their children. Are your healthy kids involved too much in the care of the less healthy child because you are too busy?

How to Say It

- **TEACH** the basics of a sibling's illness and what effect it may have on their role in the family. "Your sister has severe asthma and sometimes has a hard time breathing. If you are playing with her and she has a flare-up, you might need to see that she uses her ventilator. Or you might have to get a teacher or grown-up to help her." Rehearse scenarios that are likely to occur.

- Offer reassurance if your child has unreasonable worries or concerns, perhaps asking "Will she die?" "No, she won't die. Many kids have this type of problem. But she can get real sick if we don't have her medications. Most of the time Mom and Dad will take care of her, but there may be times when you need to tell us what is happening."

- "No, her illness is not something you can catch."

- **EMPATHIZE** with their frustrations or worries. "You had to do most of the tidying up today because your brother was sick. I bet that can sometimes feel unfair."

- "You worry when your brother has to take his insulin shots."

- "Sometimes when you get mad at your sister, you feel guilty afterward because you know she is sick."

- "It's frustrating to have to turn around and go back home because we forgot the medicine. But we want to be prepared if we need the medicine."

- "It isn't easy some days having to look out for your little sister."

- **ENCOURAGE** and praise thoughtful behavior. Be willing to overlook some misbehavior when you know your child generally tries to be helpful and responsible. "You really are gentle with your brother when he needs your help" or "It's not always easy to be patient, but you were patient right now."

How Not to Say It

- "Don't fight like that with your sister! You know she's sick!" A recent study suggested that parents are willing to make excuses for their ill child's misbehavior but do not excuse the healthy child. Watch for that and make appropriate corrections. Sick children, just like adults, may be tempted to use their illness as a strategy to avoid responsibilities and excuse bad behavior.

- "It's your job to make sure your brother stays well." If medical emergencies are possible, do not expect a school-age child to take responsibility for the safety and welfare of the ill child. It should not be his "job." It is better to say, "You are not a doctor, so it is not your fault if there is a medical problem even when you help out and do your best."

- Don't say to a whining or demanding child, "You should be grateful you have your health [that you can walk, that you don't have cancer, that you don't have diabetes]." Don't try to make a child feel guilty for being healthier than a sibling. Kids will be kids, and that means they will take some things for granted (don't we all?) and whine when they don't get what they want. It is better to say something like "It's obvious you want that toy. I know you'd like it, but I'm sorry, the answer is no." Skip the lecture and don't make any references to the child with the medical problems.

- "Your brother is not like other children." Don't emphasize the differences. Your ill child is just like other children in every way.

Medical:
When a Parent Has a
Serious Physical Illness

Larry had been feeling weak and achy for months. Sometimes he had barely enough energy to fetch the morning mail before he wanted to go back to bed and sleep. After countless medical tests and reassurances from physicians that whatever he had would eventually go away, one specialist diagnosed fibromyalgia. Larry learned that fibromyalgia was similar to chronic fatigue syndrome and Epstein-Barr. The consequence would be periods of fatigue and pain that some days would be incapacitating. Larry's first thought was that he might not be able to keep his job. His second thought was that he might not be able to coach his daughter's basketball team.

Cancer, multiple sclerosis, degenerative nerve disorders, and severe respiratory or heart problems are just a few of the common illnesses that can affect a parent. When physical illnesses are severe or incapacitating, or if recovery takes a long time, the family has to reorganize in order to cope with the situation. Day-to-day life cannot go on exactly as it had before.

Things to Consider

➤ Children should not become mini-adults when a parent is sick. They may take on some added responsibilities but should retain their status as children. They should not feel responsible for the welfare of other family members.

➤ Parents whose responsibilities are limited due to physical illness sometimes pull back even further than they should (because of depression or insecurity), or they try to compensate by becoming overly involved in areas they can have a role in. Neither extreme is helpful. No matter how ill, children will look up to the parent as both boss and comforter. Don't underestimate your value just because of illness or disability.

➤ A recent study revealed that children are misinformed and undereducated about the causes of cancer. One in five believed it was caused by casual contact. Over half worried they would get cancer. If a parent has cancer, the children need to be educated about it.

➤ You have a tremendous opportunity to teach your children a valuable lesson: how to cope well during adversity.

How to Say It

- **TEACH**. Tell your children the basics of your condition and what they can expect in the near future. "The doctors told me I have breast cancer. They will do surgery to remove the cancer, and they will give me medications for many months to keep the cancer from returning. Some days I will feel sick from the medications, so I may not be able to go to work, clean up the house, play with you, or go shopping. I will be asking you to do a few more chores once in a while."

- "You don't get cancer from being with someone who has it. Just because I have cancer doesn't mean you will get it."

- Offer **ENCOURAGEMENT**. If your prognosis is uncertain, remain optimistic. You don't need to tell children the truth if the truth will leave them worried and without answers for the foreseeable future. If a child asks, "When will you be all better?" say, "I don't know exactly when, but the medications will do their job and I expect to feel much better as time goes on."

- If a child asks, "Will you die?" say, "No. I expect to live a long life." Even if there is a possibility you could die from the illness, it is best not to say that to children until you are closer to that stage.

- **EMPATHIZE**. "It's not easy coming home from school and having to tidy up the house when you'd rather play."

- "It worries you when you see me staying in bed most of the day."

- "I'm sure it's frustrating that we have to cancel our plans for today because Daddy is not feeling well."

- "You feel sad that Mommy couldn't watch your baseball game and see you get a hit."

- "You feel excited and happy that Dad feels well enough to go to the park with us."

- **REPORT** your opinions and feelings. "I'll be glad when the medications start to work and your mom feels better."

- Reassure children that they are not the cause of the illness or responsible for its worsening. "Daddy doesn't expect you to be well behaved every minute. He understands that you can have a bad day, too. He likes it when you guys get along and don't fight, but fighting won't make his illness worse."

Smart Talk

In a 1997 study of HIV-infected hemophiliac men, 45 percent informed their children of their illness. The parents were more likely to disclose the information the older their children were or the more advanced their illness. Researchers were interested in the impact of the disclosure on the children. Results showed that the most important factor was the overall quality of the parent-child relationship, not the disclosure (or lack of disclosure) per se. The better the relationship quality, the less depression or behavioral problems and the better the school performance after the disclosure of HIV illness.

How Not to Say It

- "Will you two stop fighting? Don't you want Daddy to get better?" Don't make them feel guilty for something they have no control over. Consider the possibility that they may be fighting out of worry for their father. Talking with your kids more about how they feel about a parent's illness may do more to reduce sibling arguments.

- "Since you are the oldest child, I expect you to make sure things run smoothly in the house while Mommy is in the hospital" or "You're the man of the house while Daddy is in the hospital." Children can have more chores, but they should not be given authority (in fact, siblings may not recognize that authority). Children need to believe that parents are still in charge. "Helping out" a parent is not the same as shouldering responsibility.

- "Mom could get worse, or she could get better. We just don't know." Don't let children worry unnecessarily. It is better to remain optimistic and remind the kids what is being done to make a parent feel better. "The treatment is continuing, and some days Mom feels a lot better. We don't know when Mom will be completely well."

- "I can't take this much longer . . ." You may have many days that can be overwhelming. You don't have to pretend you are coping well when you are struggling, but you don't have to suggest to your kids that you may fall apart completely. If you need professional help or an occasional visit with friends, do that. When feeling overwhelmed, tell your kids, "Some days it's harder for me to deal with Mommy's illness. I'll be fine in a while."

- "Can't you see I'm not feeling well and can't play that game with you?" Your kids may not be able to tell whether or not you are in the mood for games. Don't discourage them. It is better to say, "Gee, I'd love to play, but I'm not up to it now. But please ask me later."

51

Money and Allowance

Twelve-year-old Paulo greatly wanted an electric guitar and amplifier. His friend's older brother offered to sell him a used guitar and amp for $400. The agreement was that Paulo could take possession of the items, but he'd have to pay $40 a week for ten weeks. All the adults agreed. The problem was that Paulo needed to earn some of the money. His parents did not allow him to take it from his college savings. So Paulo knocked on neighbors' doors and tried to earn the money mowing lawns, raking leaves, and cleaning up garages.

The first three weeks he averaged only $30. He was underpaying his friend's brother and had to make it up the following weeks. By week seven Paulo decided the guitar wasn't worth the money after all. He was allowed to drop the deal and receive back one-half of the money he had paid. The rest was considered a rental fee for the time he had used the musical equipment. Paulo learned a valuable lesson.

Things to Consider

➢ Children need to learn the value of money and that many items must be earned.

➢ Allowances are fine as long as children are expected to do some chores for free since they have a responsibility to the family. Children should be expected to save a portion of money they earn.

➢ Talking to kids about the value of money is not the same as having them understand the meaning by paying for some things themselves.

➢ Many opportunities exist to teach kids about money such as looking for sale items, not buying something you would like because it is too expensive, or having kids earn lunch money they lost.

➤ When possible, don't agree to buy your child something on the condition he pays it back later. It is better for him to earn and pay his share ahead of time and then purchase the item.

➤ Are you over your budget? Do you pay bills on time? Do you and your spouse argue about spending? If so, you will have a more difficult time teaching your kids the proper way to deal with finances.

How to Say It

- **TEACH** about the high cost of items without criticizing your child for asking for things. "You want this new brand of sneakers because lots of kids have them? I'm sure it would make you feel good to have them, but we just bought you a new pair last month. Sneakers are too expensive. After you outgrow your current pair, we can discuss what kind to get you next."

- **DO'S & DON'TS.** "It costs too much. We can't go to Walt Disney World next year."

- "I know it's your money that you received for your birthday, but you still cannot spend it to get a tattoo." Don't hesitate to say no when your values are at stake. It is your duty as a parent.

- **NEGOTIATE.** This is a perfect issue on which to make a deal with your child. How much responsibility is he willing to take on? "You want me to help pay for your trick bike when you have a perfectly good twelve-speed in the garage. You will need to earn at least two hundred dollars. What ideas do you have to achieve that?"

- "If I buy you the item on credit and you don't do your chores or don't pay me money on time, what should I do?" Get your child's opinion on the consequences of failing to do his part in the deal. If reasonable, go along with his ideas.

- **EMPATHIZE** when the answer is no. "I'm sure you're disappointed. I know it would mean a lot to have that pair of designer jeans."

- **ENCOURAGE** and praise frugal or responsible handling of money. "You had to carry your lunch money, and you didn't lose it. Good job."

- "You are doing the extra work just as you promised you would. That shows me you can be counted on to do what you say you will do."

- "When I said we couldn't buy those skates for you, you didn't complain even though you were disappointed. That meant a lot to me."

- "Your father is late paying his support payments. As soon as he pays me, I can buy this for you." It is okay to tell your child that something is not affordable because of late support payments if that is the truth and you are not at fault. (Were payments late because you were being difficult and unfair on some other issue? Then don't paint your ex as the bad guy. It is better to say that you and your ex disagree about some things, and until you work it out, the support may be delayed.) Be cautious. If the father has been mostly reliable, don't plant the seeds of animosity in your child until you know the whole story.

How Not to Say It

- "Why do you think you can get whatever you want? Isn't it time you started thinking about others?" Trying to teach your child by criticizing him is not a good idea. He'll more likely remember your criticism than the underlying lesson.

- "When I was a kid, I had to earn everything I ever got. You kids today are spoiled." You are in charge. If you want your child to earn more of what she receives, then develop a strategy and implement it. Don't criticize your child for expecting to be given everything on a platter if that is what you have taught her over the years.

- "Okay, I'll buy you this. But I expect you to help out a lot more at home than you have been. And get those grades up, too." What does "help out" mean exactly? Be very specific on what you expect. Also, it's a better idea to have your child "help out" prior to your buying the item whenever possible. "I really think you need to do more work around the house before I spend the money on this CD. It is expensive, and I do need the help. If you will help me pick up your baby brother's toys before going to bed every night, and put all dishes in the dishwasher, we can come back in two weeks and buy this."

- "I know this is expensive, but I really want it. Don't tell your father." Don't put your child in a position where to feel loyal to you she must feel disloyal to her other parent.

52

Money:
Finances Are Tight/
Explaining Loss of Job

"I wasn't laid off," Bob said. "I was downsized. Somehow that word doesn't make it any easier."

That was the beginning of Bob's financial problems. Without a paycheck he had to pay extra for medical insurance since his company no longer provided that for him. Mortgage and car payments ate up his savings within six months. Job prospects he had counted on simply fizzled. But he wanted his children insulated from anxiety.

Things to Consider

➤ When parents can no longer afford certain extra things for their children such as dance lessons or the latest video game, they can be more upset than their children. Kids can handle such setbacks, and it can be beneficial for them to realize that the family can survive belt-tightening.

➤ Men in particular view their primary role as a provider. Out of work they can feel inadequate. Now is the time to enhance the quality and quantity of time spent with the kids. Once back at work you won't have the same opportunity.

➤ Make cutting back on expenses a fun and challenging family project instead of a frustrating experience. Kids can rise to the occasion and be willing to make sacrifices. Let them feel they are doing their part.

How to Say It

- **REPORT** the essential facts. "I was laid off at work. They no longer can afford to pay me, so until I find another job, we have to come up with ways to save money."

- **REPORT** some of your concerns but remain optimistic. "It doesn't come at a good time, and I worry about finding a job that will pay well. But I believe I eventually will find a job, and we'll get back to normal."

- **TEACH** being frugal. "It would help a lot if when we buy things we ask ourselves these questions: Can we get by without it for now? Can we find it at a cheaper price?"

- Explain what the implications are for the foreseeable future. "We will probably postpone our next vacation. Maybe instead we'll take more day trips. We'll have to cut back on gifts, too."

- **ENCOURAGE** creative ways to have family fun. "Yes, we'll have to forget about eating out for a while. Even fast food is expensive. What ways can we have more fun at mealtime?"

- Praise helpful attitudes and behavior. "I overheard you tell your brother that we should not go to the movies but wait until the movie comes out in video. That was a great idea on saving money. It must make you feel good knowing you can be patient."

- **EMPATHIZE** when children desire things they can't have because of finances. "I know it was hard when most of the other kids bought their food during the class trip while you had to pack a lunch."

- Reassure an overly concerned child. "I notice you yell at your brother when he wants to buy things we can't afford. You seem extra worried. Dad and I know what we can and cannot afford. Eventually we'll have more money, so you don't have to feel responsible for your brother."

- Reassure a child if you suspect she blames herself for the financial problems. "It is absolutely not your fault that we have less money to spend. In fact, I'd give up all the money in the world if I had to just to keep you. We don't have money because I lost my job. I hope to get another one soon."

How Not to Say It

- "We could lose the house. Is that what you want to happen?" Don't make the kids feel responsible if you have to sell a house or car. Children who cooperate with being frugal still *want* more things. That's to be expected. Praise them for their help and reassure them that the family will survive even if you have to move.

- "If Dad doesn't find the right job, we'll have to sell the house and move into an apartment." Children don't need to worry about that possibility. They can be told if it seems likely that such a thing will happen, but not before.

- "No, you can't have that cereal. It's a name brand, and it's too expensive. How many times do I have to tell you that!" Actually, if you're doing your job right, some younger children may forget that the family is in a financial squeeze. Gentle reminders and a little empathy will achieve your goal. "I wish we could buy that cereal. I know you like it. But see the price? It costs two dollars more than this brand. We have to save money."

53

Moving

"South Dakota?" asked eleven-year-old Scott. "Who do we know who lives in South Dakota?"

"We don't know anybody yet," his mother said. "But that's where my job offer came from and it's too good to pass up. You know I've tried for over a year to find a job nearby so we wouldn't have to move."

"I'm not going," Scott said.

"Scott—"

"I'm not going!"

Millions of children move every year to a new home, often to a new town or state. That means leaving behind friends, classmates, and the familiar neighborhood and venturing toward the unknown. For some kids it's an exciting adventure; for others it's an adventure laced with bittersweet feelings. A few kids are miserable, but they adjust.

Things to Consider

➤ The older the child, the more likely you will meet with resistance. Preteens are forming strong bonds with friends and may be unhappy about leaving them behind.

➤ Children who cope the best during difficult transitions tend to be more self-confident and have a close, supportive family. The adjustment will be longer if a family relocates because of a divorce, if a child is not close to a parent, or if a child feels insecure.

➤ Let the children be as involved in the house hunting as possible. Their excitement may increase when they see a large backyard or a driveway big enough to play hockey.

➤ What is your attitude toward the move? If you are reluctant or over-anxious, your children will have a harder time adjusting.

How to Say It

- Unless your children really do have a say in the decision to move, it's best to state that the move will happen instead of suggesting that it might happen. They will want to know why. "Mom and I decided we need a bigger house, and we'd like to live closer to my job. We're going to start looking soon. What kind of house would you like?"

- "My company is transferring me. We have to move to another state. Dad and I decided it is best for the family if I stay with my company."

- **EMPATHIZE** without trying to persuade your child to go along with the decision. If the kids have no choice but to go along with the decision, at least help them to know you understand their feelings. "You're telling me you don't like the idea of moving. Moving can be upsetting to some people. What don't you like about it?"

- "You're going to miss your friends. I can understand that. It's sad to leave friends behind. I'll miss my friends, too."

- "This is the only house you've known. I can see why you want to stay. I have many happy memories here."

- **NEGOTIATE**—not as a means of cajoling your children into liking the decision to move (they may not like it for a long while) but to give them some choices at a time when they are feeling powerless. "Do you want your own bedroom or bathroom? Does it matter if we have a swimming pool or not? Put your ideas together and Mom and I will see what we can do to make that happen. Of course, we may not be able to afford everything, but we'll do our best."

- **ENCOURAGE**. Remind them of past times when they adjusted to new things. "I remember when you graduated from fifth grade and went to a middle school. There were many new kids and teachers you didn't know, and you weren't very happy. But then you started to get used to it and now it feels comfortable."

- State what you are looking forward to. "The area we will be moving to is so pretty. I can't wait to see the mountains from our kitchen window."

- After you've empathized, it's okay to start making suggestions as to how the kids will adjust better. "We can look for a school that has a good drama club. I know that means a lot to you."

- Expect to repeat yourself if the kids are reluctant to move. They may ask "why" many times and try to talk you out of your decision. After you've given them an explanation two or three times, any more attempts to explain won't help. It is better to empathize and let them know that the decision is final. "You keep asking me why we have to move, so I know you really don't like the idea. It is a big change and will take some adjusting, but we will move. I know I can't say anything now to make you feel better."

How Not to Say It

- "I know you're upset but the new place will be wonderful!" You've made two mistakes. First, telling a child that you know he is upset and then rushing to change feelings is not empathy. Your child may not believe you really do understand how he feels. It is better to have your child talk more about why he is upset. Second, be careful about over-sell. Is the place really wonderful? Emphasize the good points without overdoing it.

- "Look, I don't like this any more than you do, but we have no choice." If you can't find a way to be optimistic, don't expect your children to be. If you are unhappy, it is better to say, "I know exactly how you feel. I wish I didn't get transferred, either. But I know I will get used to it, and I know I will be happy there eventually."

- "We've been in the new house for a month and you're still moping around. I don't think you're even trying to like this place." Moping is just another way of complaining. Two things can help. First, putting him in touch with old friends by phone or e-mail (or even a visit to the old neighborhood, if feasible) can be a big mood lifter. Second, give him permission to mope. "I know you are still sad and frustrated that we had to move. It's okay if you want to walk around in a grumpy mood. I understand."

Making just one new friend and discovering that ties to old friends or classmates do not have to be completely severed will start to make moods improve.

54

Nagging

"I don't nag," Madge said. "I mean, I try not to. It usually starts out as a gentle reminder like 'Jason, sweetheart, don't forget your trombone. You have band practice today.' Then something happens. I repeat myself, and when Jason doesn't seem to be paying close attention, I speak louder and spread out my vowels like some opera singer. *'Jaaaayyy-suuhn!'* Before I realize it, my eyes scrunch and my lower lip curls, and the next thing you know I'm a creature from a Steven King novel—all because of a trombone. Is there a cure?"

Nagging is an outgrowth of a parent's natural tendency to repeat him- or herself because of a child's natural tendency to ignore anything that doesn't have to do with eating, playing, or video games. It is also illusory. Nagging gives parents the impression that they are doing something important, but in reality they are accomplishing very little. (Sort of like being vice president of the country.)

Things to Consider

➢ Under stress, parents nag more. Nagging may be frustration toward another that is being displaced onto a child.

➢ If affection and quality time with a spouse is less than it should be, parents may nag more.

➢ Someone who frequently nags has underlying feelings of being less in control of their life than they should be.

➢ Is your spouse also guilty of what you nag your children about? (For example, do you nag your kids to pick up their clothes, and do so loud enough so your sloppy spouse overhears?) If so, you'd do better to work things out with your mate first.

How to Say It

- **DO'S & DON'TS.** Make your kids an offer they can't refuse. Tell them what you want done and when, and (most important) tell them what the consequences will be if they don't comply. Be calm and cool.

> "Your trombone is next to your book bag. Please remember to take it. But if you forget again, you'll have to do without it today. I won't bring it to school for you."

> "You can snack while watching television in the family room, but if I have to pick up the leftovers again when your show is over, you will eat only at the dining room table for the next two days. Thanks."

> "Wake up. This is your last warning. If you miss the bus, you'll have to pay me the cost of gas for the mileage. Now what can I get you for breakfast?"

> "I've been asking you to get your dirty clothes together so I can do laundry. At the commercial I'm turning off the TV, and I won't turn it back on until you get your clothes. Thanks. Any questions?"

As you can see, the tone is not forceful or accusatory. When you are willing to apply consequences, then you don't have to nag. Let the consequences motivate your child, not your voice's decibel level.

- Praise compliance. "I asked you to set the table, and you did it right away. What a help you are."

How Not to Say It

- "How many times do I have to tell you . . ." That's nagging. It isn't necessary if you calmly apply consequences when the kids don't comply. However, you must be willing to let certain consequences happen. Will you allow your child to get a lower grade if he hands in homework late? (Or would you rather nag at him to get it in on time?)
- "If you had put your clothes in the hamper instead of on the floor, then your favorite shirt would be washed now and you could wear it. I tried to warn you." Let the natural consequences (in this case, no clean shirt to wear) do most of the speaking for you. There is no need to rub it in. It is better to say, "I wish you had a clean shirt to wear, too. If you want to try washing it now, you can."

- "After all I do for you kids, you can't even tidy up when I ask you." Your sentiment is understandable, but your words won't have anything but a short-term effect. Kids who delay following orders have learned that they can get away with it.

Smart Talk

In a study at Ohio State University of children in sixth, eighth, and tenth grades, parents and their kids were asked how frequently the children complied with helping tasks and how often they showed affection. The results showed that preteens and adolescents responded more positively when they felt more supported and connected to their parents. Girls were more helpful and affectionate than boys, and kids complied with moms more than dads. The better the connection to your kids, the less you will have to nag.

55

New Baby

Carol explained to the pediatrician how her six-year-old son, Tyler, seemed to whine for attention whenever she was feeding the new baby.

"I hope he gets over it," Carol said.

The pediatrician smiled. "Did Tyler ever try to get your attention when you were sitting and talking on the phone or with company?"

"Oh, sure," Carol said.

"So it isn't just the new baby. Tyler simply wants Mommy. It's pretty normal for children to feel that way, at least once in a while."

And so it is. Jealousy isn't fatal and it often is less of a problem for older children. Still, even when kids can't wait for the new baby brother or sister, there will be moments when they wished the stork plopped the bundle of joy somewhere else.

Things to Consider

➤ Older children may show their frustration at having less time with busy new parents by either withdrawing or acting passive-aggressively. They may get sloppier, more forgetful, or less reliable, thereby forcing parents to pay more attention to them.

➤ Having older children care for the baby (a nine-year-old can change diapers and assist with baths, for example) can help them bond—*if* the chore does not disgust them. Younger kids will want to help out but obviously require supervision.

➤ Children automatically seem older and more mature compared to an infant. But they are still kids, not mini-adults.

➤ In a blended family, a new baby can often unite the stepsiblings. They now have something in common—a little brother or sister who is genetically connected to them.

➤ In a blended family, a new baby might compel kids to give up their hopes of a parental reunion. A recent study showed that fathers who remarry pull away from their children from their first marriage if their new wife gives birth. Men seem to devote time to the "stable" family, but not the previous family. Don't let that happen.

➤ Some fathers worry more about finances after a baby arrives, and they spend more hours working. Now their older children see even less of their father, plus they have to share him with the newborn. Dads need to remember that their true worth is not their presents but their presence.

➤ Whenever appropriate, let the children be involved during the pregnancy; let them watch the sonogram, pick out supplies, etc.

How to Say It

- Older kids can be told as soon as a pregnancy becomes obvious. Enthusiasm and a willingness to let your children's feelings matter are the key attitudes. "Yes, we are having a new baby. I'm very excited. The baby should be born in March."

- **TEACH** how to handle frustrations by pretending the baby is already there. "Okay, Lynn, you pretend you are the baby, and Richie, you be yourself. Richie, make believe you are upset that I am spending all my time with Lynn. What can you say to me?"

- Praise your child for speaking up instead of acting out. "I like it when you tell me to spend more time with you. Then we can figure out a way to make it happen."

- Praise age-appropriate behavior. "You had to wait patiently before I could drive you to the game because the baby needed to be changed again. That's so helpful."

- **ENCOURAGE** speaking up by making sure it is rewarded with your time whenever possible. Otherwise, your child will learn that the surest way to get your attention is to act up. "I have about five minutes left to feed the baby. Then I'll put her down for a nap. What would you like to do together then?"

- **EMPATHIZE** when you cannot give your child the attention he wants. "I promised I'd be finished in five minutes, but the baby is cranky and won't sleep. That must be annoying to you."

- "Some older kids worry that their parents love the new baby more than they love them. Do you ever feel that way?"

- **NEGOTIATE.** "I've been so busy with the baby. What things could we do together that would make you feel better?"

- **DO'S & DON'TS.** Explain that babies require three basic things and that you must provide them. "Babies need ABC. A is for affection. Babies need to be held a lot. Otherwise, they can feel scared or get sick. B is for bottle. When a baby is hungry, he needs to be fed. He's not as capable as you are to wait for food. C is for change diapers. They need their diapers changed a lot because they can't use the toilet like you. Most of my time with the baby is spent doing those three things."

- Discuss the benefits of being an older child. "You're lucky. When you feel hungry, you can eat an apple or make a bowl of cereal. The baby has to wait for me to feed him."

How Not to Say It

- "You will love having a new baby brother. . . . I'm sure you'll be the best older sister around." That sounds nice, but it's better to let your child convey her own feelings instead of your presuming what they are.

- "You don't need all my attention; you just think you do." If he thinks he needs it, he needs it. Resist the temptation to view your older child as being more mature than he is.

- "You shouldn't say that about your baby sister!" If your child doesn't express his feelings, he will act them out. Do you have a preference? Criticizing a child for how he feels will make him feel even less important to you, and he will resent the baby even more. Empathize. "Calling your sister ugly makes me think you feel sad about something. Maybe you feel we love her more than we love you."

- "Act your age!" Actually, since regression is normal, your child is acting his age. He believes that if you act younger, you get more love and attention, and if you act your age, you get less. Once again, **EMPATHIZE** first, and then find ways to reward him for age-appropriate behavior. I know you're tired, but the best reward is your time.

Rule of Thumb: When a couple with stepchildren decides to have a baby, anxieties can be even higher. Parents may fear they will love the baby more than their stepchildren, and the stepchildren will fear the same thing. It is a good idea to announce the event privately to your biological child. That way, your child may feel more able to open up without feeling too self-conscious.

56

New Stepsibling

Put yourself in your child's shoes. First came the divorce. If your child was like most kids, he wasn't happy about it. Second was the parent's new girl-friend or boyfriend. That might be exciting or distressing, it all depends. Next came the announcement: "I'm getting remarried. Sally's two little boys will be living with me, so when you visit, you'll have two new friends."

When a divorce happens, kids lose control and consistency in their life. They had no control over the separation and no control over the new mate. But when it comes to the new stepsibling, it's a new ball game. It can be easier to fight against a stepsib than to fight the adults.

Things to Consider

➤ If you live with your stepchildren but see your biological children only on a scheduled basis, expect that your biological kids may feel jealous.

➤ Stepkids can easily displace bad feelings onto one another. They might also connect in a common bond.

How to Say It

- Discuss the upcoming first meeting ahead of time. Maybe show photos or have the kids write each other a letter of introduction. The more unknowns, the higher the anxiety. "His name is Matt. He's two years older than you and likes to play hockey. His father says he is a nice boy and easy to get along with. Here's his picture. Tell me your thoughts about meeting him."

- **EMPATHIZE** and accept the feelings. "You seem worried that you two might not get along" or "You worry that you are outnumbered and that they won't like you" or "You seem excited that Freddie trades baseball cards, too" or "You seem concerned that when you visit me, you'll be expected to spend more time with the kids than with me."

- **REPORT** your expectations. "I don't expect you and Megan to become best friends, though I hope you learn to really like each other. I do expect you guys to try to get along, just like you would with classmates."

- "Since Charlie is my new stepson, his mom and I agreed that if he misbehaves, she will be the disciplinarian. And I will discipline you. So if it looks as if I'm harder on you than on Charlie, I'm just doing what I agreed to do. What are your thoughts?"

- **ENCOURAGE** and praise cooperative behavior. "We all had a nice day together. It was especially nice watching you and your stepbrother get along so well. I give you a lot of credit."

How Not to Say It

- "How do you think it makes your stepmother feel when you fight with your stepsister?" Empathy training is a good idea but might best be saved for after you hear your child's concerns. Also, be sure your child really likes the stepparent; otherwise, he may not be interested in how she feels.

- "You guys have a lot in common. I'm sure you'll get along." Pointing out similarities is fine, but don't presume they will get along. Instead, leave room for the relationship to grow. It's better to say, "You guys have a lot in common. That might make your time together more enjoyable."

- "Your stepbrother obeyed us on the trip. Why couldn't you do that?" Don't make comparisons.

- "Of course you have to share your room. What else do you expect us to do?" Room sharing may be necessary. Don't add unnecessary resentment by failing to **EMPATHIZE** while you are being clear about the **DO'S & DON'TS**. "Yes, you will have to share a room. There is no other way. It's obvious you don't like that idea and I don't blame you. You can choose where you want the beds to go."

- "We're a bigger family now, and we'll do things together as a family." Carve out some time alone with your biological child.

57

Increasing Optimism

Jared and Kenny looked forward to receiving their new musical instruments for school band. They had each carefully considered which instrument they thought would be fun to play, and now they had arrived. Kenny chose the violin; Jared, the saxophone. Three weeks later Kenny was dutifully practicing his instrument, but Jared had all but given up.

"It's too hard," he complained.

"But you haven't tried for very long," his mother said. "It takes time."

"I did try, but when I blow into it, the sound that comes out isn't the right one. It doesn't even sound like a saxophone."

Mom was able to get Jared to practice that day, but his interest was not there. Maybe the saxophone wasn't the right instrument for him. Maybe she was expecting too much. Or maybe there was something else at the root of the problem. Come to think of it, Jared had a "why bother?" attitude about many things.

Things to Consider

➤ Optimism or a positive outlook in life requires a person to believe that resources are available to make things turn out okay. Resources may be within oneself (such as talent and motivation), or they may originate from outside (such as believing that parents or caretakers or God are looking out for you).

➤ Optimistic kids view themselves as capable and the world as reasonably safe. Thus, if they fail a test or if a friend betrays them, the setback is temporary. They believe they are still worthwhile and competent even if events turn out poorly.

➤ Optimists persevere. Pessimists quit at the early signs of difficulty because they haven't the faith in their effort. Quitting then results in failure that perpetuates the pessimistic outlook.

➤ Shy or highly active children may be more prone to pessimistic thinking because they cannot act in their world as successfully as kids more outgoing and patient.

➤ Pessimism and optimism can be learned by watching Mom and Dad.

How to Say It

- The essential ingredient to an optimistic outlook is faith that effort will more often than not result in progress or success and that all problems or setbacks are temporary. **TEACH** by giving examples a child will understand. "Do you remember when I wallpapered your room? I had to learn as I went along. It was frustrating and I made a lot of mistakes, but when I wallpaper your sister's room, I'll know better what to do."

- "When you helped train Fritz to sit and roll over, it took him a while to learn. But we all kept at it, and eventually he did learn."

- "Remember I kept throwing you ground balls so you could improve your ability? At first I threw the ball slowly, then I threw it harder and harder as you got more skilled. Hard work and effort paid off."

- **EMPATHIZE** to be sure you understand the extent of your child's concerns, then **TEACH** problem solving. "You don't want to audition for the school play because you don't think you'll get a part. But you seem sad about that, as though you wish you could get a part. You're right that auditioning is tough because there are more kids than there are parts in the play. Let's try to think of three reasons that auditioning is valuable even if a person doesn't get a role."

- "Ever since your mom and I separated, it seems to you that only bad things will happen in the future. I know that the separation was something that made you sad. That's normal. But what are some things you can trust will happen that you look forward to?"

- Give examples of how all problems are temporary. "When Grandma died, it was very hard for Grandpa to live all by himself. Even though there was no way Grandma could come back, there were many ways we could help Grandpa. That is why he spends a lot more time visiting your cousins and us. He still misses Grandma, but he's not as lonely as he was."

- "When I was out of work, we had a hard time paying our bills. While my new job doesn't pay me as much money as before, we have learned how to get by on less. We solved our problem."
- **ENCOURAGE** persistence and optimism. "You worked so hard on that school science project. Every week you would get more and more accomplished, and now it is finished. You should feel very proud."
- "When you first tried the pogo stick, you couldn't do it well. Now you can stay on it for ten minutes! Wow!"

Smart Talk

Researchers studied fourth, fifth, and sixth graders who had experienced at least four major stresses since birth (such as poverty or divorce). Some seemed resilient, able to bounce back and cope effectively with daily life, while others seemed to struggle. A key difference was outlook. Optimistic thinkers reported feeling less stress overall and less depression, and they felt more competent. When outside stress was high, those kids with positive expectations about the future did not think of themselves in a negative light even when they faltered.

How Not to Say It

- "Cheer up!" Telling a child he should feel better when he clearly feels depressed or cynical won't help. He'll just think you don't understand. Positive phrases should be saved for after you have empathized and given examples of past successes or reasons for optimism.
- "You can do it!" This is fine for a child who already believes in herself and just needs a pep talk. But if your child shows signs of pessimism, it's better to understand first her reasons for thinking that way and then gently remind her of past successes she is overlooking. Pessimists have distorted thinking. They ignore positive evidence and hone in on evidence that supports their negative outlook. They have to be shown over and over that they can do it, not just be told.

- "You have a bad attitude. You don't see other kids quitting this soon, do you?" Your negativity is showing. It doesn't sound as if you have as much faith in your child. It is better to let her know that her attitude makes some sense but is not helpful. Remind her of past efforts that succeeded and let her know you have confidence in her ability to try hard.

- "Why do you have to be so negative? Can't you look at the bright side?" These questions are not helpful to kids. They may be unable to figure out why. Or if they can come up with reasons, you have just prodded them to defend their style of thinking, not change it.

58

Parental Emotional Problems: Depression, Fears, Compulsions

Tammy's mom has obsessive-compulsive disorder. Her fear of germs is so strong that she washes her hands forty or more times a day. Sometimes she won't attend Tammy's ball games for fear of contamination.

Lyle's dad is severely depressed. He has just returned to work after a six-week leave and is feeling better. Still, he gets little enjoyment from things, never horses around with the kids, and seems tired and unmotivated.

Hilary's mom gets panic attacks. She is so frightened of them that she has stopped driving for fear she will get into an accident while panicking. Hilary can't understand why her mom won't go places with her anymore.

Right now 15 percent to 20 percent of the population suffer from depression or an anxiety disorder. The good news is they can be treated. But until a person has made significant improvements, their emotional problems can be a strain on them and their family.

Things to Consider

➤ In most cases, the problem can go away. In some, the problem may persist but be manageable.

➤ Once aware that something isn't right, children need to be educated as to the nature of the problem and the effects it will have on their life. They need to be reminded that it is not their fault and that in all likelihood the situation will improve.

➤ These problems are not cured by willpower. People suffering from depression or severe anxiety wish they were not feeling that way.

➤ Provide as much consistency in your child's life as possible. Regular mealtimes, favorite TV shows, bedtime stories, etc., offer comfort and reassurance that all is basically the same.

How to Say It

- **TEACH**. Explain the disorder in simple terms. "Just as some people are afraid of spiders and get really scared, your mom gets really afraid of germs, so she washes her hands too much. She realizes she shouldn't feel that way, but right now she can't help it. She is seeing a doctor to help her get over this problem, though."

- "Severe depression is more than feeling sad. The person gets no pleasure from anything and begins to feel as if nothing will help. It can take a few months sometimes to improve, but medications help a lot."

- Establish a plan of how the family will contend with the problem. "If your dad had a broken leg instead of depression, we wouldn't expect him to do all the things he usually does. Until he feels better, I'll need a little more help around the house. Is there some chore you'd be willing to do?"

- Reassure the child that matters will improve and she is not at fault. "Dad is not depressed because he's tired of being a father. His depression has nothing to do with you. There is a chemical in his body that he needs more of to feel better. The medicine is helping with that. He will definitely feel better. It just takes a little time."

- "You are not bothering Mommy with your problems. She wants to do things for you. She just can't right now. It's okay to ask her for things, but understand she may have to say no sometimes."

- Forewarn kids to upcoming changes in their routine. If they know what to expect, they have time to prepare. "Dad will be seeing a doctor called a therapist who will help Dad with his problem. In fact, we will all go together some times so we can all talk about what is happening and get our questions answered."

- **EMPATHIZE** with a child's feelings. Then offer **ENCOURAGEMENT**. "You worry that Mommy will never get better. A lot of kids might worry like that. But Mommy's problem is one that will get better."

- "You seem a little embarrassed when your friends come over and ask why your dad is not working. That's okay. It's no big deal to tell them he isn't feeling well but hopes to be better soon."

- "You're angry that we can't go on vacation this year because Mom isn't up to it. I'm disappointed, too. Can you help think of fun things we can do as a family when Mom feels better?"

Rule of Thumb: Talking matter-of-factly about the problem and how it might affect each person in the family will probably increase emotional closeness and overall family communication.

How Not to Say It

- "Nothing's wrong." If it is becoming obvious that something is wrong, tell the kids. Otherwise, they will be confused.

- "Stop doing that! Don't you understand your father's depressed?" If the kids are making a disturbance, a simple request to stop may suffice. If they persist, their behavior may be a sign of their own emotional insecurity about the parent's problem. If so, it is better to take them aside and inquire how they are feeling about the situation.

- "If you kids would stop fighting, maybe your mother wouldn't be under so much stress." Don't suggest that your children are in any way to blame for the problem.

- "Sometimes I just want to scream!" You're entitled to feel overwhelmed, but showing that to your kids will make them more anxious and perhaps afraid to speak up about their own concerns. If you say or do something you regret, let the kids know you made a mistake. "When I said 'I want to scream!' I guess I was feeling frustrated that things aren't better yet. But the truth is we have a lot to be thankful for despite the problem. Next time I'll try to simply say that I wish things were all better."

59

Parental Emotional Problems: Addictions and Bad Temper

Krysta couldn't think of a good enough excuse to prevent her neighbor and classmate Amy from coming to her house after school.

"I just want to stay fifteen minutes," Amy said. "My mom isn't home yet."

Krysta's heart started to pound. What if her father was drunk? His car was in the driveway. She imagined him sitting in front of the TV with a drink in his hand, swearing at the sports commentator. She arrived at the front door, took a deep breath, and opened it. . . .

While addictions and even severe problems with one's temper are listed as actual disorders, they tend to be problems that the person denies he has. Or else he admits to the problem but minimizes its negative impact and tends to blame others for making it necessary for him to do those things. Unlike disorders such as depression or phobias, an addict or a "rage-aholic" often will not seek treatment, so it is hard for family members to remain supportive and optimistic that the situation will improve. What do you say to a child whose parent has a serious disorder such as alcoholism, drug addiction, or gambling but who refuses to get the kind of help needed?

Things to Consider

➤ If you are the nonaddicted parent, the effectiveness of anything you say to your kids will depend on the extent you feel helpless or angry. The more you must submit to your spouse's ways, the more hopeless you feel; or the more resentful you are, the more your communications will have a neutral effect at best. More likely you will say the wrong thing and add tension and misery to an already difficult situation.

➤ If your partner is not getting help, you must. Seek out a therapist or try organizations such as Al-Anon. They can give you a sense of influence over your life. You need to feel empowered, not helpless.

➤ Divorce or separation is scary and a sad outcome for any marriage that once had promise. If your partner refuses help, you must weigh the impact on your family of divorce versus remaining together. Since you cannot change your partner's behavior, you must decide what you can and will tolerate.

How to Say It

- **TEACH** about the disease/disorder. "Your mother has alcoholism. She cannot control her drinking. She gets drunk and is unable to care for us the way we want."

   "Your dad has a very quick temper. He doesn't like it when he loses his temper but he has a hard time controlling it."

   "Your father is addicted to gambling. He has a strong urge to gamble our money and he cannot control it. That is what you have heard us fighting about."

   "Addictions make people have mood swings. Some days your mom will feel happy and other days she'll be angry and miserable. It's not your fault on those days. You aren't making her feel bad, her addiction is."

- Give practical advice. "If your dad is drinking . . . [If we are arguing . . . , If Dad's temper is getting out of hand . . .], leave the room and go to a neighbor's house. Call before you come home to see if it's a good time. You should not have to put up with this behavior."

- **EMPATHIZE**. This is essential not just for your child but for you. Empathy requires that you not deny a problem exists. Unfortunately, spouses of addicts often have their own level of denial. It can be easier to minimize a problem than face it. "It embarrasses you when you come from school with friends and your mother is asleep on the couch with beer bottles next to her. I don't blame you for feeling that way. It probably makes you feel sad, too."

   "It's scary listening to Mom and Dad fight all the time about gambling."

   "You worry that things will always stay this way."

   "Your father could get help, but he won't. Part of the disease is that he believes he doesn't have a problem. It's frustrating, isn't it?"

"Your father admitted he drinks too much, but he refuses to get help. That is his problem. I know you worry about him when he drives a car."

- Some children will try to be perfect and well behaved when they live in a dysfunctional family. They do this so as not to add more stress to an overstressed situation. However, don't mistake their good behavior (high grades in school, never in trouble, overly responsible) for healthy adjustment. They are hurting inside but won't let others know. "You are doing so well in school despite our problems. Sometimes I think you are sad inside but don't want to talk about it."

- Don't play into denial by making the problem a secret to outsiders. "You feel embarrassed that Mom gambles. It's okay to tell your friends about it. Your friends might find ways to help you feel better."

- Clarify expectations. "If your father won't get help by next week, I have plans for us to get a separation. I will not allow things to continue the way they have been."

- "Your dad's temper is too much for me. I'll be speaking to a therapist—a doctor who will help me decide what I can do to help you and me handle the situation better."

- **ENCOURAGE** normal, healthy activities. Praise when appropriate. Kids with addicted parents often suffer poor esteem. "I want you to take swimming lessons. I know you love swimming and are so good. I'm proud of what you've accomplished."

- **ENCOURAGE** talking to you about their worries. "Dad won't listen to your concerns. I'm sorry. I wish he would, but he can't. However, I can listen and will do my best to help you and me get through these hard times."

- As much as possible, smile, laugh, and have fun with your kids. They need the relief.

How Not to Say It

- "The person with the problem is your mother. Maybe if you talk to her, she will take her problems seriously." Children should not bear that responsibility. If the addicted parent or the one with the bad temper is not getting needed help, the other parent must take steps to protect the kids even if that means separating.

- "If we are all patient, things will improve someday." Don't kid yourself. Until the addict wants help, it won't occur. Your patience may show him that his intolerable behavior is tolerable. It is better to say the truth: "There is nothing we can do to solve Daddy's problem. We can be patient and loving and we can complain, but nothing we do will help. Only Daddy can get help when he decides."

- "Maybe I'll get a divorce." A divorce may be the natural consequence, but it is best to tell a child when you are pretty sure it will happen and happen soon. Don't leave your child hanging.

- "Don't complain about your father. How many times have I told you that I can't do anything about his problem?" You are angry with your child because her comments are revealing your own helplessness. A child who stops complaining isn't showing healthy adaptation. Your child may be going numb or learning that her feelings don't matter to either of her parents. Then you can expect acting out (mischief, petty crimes, poor school performance) or acting in (depression, self-criticism). At all times keep the lines of communication open even if you've heard the concerns before.

- "If she really loved you, she'd get the help she needs." It is only after they have been sober a while that addicts realize how hurtful their behaviors have been.

- "Your father loves you very, very much." If the addicted parent is not showing much love, don't try to persuade a child he is loved very much. It is too confusing. It is better to say that your child deserves to be shown love because he is a good and wonderful child.

- "How dare you tell the teacher!" Stop the secrecy. Outsiders need to know, especially a child's teachers. If they know what is happening at home, they can try to intervene so your child will have additional emotional support.

Rule of Thumb: Healthy adaptation to an addicted parent is not one of accommodation. Patience and understanding are necessary but not tolerating the status quo. Well-meaning spouses "enable" pathological behavior by tolerating it over time. By not tolerating the behavior, the person will get the help he or she needs, or the family may need to break up.

60

Peer Pressure

Craig attended seventh grade in a parochial school where uniforms were required. The children were allowed to wear shorts as part of their uniform until November. In late October, despite morning temperatures that were at freezing, Craig waited at the bus stop wearing shorts. Why? "Because most of the other kids are still wearing them," he said.

Ellen was in Craig's class. She is one of the 19 percent of seventh-grade students who admit to having engaged in sexual intercourse at least one time (according to a 1992 survey of students in Cedar Rapids, Iowa).

Anthony, age eleven, wants an earring, bleached blond hair, and a colorful underwear waistband that peeks out over his baggy pants—just like his new friend, Rich.

The influence of peers on growing children's attitudes and actions cannot be overlooked.

Things to Consider

➢ Preteens and adolescents improve their self-image by conforming to some peer group standards. With luck, those standards aren't so outrageous that parents will faint.

➢ At the same time, kids need to carve out a unique sense of themselves. Going along with new fads and trends is really a young adolescent's way of discovering who he is and new facets of his personality. It helps when parents don't overreact.

➢ Don't underestimate the impact of your values on your developing child. The majority of older kids and teens want to come to their parents to discuss problems and issues. Your opinions and values do count. (It just won't seem like it.)

➤ The goal is to help your child be confident enough to do what is right despite what his peers are doing.

➤ Do you cave into peer pressure because you want to be accepted by a group or don't want to displease others? Do you sometimes do things you shouldn't (speed, eat the wrong foods, swear in front of your kids while talking to friends, etc.) and comment that it's not a big deal because most people do it?

How to Say It

- **TEACH** about peer pressure but don't lecture. Examples from your life might be more interesting and useful. "A bunch of my friends had this pack of cigarettes and started smoking. They wanted me to try. I did take a puff, but I felt funny doing something I knew I shouldn't, so I stopped there. My friends teased me for a while, but then they stopped."

- "It's easy to go along with a crowd. The harder thing is to do what's right even when everyone else says it's okay to do what is wrong."

- **TEACH** ways to say no. "When your friends want you to do something you know is wrong, tell them 'I don't want to' or 'That has no interest to me,' and then walk away."

- **EMPATHIZE** with the need to feel like part of the crowd. "Everyone wants to feel accepted by a group of friends. It can feel awful when it seems as though you don't fit in."

- "Kids who say no to their friends and are able to resist pressure to do bad things feel a little unsure of themselves at first. But eventually they realize they are doing the right thing."

- **DO'S & DON'TS.** Now is the time to make clear to your children what you want or don't want them to do. The dilemma is how to state your view in a way that won't cause them to refuse to discuss the issue later on. You always want them to come to you with their concerns. "I'd be failing my job as a parent if I gave you the impression that drinking is okay. It is not. You are too young. But I'd also be failing my job as a parent if I made you feel afraid to talk to me when you feel pressured to follow the crowd."

- **ENCOURAGE** independent thinking. "In situations where friends are pressuring you, ask yourself: Is it illegal? Is it dishonest? Is it mean? Then decide for yourself whether you want to be someone who does those things."

How Not to Say It

- "I don't like the looks of your friend." Your growing child may not respect your making snap judgments on appearances only. Have the friend over and get to know her. You'll have more information to support or disprove your original view.
- "Why do you have to do things just because everyone else does?" You are coming dangerously close to repeating what parents of every generation have said: "If your friend jumped off a bridge, would you jump in after him?" What you want to do is get your child to realize he can be an independent thinker without alienating him. Questions like the above are accusatory and off-putting. Say something empathic like "It seems important to you to do exactly what others in your class are doing." You are planting a seed and opening the door for more communication later.
- "Don't you have a mind of your own?" Besides being harsh and critical, this comment is paradoxical. What you are really saying is "If you do what I want you to do, then you have a mind of your own. If you do what your friends want, you don't have a mind of your own."
- "Someone at your school got suspended for smoking pot? Good. Don't ever let me catch you smoking pot, or you'll never forget it." It is essential to be clear about your values, but you also want to be approachable.

61

Perfectionism

Sandy sat at the dining room table in tears. She'd been drawing a picture to give to her grandmother, and she made a small mistake. "It's no good," she cried. "I have to do it over again."

Sandy also had a nervous stomach. While she was a straight-A student, school made her uneasy because she always worried she might not get a high score on any of her tests. School projects often became a nightmare for her. She'd redo them until she felt they were perfect, but that meant she was still at work on them the night before they were due.

Things to Consider

➤ Perfectionistic kids (and adults) tend to be worriers. They worry about things that could go wrong, they worry about failure, and they worry about their parents. They look at negative possibilities and turn them into likely probabilities.

➤ Perfectionism is a misguided way to control anxiety and worry. A perfectionist tries to make his life perfect as a way to feel good.

➤ Perfectionists tend to be self-critical. Since they are imperfect and make mistakes, they judge themselves harshly. Helping a child to be less of a perfectionist takes time. (Parents, don't be too hard on yourselves if your efforts don't bring quick changes.)

➤ Certain parenting styles can contribute to perfectionism in kids. Parents who are overly strict and who believe that children must prove themselves worthy of love can prompt some kids to become perfectionists.

➤ In dysfunctional families such as those where at least one parent is alcoholic, one of the children (often the eldest) tends to "grow up early" and take on added responsibilities. These children often try to keep the household peaceful. They try to be overly good and helpful, and can develop perfectionistic tendencies. They won't change unless the parental problems improve.

How to Say It

- **TEACH** a child to deal with uncertainties by thinking rationally. Have your child say aloud during tasks such reassuring comments as "I'd like to get a perfect score, but it isn't terrible if I don't," "It's okay to make mistakes; everybody does," "I can do my best without having to be perfect," and "My parents love me no matter what."

- Use this analogy: "You've heard of guard dogs that protect their owners by barking at everybody, even friendly people. The guard dog worries too much. The part of you that worries is like a guard dog that barks. We want to train that worry part of you to worry (bark) less."

- Since perfectionists tend to do tasks at the last minute, help your child structure his time so that certain school projects are completed early. Resist the temptation to let your child check and recheck his work. "Your science report is due in three weeks. Let's figure out a schedule that will help you finish your report in two weeks."

- Offer **ENCOURAGEMENT** by pointing out the many worries that don't come true. "You worry that Daddy will get hurt, but he comes home from work every day and isn't hurt." "You worry that we will be mad at you if you don't get an A. Guess what? We're not mad at you, and we want you to enjoy doing your work."

- Identify tasks your child does where she is not a perfectionist (certain games, playing with dolls, doing certain chores, etc.). Point out that your child probably enjoys those tasks. "I noticed you weren't trying to play with your toys perfectly. You just had fun. If you don't try to be perfect at school, you might enjoy studying more."

- **REPORT** times when you make mistakes, and show that you can have a positive attitude. "I forgot to pay a bill on time, and now I have to pay a late fee. I'm usually good about paying bills on time, but on this occasion I forgot. No big deal." (You may want to purposely make mistakes—spill something, forget something, etc.—so you can demonstrate an "it's no big deal" attitude.

How Not to Say It

- "I see you spelled three words wrong on your test." Praise the overall grade and don't focus on critical details.

- "Hurry up!" "I'm very disappointed in you." "You know better than that." These phrases inflame perfectionistic tendencies. Watch your language for any signs of urgency, sharp criticism, or fault-finding. It is better to praise desirable behaviors.

- "Damn! I took a wrong turn!" Don't criticize yourself for making common mistakes. Your child will overhear and learn the wrong message.

62

Perseverance

Lee's parents could tell that their son was not enjoying piano lessons. Getting him to practice was an ordeal. They discussed the idea of letting him quit. Why should they force him to do something he hated? On the other hand, they had purchased a piano and had paid for months of lessons. Shouldn't he do his best for the time being?

It is a truism that the most successful people have experienced many failures. They succeed because they persevere. People who give up when the going gets tough have a tendency to develop depression and poor self-confidence, which makes it more likely they will not persist when future tasks become challenging.

If you want your child to persevere, you must be willing to let her fail. Then you must show her how to cope with failure—not by withdrawing from the task but by learning from mistakes and pressing forward. Overprotective parents may try to shield their kids from failure and miss teaching them a valuable lesson. But pushy, ambitious parents won't help their child persevere, either. Such parents are overly critical and value outcome more than effort. Children of these parents learn to fear making mistakes and consequently accept fewer challenges. They play it safe so as to not risk failure and rejection, and never learn how to dust themselves off and persevere.

Things to Consider

➤ Overprotective parents operate from fear. To ensure safety they keep their children from taking appropriate risks or give them permission to give up.

➤ Overly ambitious parents also operate from fear. They fear inadequacy and overcompensate by pushing their kids (and often themselves). They confuse "cracking the whip" with encouragement.

➤ Kids give up trying because they know someone else will do it for them or because they believe they do not have what it takes to succeed. While practicing a skill (such as long division) can enhance perceived competence, a more important skill is coping with frustration and anxiety when things don't go as planned.

➤ Perfectionistic kids won't persevere unless they feel assured they will succeed. They need help learning to see the value of failure and making mistakes.

How to Say It

True self-esteem does not develop from glowing accolades. It emerges from knowing one is truly loved and from succeeding at challenging tasks. Parents first need to examine why a child is not persistent. A good strategy is to identify tasks where the child did persist and find out what made that task different from one where the child gave up.

- "I noticed you kept practicing your flute even when you made mistakes. But you gave up playing basketball. What made it easier for you to practice the flute?"

- **EMPATHIZE.** This is a good way to help your child uncover his reasons for wanting to give up. "You seem frustrated with math. I'm wondering if you don't like it because you don't understand it."

- **DO'S & DON'TS.** If you invested money in an activity that your child really wanted to participate in but now he's showing no interest, you can insist he follow through. "We just bought you a uniform and paid the Little League fee. Now after three games you want to quit. I'm sorry, but you need to play for at least another month. If you need help, I'll be very happy to spend time practicing with you." The goal is not to punish your child, but teach him that his decisions do have consequences and that you won't always bail him out.

- **TEACH** how you persist at tasks despite setbacks. Give examples of famous people. "Even your favorite baseball player strikes out. He gets a hit only one out of three times at bat. What would you think of your favorite player if he quit because he didn't like striking out?"

- **ENCOURAGE**. This is most important. When you see your child correct a mistake or stay with a task that is frustrating, praise him. "You reread the chapter in your history book when you didn't know the answer to the question. When you still couldn't find the answer you looked it up in the encyclopedia. I'm very pleased and impressed. You showed you would not give up even when the task got difficult."

- Praise emotional control. The more agitated a child gets, the less likely she will complete a difficult task. Kids who can learn to control their emotions will persevere. "I saw you get frustrated with your homework. Then you took a break and threw the ball around with the dog before you went back to your work. Good for you. That was very smart to realize you needed a few minutes to enjoy yourself."

How Not to Say It

- "You promised you'd practice the piano if we bought you one. Well, we bought you one, and now you say you are bored. Tough." It may be a good idea to insist that your child follow through on his promise. However, a better approach would be to empathize with his feelings and try to learn underlying reasons why he has changed his mind.

- "Okay, we'll let you quit baseball, but don't expect us to pay for any other sport you want later on." This is unrealistic. Chances are you will oblige him later on. It is better to have consequences for his decision. Maybe he needs to earn back the money you spent on baseball equipment by doing extra chores.

- "Okay, we'll let you quit baseball even though we paid a registration fee. You can play soccer instead. But you'd better not quit that." What will happen if he does quit soccer? Kids will persevere more if they must pay a price for giving up. Perhaps the child could earn money to pay the registration fee.

- "You knew three months ago that your science fair project was due next week. Why are you just starting it now?" Kids procrastinate, at least in part, because the ability to be completely self-directed rarely develops before adolescence. Children need help learning to structure their time wisely. Parents need to be on top of their children's school assignments for that reason.

Smart Talk

Can Intelligence Be Improved?

Regardless of how smart or talented (or less capable) a child is, it is her *belief* of how smart or talented she is that will make a difference in perseverance. "Helpless" children believe that failure is due to lack of ability, so they do not persevere. "Mastery-oriented" children believe that if they keep trying, they can get smarter or succeed on a task. They persevere even when the task is challenging and mistakes are made. Easy success in school is not necessarily a good thing if your child never learns how to handle failure. Poor success is not necessarily a bad omen if the child attributes failure to lack of effort (not studying hard enough, etc.) rather than lack of ability.

Interestingly, a child with a helpless mind-set won't necessarily persevere after some successes. More important for that child is learning to use negative feedback as a message about effort and not a message about ability. If your child gives up easily, point out ways that her effort was low, not her ability, and help her use negative feedback (a poor test grade, etc.) as a clue to changes she can make that will make her smarter. (Students who don't think of themselves as smart but who believe they can become smarter perform much better than they did on previous tests.)

Praise effort lavishly. Praise outcome a little less.

63

Pets

The chant is universal and goes something like this: "If you kids want a dog, then you will have to take responsibility for it. I expect you to make sure it is fed and that you play with it. You'll have to clean up after it, too."

Of course, all kids agree to these conditions until the puppy has lived with them for, oh, two days, and then the kids slack off. What should parents say when the children want a puppy or a kitten or some other pet that requires care and feeding?

Things to Consider

➤ Don't get a pet unless you are prepared to do much, if not most, of the work involved. Yes, some children will eagerly take on the responsibility for pet care, but even they get bored.

➤ Kids can help with pet care and might even be reliable, but chances are they will need reminding.

➤ Research shows that pet ownership improves a child's sense of autonomy (taking care of himself) and self-confidence. This seemed especially true of children nearing adolescence.

➤ Cat owners will disagree, but when it comes to enhancing a child's self-esteem, dogs do the trick more than cats. The reason? Dogs are better able to give the impression that they like their owners.

How to Say It

- Skip the lecture about responsibility. Do make clear any expectations that you intend to truly enforce. "Okay, we can get a dog. But understand that twice a week I will send you into the yard with a pooper-scooper, and you will clean up after the dog—even if it's winter or you're in the middle of your homework."

- **EMPATHIZE** when kids don't want to take on responsibilities they had promised, but state **DO'S & DON'TS** clearly and calmly. "I know you want to ride bikes with your friend, but you promised you would give Pepper a bath before dinner. The hose is all set along with the shampoo. It will take ten minutes. I know you are annoyed, but I appreciate it when you keep your promises."

- Take advantage of opportunities to **TEACH** or **ENCOURAGE** values such as kindness, self-sacrifice, and compassion. "Scamp isn't feeling well after his operation. It's really nice of you to spend all that time petting him and making sure he is comfortable. That shows kindness and compassion."

- "You said it would be okay to stop buying those candy fruit snacks you like so that we could buy Fluffy a new pillow. That is very thoughtful."

How Not to Say It

- "We can get rid of this animal if you don't intend to take care of it." Since kids (and most adults) view pets as part of the family, you might as well be threatening to throw Grandma into the street. Praise appropriate pet care and expect that you might have to do a lot of the work, and you'll do fine.

- "Look at how the puppy chewed up the leg on the chair. Weren't you watching him?" That's what puppies do. Unless you place the puppy in a safer place, expect things to get chewed and don't blame the kids.

- "This isn't my cat, it's your cat." Children cannot take full responsibility for the welfare of a pet. They can help out, but you must be prepared to be the responsible one. Otherwise, it's better not to have the pet in the first place.

64

Concerns About Physical Appearance

Mark was noticeably overweight compared with his fourth-grade friends. While he occasionally was teased, most of the time his weight was not an issue.

Linda had braces. She hated them but understood the reasons they were necessary. She also endured some mild teasing, but her friends generally paid no attention to her braces.

Neil was short for his age. In fact, he was the shortest boy in his fifth-grade class. His parents noticed he was generally happy but that he got frustrated more easily. He hated being teased.

All of these children were noticed in some way for their appearance. Girls who are the first to develop breasts in their class may feel very self-conscious. Children who wear glasses sometimes feel the same way. We can't protect our kids from being teased about their appearance, but we can talk to them in a manner that might soothe the hurt feelings and provide them with a sturdier sense of esteem.

Things to Consider

➤ Concern about weight and body size tends to show up in girls more than boys and in white children more than African Americans.

➤ Children as young as preschool age believe that "fat is bad." Most preadolescent girls believe they are overweight, often because of fashion magazines and commercials that depict very thin models.

➤ Studies of children who are short in stature show mixed and contradictory results in terms of social, emotional, and academic functioning. That means short stature does not automatically mean a child will have difficulties. Height becomes more of an issue when children enter adolescence. Short children do better when their parents foster competence and self-reliance.

➤ Shorter children tend to avoid group activities such as basketball where they will feel self-conscious. They prefer more solitary sports such as swimming or hiking.

➤ One study showed that almost one-quarter of short-statured children repeated a grade, mostly because parents felt the child was immature. However, repeating a grade did not seem to change any academic or social skills.

How to Say It

Prevention is the best medicine. No matter what their appearance, skills, intelligence, or health status, children from loving homes with involved parents or caretakers who are firm but warm will be able to withstand most difficulties. Still, some ways to speak to them may be better than others.

- If your child's appearance bothers him, **EMPATHIC** statements may help him feel understood. Empathy does not mean you agree with your child's assessment, only that you understand why he might feel the way he does. "It bothers you that a kid in your class called you a name because you are not as tall [wear braces, are overweight, lack a certain skill, etc.]. I can't blame you. No one likes to be called names."

- "You think if you weigh more than the other kids, you might be laughed at."

- "You wish you were taller [more athletic, didn't have freckles, had a better singing voice, etc.]. Many kids wish they looked a little different from the way they do."

- **TEACH** coping with frustration or hurt feelings. Help them challenge their negative expectations. "Some kids aren't that smart, but still they have friends. Some kids aren't as good at basketball as other kids. Some kids are popular, some are not so popular. But they all have friends at school or in their neighborhood. Being well liked doesn't depend on how you look."

- "Haven't you ever seen kids who aren't that tall playing with their friends at school?"

- "We can start an exercise program for you, and we can make sure you don't eat any sugar. But some kids still can be very thin without trying and some gain weight easily. It isn't fair, but that's how it is sometimes."

- **ENCOURAGE** whatever skills your child possesses. Children with physical disabilities or limitations should be taught as much self-reliance as possible. "Let me see if you can do that by yourself. I bet you can."
- "See what you can accomplish just by trying hard and sticking to it?"

How Not to Say It

- Don't encourage obsessive preoccupation about appearance. "Don't eat that. Do you want to get fat?"
- "Make sure your clothes and hair look right. You want the boys to like you, don't you?"
- "Why do you keep wanting to lose weight? You look fine." Don't dismiss your child's concerns with platitudes, especially if she is very focused on being thin. Girls are at higher risk for eating disorders than boys. Instead, inquire further into your child's concerns. "You lost weight but still don't seem satisfied. You worry a lot about how you look, don't you?"
- "Don't let the other kids bother you. What do they know?" It isn't easy to ignore the scrutiny of peers. Your child may get the impression that you just don't understand.

(See chapters on bullying and teasing.)

Smart Talk
Dads, Listen Up!

In a study at Loyola University, about five hundred fifth- through ninth-grade students were "beeped" several times a day and asked to write down what they were thinking, feeling, and doing. One purpose was to determine how much the parents were involved in their children's experiences. The more a father was involved with his job, the less involvement he had in his daughter's life than his son's. In fact, the more satisfied a father was with his career, the less self-esteem his daughters had—presumably due in part to the father's reduced involvement. Girls very concerned about their appearance especially need a father's involvement in their lives.

65

Puppy Love

Eight-year-old Craig and his mom were buying school supplies. Craig grabbed an extra package of construction paper.

"We don't need any more paper," Mom said.

"It's not for me. It's for my teacher. She ran out of it."

"But the school will buy her the paper she needs," Mom answered.

Craig's face was downcast. "Okay," he said glumly.

Mom sensed what he was feeling. "Listen," she said. "Soon it will be Hanukkah and Christmas. I'm sure we can find your teacher an appropriate present."

Craig looked up and grinned.

Kids will develop crushes on their teachers, their schoolmates, or celebrities. It is the first stirring of romantic feelings that can confuse a youngster. A parent's job is to accept these feelings for what they are—normal emotions that should be neither trivialized nor a cause for concern. They are just additional signs that your child is growing older and that someone other than parents can be the object of his affections.

Things to Consider

➢ Infatuations are safe, distant ways to rehearse for the romantic moments that high school dating will probably bring.

➢ Initially, these feelings can confuse a child who may not understand why her heart beats rapidly when she sees a certain boy.

How to Say It

- Show interest and try to elicit more information about your child's feelings. **EMPATHIZE**. The goal is to let your child know that her feelings are normal, that you are interested, and that you can be someone to talk to whenever necessary. "It sounds as if Michelle is very special to you. What do you like about her?"

- "I remember liking my fourth-grade teacher a whole lot. I wonder if you feel the same way about your teacher."

- "It's kind of nice and exciting to imagine having Ricky Martin as your boyfriend."

- **TEACH** when appropriate. Since girls tend to mature more quickly than boys, some preteen boys are in the predicament of receiving phone calls from girls who like them. The problem is that the boys are not so interested. "Lisa called you. I think she kind of likes you. You can be polite to her but you don't have to feel obligated to stay on the phone for long if you feel uncomfortable. It's okay to say 'I gotta go.'"

- "I noticed you've written the name Jennifer on your notebook. Maybe she is someone you like. That's nice."

- **DO'S & DON'TS**. Guidelines about dating may be necessary if your child brings up the topic. If you mention it before she does, it might come across as a criticism. "No, you can't ask him for a date. You are too young. But you can invite him over to the house along with some other friends for a holiday party."

- **ENCOURAGE** appropriate expression of those early infatuation feelings. "I saw a poster of your favorite singer in the mall. Would you like one for your room?"

How Not to Say It

- "You're too young to have those feelings . . ." Don't trivialize your child's feelings. She will have them regardless of your opinion, and you may only succeed in preventing her from talking about them with you.

- "Don't be silly. You'll never meet Ricky Martin, let alone date him!"

- "It's called puppy love. They call it that because it's not the real thing." The feelings are real to your child, however innocent and immature they might be.

- "You can dream all you want, but you're too young to date so don't even think about that possibility." He might be too young to date, but it's better not to sound critical. He'll just think you don't understand.

- "Is he your boyfriend?" If said teasingly, this is definitely a put-down. If said sincerely, are you condoning having a boyfriend (or girlfriend) at that age? Many sixth to eighth graders who "date" are at risk for experimenting early with sex. Television, MTV, movies, and advertising are all very sexually suggestive (and explicit) and often give preteens the idea that having sex is acceptable. The older your child is when he/she begins dating, the more likely that sexual experimentation will be postponed.

66

Quarreling with Siblings

Imagine (it's not hard) that as you enter your house after a hectic day, you hear your beloved children screaming at each other. What would you do?

(a) Get back in the car and find someplace less stressful to be, such as a traffic jam.

(b) Hide in the bathroom until it blows over.

(c) Wait for your spouse to intervene (unless he is hiding in the bathroom, too).

(d) Yell at the kids for yelling at each other.

(e) Calmly and respectfully discuss with the children the effective ways to resolve arguments.

If you answered "e," you are either lying, a member of the clergy, or you just won $200 at the office pool and are too numb from excitement to really care what's going on.

Siblings will fight with each other. It's guaranteed. The best that parents can hope for is that the quarreling will be infrequent and not explode into *Wrestlemania: The Final Armageddon*.

Things to Consider

➤ Parents are rarely consistent when it comes to intervening in their children's arguments. Since most interventions will work once in a while, it can be confusing to know which intervention is best. Ideally, parents will try to teach their kids effective ways to discuss their differences and resolve disagreements. That requires some patience on the parents' part and a willingness to let the kids handle some situations by themselves.

➢ Do you tend to blame one child more than the other? Such blaming may be warranted but it could also be a clue to your bias. Do you tend to rescue the underdog? Does the more troublesome child remind you of someone you have issues with—such as your spouse? Do you expect the older child to act more maturely even though he is only seven years old?

➢ The more tense or unsatisfying the marital relationship, the more you can expect spillover into how you intervene with the kids. You may be harsher and less patient with them or too lenient.

➢ If you believe your spouse is too lenient, you may overcompensate and be stricter. Neither one of you may be handling the situation objectively.

➢ Hormones can make kids more irritable. At ages six to nine, the *adrenarche* phase of development begins. Levels of sex hormones increase and can cause moodiness, although no physical signs of puberty will be evident.

How to Say It

- The goals are to halt the potential for violence, calm down the kids just enough so you can help, and **TEACH** them to solve problems effectively. Don't immediately intervene (unless they might hurt each other). They may be able to resolve matters themselves. "Do you want me to help you solve this argument?" If they say yes, you have leverage as the invited guest. If they say no, give them a chance to figure things out on their own.

- Most arguments have to do with teasing and hurt feelings or unfairness. Step one is help them define the problem. "You are arguing over who sits on the loveseat while watching the movie. Why do you both think you have the right to sit there?"

- Step two is to brainstorm possible solutions. "Let's figure out three ways you might agree to solve this problem. John, you go first. What could happen that would make your sister think it was fair?"

- Step three is to agree on a plan. "Okay, John will sit on the loveseat for half an hour, then Jane will use it."

- Next argument, be a coach rather than a teacher. "Let's see if you guys can remember the steps to solving problems. You try to handle it yourselves, but I'll be available if you need assistance." Better still, when the kids are getting along and in a good mood, have them playact an argument followed by a try at calm problem solving. The rehearsal will help and may even be fun.

- Be cautious about taking sides. Siblings are experts at provoking each other in silent, subtle ways so that they appear to be innocent to the observer. "I don't know who started it, but I expect you two to find a way to solve it without arguing."

- Change the environment. "I want you two to sit at the kitchen table and don't leave until you have settled the problem." The change of scenery can help modify their feelings.

- **ENCOURAGE** any effort at problem solving. Praise desirable behavior. "Wow. I left you two alone, and you figured out a way to solve the problem. I'm impressed!"

- **EMPATHIZE** by digging deeper. Perhaps what's troubling one or more of the kids is not their sibling. Have they had a bad day at school? Did she lose the big game? Did his best friend move away recently? Are the parents not getting along? If you suspect an underlying issue, talk to that child privately. "I know your sister bugs you, but I was thinking that maybe you were still upset that Grandma is in the hospital. Tell me what you think about that."

- Say nothing. Grade-school children have had some experiences successfully resolving problems with friends. Grit your teeth, count to twenty, and see if your kids can manage without your help. If they can, everyone is better served.

How Not to Say It

- "Haven't I told you not to fight?" "Won't you kids ever learn to get along?" "What did I just tell you three minutes ago?" Every parent says these things at one time or another, but rarely do they help. It might stop the argument temporarily, but it doesn't show them how to solve the problem.

- "Who started it?" Never in the history of parenthood has a child answered this question accurately.

- "Wait until your father [mother] gets home." Handle the situation yourself.

- "If you don't stop arguing, I'm turning off the TV for the rest of the night." Try not to come up with arbitrary punishments. It's always better if the kids know ahead of time what the consequences will be. Or you might try saying, "It's too loud in here with you guys yelling and the TV blaring. If you can't discuss things more calmly, I will turn the TV off until you do. Thanks."

- "If you two don't fight, we will go out for ice cream later." Once in a great while this is okay, but some parents overuse it. Besides, what if they do fight and you tell them they'll get no ice cream? Now they have no incentive to get along. It is better to praise them frequently for cooperative behavior, teach problem solving, and apply quick and fair punishments when necessary. That will improve the odds that they will try to cooperate further.

67

Refusing Lessons

Marty wanted to take karate lessons real bad. His parents wisely signed him up on a temporary basis, just in case he later changed his mind. After three months, Marty still wanted to continue, so his parents paid for a year in advance (it was cheaper than paying month to month). But when Marty's friend John quit karate, Marty lost his interest as well. Should his parents force him to attend? How can they teach him accountability if they let him back out so easily? What should they say if he whines and complains that he hates karate?

Things to Consider

➤ Extremes are not advisable. Committing a child to a year of piano lessons when there are doubts she will persist or allowing the child to give up as soon as she loses interest can cause more problems.

➤ Make sure you are not trying to push your child into living out your dreams.

➤ Do you give up quickly on interests? Or do you stay in a miserable job out of a sense of duty? Either way, you may over- or underreact to your child's unwillingness to keep a commitment.

➤ Is your child's lack of interest playing into a power struggle between you and your mate (or ex-mate)? If you think your spouse is too lenient on the kids, you may insist your child stick with dance lessons. If you think your spouse is too strict, you may side with your child and say there is no point forcing him to do what he does not want to do. In either case, you are not necessarily seeing what is best for your child. You are simply opposing your mate.

How to Say It

- **REPORT** your expectations ahead of time. "I know you may decide that you don't like music lessons. That's okay before two months are up, but after two months you cannot change your mind."

- "We will buy you this inexpensive keyboard for practice. If you still want to take lessons after a year, we will buy a piano."

- **NEGOTIATE.** "If you really want an electric guitar and I buy one for you, you will have to pay half the cost of the guitar if you decide to stop taking lessons—unless you can think of some other way that is fair."

- Explore your child's reasons for wanting to quit. He might dislike a child in the group; maybe others laughed at him or maybe the teacher yelled at him, and he feels uncomfortable. Once you know the real reasons you may be able to resolve the problem without ending the lessons. "I know you promised you would stick with the lessons. Since you've changed your mind, I'm wondering if something happened that you haven't told me."

- **EMPATHIZE** when your child protests he has lost interest, but stick to the **DO'S & DON'TS** you agreed to. "You feel frustrated that you can't switch instruments. I can understand that. But you promised you would stick with the trombone, and we did buy you one."

- "Since we've paid for the trombone, I'm not willing to buy another instrument until we can sell yours. If you practice and keep up your lessons, I'll put an ad in the paper."

- **ENCOURAGE** those aspects of the lessons where your child does persist. "I know the warm-up exercises and stretching exercises are boring. That's one reason you want to quit dance lessons. But in three months you've learned how to tap very well, and I know you enjoy that part."

How Not to Say It

- "All right, all right. You can stop your lessons. But don't expect me to fork over the money the next time you want to learn something new." Don't give in to whining. If your child really is miserable taking lessons or is in over his head, you should probably cut your losses and chalk it up to immaturity. But it is better to end the lessons after he agrees to attend for one final month (or week).

- "But your grandmother was so excited when I told her you were taking horseback riding lessons." This addresses your reasons for wanting your child to hang in there but does not address her reasons for wanting to stop. It is best that a child take lessons in something that is not required by school and that she thinks she'll enjoy, not because it will please an adult.

- "How was your lesson today?" "Okay." "That's good." If you can't generate more enthusiasm for your child's efforts, don't be surprised if his enthusiasm wanes.

68

Refusing to Talk

"I can't get him to open up," Joy said to her husband. "You try."

"Maybe we should leave him alone," Al said. "He's old enough to sort through things by himself."

Joy sighed. "He's ten years old. The Dalai Lama he's not."

"All right, I'll give it a try. But I know what he'll say: 'Nothing's the matter.' Then what do I do?"

Getting kids to tell you what's on their mind can sometimes be a frustrating task. The first thing to think about is whether this is something new or a chronic pattern. If it's recent, you can probably make headway using empathy and intuition as you probe for what might be bothering your child. If it is a long-standing pattern, change your approach. Whatever you've done before hasn't worked.

Things to Consider

➢ Around age ten or so, boys tend to move away psychologically from their mothers and look more to their fathers for advice. But many men are not talkative. Some fathers are either psychologically or physically absent. When boys have no one to turn to, they learn to manage their feelings and problems on their own. That may teach self-sufficiency, but it also results in a boy who grows up to be a man uncomfortable with discussing feelings.

➢ If something is bothering your child, it likely has to do with self-esteem or issues of competence or incompetence. It may also concern issues of fairness or unfairness. Probe those areas first.

➤ Children do not possess great insight into why they feel the way they do. (Rising hormone levels present yet another complicating factor.) Asking "why" or "what" questions may not get you anywhere when you are probing for insightful answers. Questions with yes or no answers can help when a child is confused. (Note: One study showed that on average, dads asked more "wh—" questions while moms asked questions that yielded yes or no answers.)

➤ Hasty reassurances ("You shouldn't feel that way . . .") sound helpful but can actually make him feel dismissed or disqualified. Hold off on pep talks until you are sure you understand your child's concerns and have tried to empathize.

➤ Regular and meaningful "talk time" with your children—more than the simple exchanges that occur as you pass each other in the kitchen—will increase the odds that your child will want to discuss more upsetting or personal matters with you.

➤ Some children are sensitive to marital and family problems and do not want to add to a parent's burden by discussing their personal issues.

➤ Children who must take on added responsibilities of caring for younger siblings because of family strain may learn to keep their own problems to themselves.

How to Say It

- Probe but don't be pushy. Back off if your child is adamant about not talking. "I notice you've been very quiet ever since you got home from school, but when I ask what's wrong, you shake your head and say nothing. I'm thinking it might have something to do with the test you had to take." If your child just shakes her head no, she hasn't actually told you to back off. Keep up the probing, gently, until you get a clear message that she doesn't want to talk.

- Use **EMPATHY** by reflecting back your impressions. "I can see that talking about things isn't always something you like to do." (The use of the word *always* implies that he does open up once in a while. It is a good idea to use language that suggests your child might choose to open up later.)

- "Now doesn't seem to be the time you'd like to talk about it." (Implication: He will talk about it later.)

- "Maybe you want to think things over yourself. I have faith that if you need help with something, you'll talk about it when you are ready." Often, reluctant children do want to talk but are worried about doing so. Maybe they worry that you will be upset, or perhaps the topic is embarrassing. Saying you have faith in them helps. It gives them a gentle pat on the back, respects their privacy, and shows that you are approachable.

- "When you're ready, I'm here."

- "Is this something you'd rather talk about with your mother?" (Implication: Your child will want to discuss it with somebody.)

- "I can remember when I was your age, I didn't always know if I wanted to talk to my parents or not. But it always worked out better when I did."

- Have you been a good listener? If your tendency has been to criticize or trivialize your children's concerns, perhaps that is a reason for their reluctance now. "I know that in the past I haven't always been the easiest person to talk to about things. If that is your reason for not talking, I understand. I wouldn't want to talk to me, either. But I'm hoping you'll give me another chance." Such honesty and self-deprecating humor may shift the tone just enough to make it more likely he'll talk to you.

How Not to Say It

- "How do you expect me to help you if you don't tell me what's going on?" The idea is right, but the tone is wrong. A better approach: "I'd like to help. I'm at a loss to know what to do. Please tell me what's going on."

- "I'm not leaving until you tell me what's bothering you." State firmly that you are concerned but give your child room to take his time, mull things over, and perhaps come to you later.

- "You had your chance. If you need to talk, find someone else."

- "Do you really think you can solve all problems by yourself?" Actually, resilient children do solve some problems by themselves. Your role is important, but sometimes you can stand back and let your kids handle things themselves.

- "You're like your father. He doesn't talk, either." Making critical comparisons won't help.

- "I'm asking you a question! Don't sit there and say nothing. Talk to me!" Your frustration is understandable. It is better to **REPORT** it than to show it. "I'm frustrated. Something is on your mind that seems to be bothering you, and I'd like to see if I can help."

- "Finally you spoke up! Why couldn't you do that earlier? It would have saved me a lot of aggravation." It is better to praise him for confiding in you.

69

Running Away from Home

Amelia's parents received a phone call from the mother of Amelia's best friend. Apparently, Amelia showed up with a backpack full of clothes and wanted permission to stay for the weekend—"or maybe longer."

What was a twelve-year-old girl running away from home for?

One-quarter of a million kids under age thirteen will run away from home this year. The number is higher for teenagers. A 1998 study of teen runaways found that the majority left home because of perceived physical or emotional abuse. Those adolescents reported that running away was a last resort—not merely a bold attempt to annoy their parents—and many wanted an opportunity to reconcile with their families.

Things to Consider

➤ Err on the side of caution. Presume that running away is a sign your child has significant concerns.

➤ Most runaways end up at the home of friends or relatives.

➤ Younger children who run away simply because they are angry with a parent must be warned of the dangers of running away.

➤ Verbal and physical abuse are the reasons many children run away. Secondary reasons include inability to communicate with a parent, a chaotic household, or to accompany a friend who is running away from home.

How to Say It

- Use news reports of runaway children as an opportunity to **TEACH** ahead of time how serious and dangerous running away from home is. (Don't worry that you might give your child ideas he otherwise would not have.) "Most kids don't run away from home. When they do, it is often because there is a serious problem at home and the child does not believe he can talk things over with a parent. I want you to understand you can always talk to me. And I want you to understand that running away is very dangerous."

- If your child is threatening to run away, take time to consider what the underlying problem might be. "You rode your bike when I told you not to, so I punished you by not letting you ride your bike for a day. Now you are threatening to run away from home. I'm worried that something else might be bothering you. Let's talk about it."

- If your child threatens to run away, don't be intimidated. Use **DO'S & DON'TS.** "If I think you have run away, I will call the police. I will also speak to every one of your friends and their parents in order to find you."

- If your child threatens running away and is argumentative and trying to push your buttons, don't get sidetracked into more areas of conflict. Use words such as *nevertheless, but, still,* and *regardless* that will pull you back to the discussion at hand. "Regardless of your anger at me about not letting you go to the dance, I will call the police if you choose to run away," or "Still, despite your problems, I will call all your friends' parents to help find you if you choose to run away. We can solve your concerns in ways other than running from home."

- "Tell me what problem you will solve by running away from home." Running away is an attempt at resolving or escaping from some problem.

- If your child does bring up a concern, take it seriously. **EMPATHIZE** when appropriate. "You don't get along with your stepfather, so you want to leave home. I can imagine how hard it must be for you when you argue with him. Let's talk about ways that will help you two get along."

How Not to Say It

- "Run away if you want to. You'll be back." In the 1960s, *The Andy Griffith Show* was a popular television program. In one episode, the young son, Opie, decided to run away, and his father used "reverse psychology" and allowed his son to leave. Of course, the boy returned. There are too many dangers in today's society, however, to take that chance.

- "That's not a reason to run away . . ." You're missing the point. Your child evidently thought it was a good reason. It's better to listen to your child's concerns and take appropriate steps to solve those concerns.

- "You'll never amount to anything if you think you can just run away from your problems." Personal attacks on your child's character will add to her resentment. Criticize the behavior, not the whole being of the person. "I know when you think things through, you'll understand why running away is risky."

If your child ran away because of physical, sexual, or verbal abuse, steps must be taken immediately to halt the abuse; otherwise, the risk of running away in the future is high.

70

Saying "I Love You"

Linda told a story about one day when she was a little girl. Her father had come up behind her and put his arm around her. "You know," he had said, "every time I hear you humming in the morning I thank my lucky stars I have you."

It was a memory that always brought a tear to her eye. Her father had died not long after in a farming accident.

On average, adults who believe their parents loved them as children are not always able to admit that their parents showed them love. Many children have to read between the lines. They "know" a parent loves them but they do not always feel it. Telling children you love them is meaningless if your love is not demonstrated. However, showing love without saying "I love you" at least once in a while can cause some doubt or anxiety. Children need action *and* words.

Things to Consider

➤ Many marriages are less than satisfying because one spouse (often the husband) will rarely say "I love you" even though he may work hard and be devoted to his wife in other ways. Words without action are meaningless. Actions without words are meaningful but not intimate.

➤ You don't need to be a poet or sound like a greeting card. Think about the little things you love about your children and then tell them. If you repeat it once in a while, it might take on even more meaning to your child because it is unique and for him or her only.

How to Say It

- "My love for you is bigger than the sky. . . . No, bigger than the universe."
- "No matter what you do, no matter where you go, I will always love you."
- "I love you, son. Always remember that."
- "I'm not good at saying this, so listen up. I love you, and I always will. Now finish your breakfast."
- "You mean the world to me."
- "Do you know what cherish means? I cherish you."
- "It makes my day just being with you in the morning before you head off to school."
- "Just having you in my life makes life worth living."
- "If I could go back in time and do things differently, I'd still want you as my son.
- "Good night. I love you. God bless you."

How Not to Say It

- The only wrong way to say it is not to say it.

71

School:
Attending a New School

"I began my new job as a hospital nurse three weeks before my daughter started first grade," Marcie said. "It helped me understand what my daughter might be experiencing on her first day at school.

"First, I knew that my job was very important, so that made it all the more nerve-racking even though it was also exciting. Second, I barely knew anyone and didn't know my way around the hospital. That made me nervous. I watched other nurses do their work with ease, and I wondered if I really was up to the job. I had much more sympathy for my daughter, that's for sure."

Starting school or transferring to a new school can be an adjustment for most kids. It need not be traumatic, and once the children have adjusted, they can feel proud that they coped well. But until the transition has been successful, parents can make a difference in how well their kids adjust.

Things to Consider

➤ Ideally, avoid transferring your child to a new school in midyear. The curriculum is well under way by then and it might be harder for your child to catch up. Also, social groups may already have formed, and your child may have a difficult time establishing new friends.

➤ Adjusting to a new school will be harder when your child is adjusting to other changes such as parental separation or divorce or serious illness of a family member.

➤ Children will miss their friends from their former school. First-time students will be more anxious about the new environment.

➤ Anxiety is always higher when the number of unknowns is high. A visit to the new school is essential to reduce anxiety. If that is not possible, one parent might videotape the school or take snapshots. Or check to see if the school has a web page. A message from the principal or future class-mates will ease anxiety and bring a smile.

➤ If your child is having some difficulty adjusting, ask her teacher to provide extra kind and encouraging words or introduce other kids to your child during lunch or recess.

➤ Find out from the teacher which student in your child's class was new to that school a year before. Seeing how that student has adjusted can encourage your child.

How to Say It

- Kids need practical information about their new school—what it looks like, what a typical day will be, the number of hours spent there every day, etc. The clearer the image, the better. Once those facts are provided, the focus should be on your child's expectations. **EMPATHY** will help you probe. "I bet you'll be glad when you're all settled into the school and know where everything is."

- "What are you looking forward to the most, and what are you nervous about?"

- Encourage expression of thoughts and feelings. Performing some physical activity with your child while talking (play catch, ride bikes, go for a walk, jump rope, etc.) can make the dialogue feel less formal and serious. "How about throwing the ball around for fifteen minutes? You can tell me all about your day, and I'll tell you about mine."

- Children may wonder "What if I don't make any friends? What if they make fun of me? What if nobody asks me to play with them during recess?" Be ready to provide guidelines on coping with specific fears. But first try to discover why your child is fearing those things. "Many children worry about those things. What makes you worry about them?"

- "But the truth is you have always made friends. Once people get to know you, they do like you. If you want, we can have a party at our house soon, and you can invite your classmates."

- "Let's rehearse what you can say if you want to play with a group of other kids."

- **ENCOURAGE** by pinpointing successes in coping as your child progresses through his first weeks of school. "Already you can tell me many of the teachers' names, and you have made two new friends. That must make you feel good."

- "It's only been a few weeks. It often takes longer to become comfortable with a new school. You're actually doing fine."

- "If you notice any new students who have just arrived, you can be the expert. You can tell them to come to you if they have questions, and you can show them around. How does that sound?"

- "We'll make sure we e-mail your friends at your old school, and you can tell them all about your new teachers."

Rule of Thumb: Most children are fairly well acclimated within three months. Remind yourself that your child will eventually get used to the new school.

How Not to Say It

- "This is no big deal. You'll be fine once you get used to it." You are closing off room for discussion. Encouraging your child should not be done at the expense of understanding and responding helpfully to his concerns. Encouragement is best when preceded by some empathy. "It's normal to feel nervous and a little excited. But I know as time goes on you'll feel more comfortable and less nervous. What could happen that would make you feel better?"

- "If you don't improve your attitude, no one will want to play with you." Scaring your child into a positive attitude is a contradiction.

- "You're making your little brother afraid to go to school. Try to be more positive." It's not your child's responsibility to prepare his younger sibling for school. Remember, your younger child is also watching you. Your role is more important.

- "I'm tired of hearing you complain." Often, children (and adults) whine or keep complaining because they never really felt listened to the first time. It is better to assume there is something you've missed about what's troubling your child. Also, encourage your child to list the things he likes about the new school in addition to listing his complaints.

- "Just introduce yourself to some kids" or "Just talk to the teacher if you have any questions." Kids who are nervous about the new school may need coaching on how to approach others. Don't just tell them, show them.

72

School:
"My Teacher Is Mean!"

Most kids will complain about a teacher sooner or later. Often the issue is one of perceived unfairness: The assignment was too hard or not enough time was given to study for a test. Children who report the most teacher unfairness also tend to be children with the most discipline problems. A child's view of his teacher is important. Dropout rates of high school students are highly correlated with belief that teachers are unfair or uninterested. According to an article in the *American Psychologist,* teachers view low-income students less positively and with lower achievement expectations, often basing their opinion not on scholastic abilities but on speech patterns and style of dress. These views can develop as early as kindergarten.

Parents shouldn't dismiss a child's concerns about a teacher, and shouldn't automatically regard their child's opinions as accurate. The goal is to uncover the true reasons for the child's views and take steps to improve the situation. Usually, greater involvement in your child's study habits and improving his ability to be well behaved will pay dividends.

Things to Consider

➤ Find out if having a "mean" teacher is adversely affecting your child's school performance. If not, having to cope with various adult personalities may be a fine lesson in life.

➤ Sometimes adults and children complain about someone when in fact it is someone else who is the real problem. (For example, a parent who complains that her children do not appreciate her might really be feeling unappreciated by her husband.) So a child who says a teacher dislikes him may also be feeling disliked by a friend. Probe for possibilities.

➤ A teacher's expectations can affect how well or poorly a child performs, though this effect is small. A recent study showed that the most powerful teacher expectation occurred when teachers *overestimated* the abilities of low-performing children. These kids rose to the occasion and did better than past test scores would have predicted.

➤ The best teacher will challenge your children to perform well and will not be content with mediocrity.

➤ Your expectations are more important than the teacher's. You set the standards of excellence. If a child is having trouble with schoolwork, look first on the home front. Have you taught good work habits? Do you check your child's schoolwork daily and monitor homework? Do you instill respect for authority? Do reading and writing come before TV and video games? If you've slipped up on these, don't be quick to judge your child's teacher as mean. She just may have higher standards than you do.

How to Say It

- The immediate goal is to get your child to explain as fully as possible why he thinks a teacher is mean. Elicit as much information as possible before you draw any conclusions about the accuracy of the claim. "What did your teacher say or do that made you think he was mean? . . . Anything else? . . . Has this happened before or was this the first time?"

- Find out if your child is troubled by the belief that the teacher is mean. "How much does it bother you? A little? A medium amount? A lot?"

- Explore alternative interpretations. "Sometimes teachers and parents do things kids don't like, but they do it because it is good for the children. Things like getting you to bed at a reasonable hour, not letting you eat too much candy, being sure you do your homework, and having you help around the house. Is it possible that your teacher thought he was being helpful?"

- Brainstorm solutions. Often, teaching your child to be more polite, inquisitive, and reliable with assignments can make the difference in a teacher's appraisals. "Are there times your teacher is not mean? Are there students your teacher is nice to? If so, what happens to make your teacher nice at those times?"

- If it seems to you that your child's teacher may simply be stricter than past teachers, **EMPATHIZE** with your child's feelings but **ENCOURAGE** obedience. "It isn't always easy having a strict teacher. Sometimes it feels unfair. But by being strict she is more likely to spend time on your lessons, and that is a good thing. Besides, she believes you have what it takes to follow her rules. She has faith in you."

- "I remember having a mean teacher when I was in sixth grade. Would you like to hear how I handled it?" Such stories can help your child cope and make him realize it is not necessarily a horrible thing to have a grumpy teacher.

- "You can always talk to me about your teacher. If necessary, I will talk to your teacher about the best way to handle matters. Do you have any thoughts about that?" Older children may prefer that you not say anything to their teacher. You must weigh that concern with their other concerns.

Smart Talk

How to Say It to Your Child's Teacher

If you have a concern about the teacher's methods, you may be interested in these three guidelines by author and former Secretary of Education William Bennett offered in his book *The Educated Child:*

1. *Gather the facts.* Your child may not be the best reporter of facts. Keep an open mind and don't automatically presume the teacher is at fault.

2. *See the teacher as an ally.* Assume the best about the teacher—that she wants your child to learn as much as possible. View her as on your team, not as an adversary. Treat her with respect.

3. *Follow the chain of command.* Don't automatically run to the principal. Try to work things out with the teacher. Once you do go above the teacher's head, you may never have a good relationship with that teacher. Choose your battles wisely.

To prevent difficulties with teachers, you may also want to do the following:

Be polite and gracious in all correspondence. Say words of genuine appreciation whenever you can. Teachers can use pats on the back.

Be involved in the school as much as possible so teachers know you. Volunteer at functions, chaperone a trip, help out with a holiday class party, give a talk to a class on a topic of interest, and so forth.

Follow up later on with a note of thanks after a problem has been resolved.

How Not to Say It

- "If your teacher was mean, she had a reason." Showing support for teachers is usually a good idea, but it's better to first probe for reasons why your child feels the way he does. "Oh? You think your teacher is mean? Tell me more."

- "You must have done something wrong." Again, don't jump to conclusions. This kind of comment closes off communication instead of enhancing it.

- "Your teacher sounds like an idiot. He had no right to say those things." There are two sides to every story. You are better off giving the teacher the benefit of the doubt. Your child will not respect her teacher if you show disrespect.

- "That's life. You have to learn how to deal with mean people." You are blocking off communication and missing an opportunity to probe for other problems.

73

School:
Homework Hassles

Joshua hovered over his math homework, writing furiously. He had five minutes to finish before his bus arrived.

"Mom!" he called. "Will you help me? I can't do this problem!"

"You told me you finished your math last night," Mom said.

"It was mostly finished. Will you do this problem for me? I'm going to miss my bus."

"No. You know how to do that—"

"Please!" Josh said. "I don't have the time!"

"You should have thought of that last night when—"

"Mom, you're not helping me!"

Helping your child to develop proper study skills will save you and him lots of needless aggravation.

Things to Consider

➤ There is no accepted standard for the amount of homework a child can reasonably expect to do on a daily basis. However, a common formula is to allow ten minutes a night for a first grader, and ten minutes per night added for each grade level. Thus, a fifth grader might average nearly an hour a day of homework while an eighth grader may average ninety minutes or more. (Note: Children watch between three and four hours of TV per day. Something is wrong.)

➤ Children often try to do other things while studying, such as watch television or talk on the phone. If so, they may spend double or triple the time it would take them if they simply sat at a desk and quietly did their homework.

➤ Unless you know what the homework assignments are and when they are due, you cannot help your child organize his time. One fourth-grade boy—with good intentions—began reading a book the night before his written book report was due. He completely underestimated the amount of time required to do the assignment.

➤ If your child rarely has homework or is able to complete it in school, she is not being challenged. You are doing your child a disservice to allow that to continue.

➤ Spelling words, historical facts, geography, etc., can be reviewed in the car when driving to a store. It's a great idea to use words or facts that the child has already been tested on to demonstrate how material can be forgotten unless it is reviewed. This technique is especially helpful for students who take comprehensive exams at the end of a quarter.

➤ Your children will eventually discipline themselves to do homework if you value such discipline. Do you do your work on time? Do the kids see you postponing necessary work and wasting time? Do they see you reading books and eager to learn new things?

➤ You will have made a huge, positive step when your children ask permission to watch television instead of your asking them to turn it off. TV should be an infrequent privilege, not a daily right.

How to Say It

- The most important thing to **TEACH** (repeatedly) is that you value education and you value homework as an essential tool for educating your child. Of course, most kids would rather play than do homework. You can **EMPATHIZE** without losing sight of your values. "I know that you'd rather not have any homework. I remember feeling that way, too. But I want you to learn as much as possible because I know you will have more choices when you get older if you do the best you can in school."

- Children need help persevering when assignments get difficult. For that to happen, they need to believe they have what it takes to succeed. At least they need to believe that solid effort will most often yield solid results. Praise specific study skills and praise effort. "You came right home from school and immediately went to your desk to do homework. That was smart. I noticed that you reviewed your chapter when you didn't know how to answer the homework problem. That was a smart idea, too."

- "I can see that you tried to figure this problem out yourself before you asked me for help. That shows good effort."

- "If you try hard, most of the time you will do pretty well. If you try but not very hard, sometimes you will do okay. If you don't try, you won't do well."

- When assisting a frustrated child with her homework, parents make one of three mistakes: They, too, get frustrated and therefore aggravate the situation; they do most of the work for the child (big mistake—it rewards whining and procrastination); or they pull away and offer less help. The better approach: "I can see that this is frustrating for you. I can do the first part of the problem for you and you can finish it, or you can do the first part and I will finish it. Which do you prefer?"

- "It seems as if no matter how I try to help, you are still frustrated. Maybe we both could use a five-minute break. How about a game of Go Fish?"

- Have your child speak aloud his thinking process as he works through a problem. That can help you detect where his confusion might lie. "Let me show you what I mean. I'll talk out loud while I do this addition problem. Six plus four is ten, so I put down the zero and carry the one . . ."

- Don't make overseeing homework a chore. If it's an aggravation for you, then your child will be less likely to enjoy it or less likely to ask for help when needed. "Oh, good. It's time to look over your homework. Let me finish drying my hands, and I'll be right over."

- "If you have a homework question, you can always come to me. If I am busy, I'll quickly stop what I'm doing and answer your questions." Show by your actions that homework issues are very important to you as a parent.

How Not to Say It

- "Did you do your homework? Good." Ask what the homework was and then check it over. Show an interest. It's an opportunity to catch mistakes or praise good effort.

- "You didn't have any homework today? Oh." Be more curious. Did your child have homework but finish it in school? Is not having homework typical? If so, the teacher is being negligent.

- "Okay, I'll do it for you this time. But next time you'd better have your assignment finished the day before it's due!" The problem here may be as much yours as the child's. If you are on top of his assignments, you'll be able to remind him ahead of time to get to work. Catching up on homework at the last minute is sometimes inevitable but should occur very infrequently.

- "Why didn't you tell me you had a science project due on Monday? Now we'll have to spend the entire weekend working on it!" Get your child into the habit of telling you what his assignments are daily. Some students must write their assignments in a book that you should have access to. If you don't inquire regularly, some assignments will slip through the cracks. Even bright children don't organize their time well and may underestimate how long a project takes to complete.

Smart Talk

Homework is even more of a hassle when parents disagree on how much help to give their child. Be careful about spousal power struggles. The husband who thinks his wife is too lenient may oversee homework in a strict, harsh way in order to compensate for his wife's leniency. But the wife may overindulge her child as a way of overcompensating for her husband's military style of teaching. In neither case is the child being truly helped. If this describes your marriage, begin with the premise that the best approach is what works for your particular child. Ideally, you want your child to be able to do as much of the work on her own but be able to ask for help when needed. Homework should be challenging but not too frustrating or overwhelming.

School:
"I'm Afraid to Ask Questions in Class!"

Mickey was a capable seventh-grade student. But when he was struggling with his homework, his parents discovered he had questions he could have asked the teacher but didn't.

"I feel funny asking questions," Mickey said.

His parents discovered no compelling reason for Mickey's reluctance. He was reasonably bright and never had an embarrassing incident in school that might make him shy. What could they do?

Things to Consider

➤ Children who are reluctant to ask questions in class are usually either shy or fear looking foolish. A parent-teacher conference can help. A teacher can praise children for asking questions and make sure such inquisitiveness is rewarded.

➤ Preteens get extremely self-conscious. A child who is worried about pimples on his face or how his hair looks may not want to call attention to himself by asking questions in class.

➤ If anxiety is at the foundation of a child's reluctance to ask questions, practice is essential. The only way to challenge their belief that something bad will happen if they ask questions is for them to ask questions and discover that the consequences are positive.

Smart Talk

Seeking help in a classroom is associated with better grades and improved confidence. Still, many students do not ask for help when needed. An extensive body of literature reveals the following findings:

Kids who feel competent are more likely to ask questions when needed. They are less concerned about looking foolish.

Younger kids, if taught that asking questions will help them learn, will ask more questions. Older children (seventh grade) will also weigh the costs of asking questions (appearing stupid, being criticized for not knowing something, etc.).

Children who need the most help (who are less capable) are least likely to ask questions. For them, asking questions only affirms their lack of competence.

Sometimes asking questions is a sign of *dependency* on the teacher. Asking for answers instead of asking for information that will help them understand material better is a clue to that dependency.

If asking questions is viewed as a reflection of inability or inadequacy, children are less likely to ask. If asking questions is viewed as a way to become more knowledgeable and competent, children are more likely to ask.

How to Say It

- **TEACH** that seeking help in a classroom will help the child learn and develop greater knowledge and skill. Discourage the belief that asking questions is a sign of lesser ability (it isn't). "It is a well-known fact that children who ask questions learn more and do better in school."

- "Asking a question is a way of showing that you want to learn more. Teachers like that attitude."

- The goal is to encourage your child without being pushy. A reluctant child will not feel more at ease if you get demanding, and a shy child needs gentle coaxing. "Let's make a list of three or four questions you could ask your teacher. Then you tell me which of those you'd be willing to ask tomorrow."

- "A good time to practice asking questions is right when the class begins. The longer you wait, the more you might decide not to ask."

- "A simple question to ask your teacher might be: 'Could you repeat what you just said?'"

- "Let's rehearse speaking up. When we're at the restaurant, you can ask the waiter if they serve curly fries with the burgers."

- "Asking a question does not mean you are stupid. If you watch, you'll see that the smartest kids in the class ask questions. In fact, because they ask questions they do better in class."

- **ENCOURAGE.** "Your teacher told me you asked a question in class today. Good for you. Tell me what it was like."

- "Tell yourself, 'The more questions I ask, the smarter I am.'"

How Not to Say It

- "I expect you to ask at least one question in class tomorrow." If your child is fearful, making an order won't clear up the fear. **DO'S & DON'TS** are inappropriate in this case.

- "It's silly to be afraid to ask questions." If your child has some anxiety, you have just informed her that you really don't understand. You are not offering encouragement when you tell your child she is wrong to feel the way she does. It's better to understand, if possible, what her fears are and then offer some practical advice on how to overcome them.

- "If you don't start asking questions in class, I'll have to discuss this with your teacher." You make it sound like a threat. Your child should view you and her teacher as allies who only want to help. Say instead, "It is important to me that you feel comfortable asking questions. If you have difficulty, I'll chat with your teacher and together maybe we can help you."

- If a child asks you a question from his homework, don't respond by saying "I thought you knew that already. Why don't you know that answer? Did you forget?" Any comment by you that equates asking questions with poor ability or forgetfulness may prompt your child to stop asking questions.

School:
Poor Report Card

Jamie got a B in fourth-grade social studies. Across the county border in another school district, fourth-grader Laura earned a B for social studies. Is it reasonable to assume that these students learned pretty much the same thing and have about the same level of intelligence?

Absolutely not.

The truth is that the meaning of test scores, grades, and report cards varies from district to district. Teachers have varying standards, too. Some teachers grade on a curve, which means some students will get an A regardless of how well they understand the material. The self-esteem movement has prompted many schools to use more ambiguous measures of performance that toss out letter grades in favor of descriptions such as "Satisfactory" or "Improving." Some parents complain so much if their bright child receives a low grade that teachers relent and raise the grade to something more acceptable.

Ironically, a child with a "good" report card may be in more academic trouble these days. Parents unwittingly assume that an A or B student is doing well. In fact, the student's performance may be mediocre but the grades are inflated. That student will be in for a rude awakening if she attends a high school or college with more demanding standards.

Things to Consider

➤ If you do not know what specifically was taught and what the standards were for achieving the grades, the grades on the report card have little meaning. Talk to the teacher and find out exactly what an A means.

➤ Academic performance is not just a matter of ability. Research shows that involved and supportive parents who take a strong interest in their children's school performance will motivate their children to work harder.

➤ If a poor report card was a shock, you haven't been keeping tabs on your child's schoolwork during the quarter.

➤ Research also shows that the child's perception that his teacher "cares" can motivate him to work harder and perform better. What is a "caring" teacher? Someone who tries to understand a student's point of view, teaches him according to his individual abilities, and has expectations that the child will perform to the best of his abilities. (Good news! Kids want to be challenged to do their best! So why do some schools, teachers, or parents tolerate less?)

Smart Talk

Should You Pay Your Child for Good Grades?

Generally, no, you should not pay for good grades. While an occasional monetary reward may motivate a child to perform better, this practice has a number of pitfalls. First, it often reveals a lack of parental confidence that the child can get good grades any other way. It may also be a sign that the parents are not taking time to discover underlying reasons for poor school performance. Plus, it is based on the principle that the money is a motivator. What if it loses its appeal? Or what if the child requires a lot more of it to be motivated? Money should not replace parental involvement. If a parent insists that money is an appropriate reward, it should be accompanied by much praise ("You do well when you put your mind to it" or "You are doing a very good job on this report").

How to Say It

- When grades decline, don't first presume the child is lazy. A new school or a different teacher may have stricter standards. "Is the schoolwork getting harder for you?"
- "What has changed that makes getting better grades harder?"
- Try to figure out a plan of action. "What could you do differently that would make your grades improve? Any ideas?"

- Clarify that grades are important and that you will help your child become more organized and more prepared for tests. "It seems that your grade was based on homework plus test scores plus class participation. You did well on tests, but I know you sometimes were late with homework. That will be our first priority."

- Set a clear goal. Telling a child to "improve" his grades is vague. "What grade would you want to reach by your next report card? . . . To achieve that I'll review your homework every night and quiz you during the days before a test. What do you think?"

- Offer realistic **ENCOURAGEMENT**. "I've seen you get better grades. I know your work is harder this year, but I also know that when you take the time to learn something, you usually do well."

- "If you don't do well on a test, what do you think is the main reason?" Kids who attribute failure to lack of ability decide it isn't worth trying hard. Kids who attribute failure to reasons other than lack of ability (didn't study hard enough, etc.) usually perform well overall.

Rule of Thumb: A continuous decline (or sudden drop) in school performance signals a problem. Depression, anxiety, substance abuse, or family conflicts are common causes.

How Not to Say It

- "What am I going to do with you? Don't you want to be successful in life?" Frustration is understandable. It is better to search for underlying problems or at least convey that your child has the ability to make a solid effort.

- "You can forget video games until your grades improve." It might be necessary to curtail TV or video games. If so, it shouldn't be a form of punishment but rather a common-sense assessment of the obstacles to your child's best performance. A better way to say it: "I've noticed that you spend at least three hours a day on TV or video games. Much of that time needs to be spent studying. From now on you can play those games only after I've checked your homework and you've studied your lessons. The most important thing is for you to do the best you can in school."

- "Are you stupid or something?" A comment like this is not only inappropriate and unhelpful, it is a signal that home life may be tense. Inflammatory comments suggest that at least one of the parents is unhappy or angry and that there is spillover onto the children. An honest self-appraisal may prompt parents to improve their own life or seek counseling.

Smart Talk

Parents' influence on their children's school achievement is more profound than you might think. Recent research has demonstrated the following:

Parents' perceptions of their sixth-grade child's abilities in math and English were better predictors of that child's future performance than were the child's past grades.

Children who doubt their abilities do not persevere in difficult tasks. High-achieving children who nevertheless *underestimated* their academic abilities (had low confidence) were also viewed by their mothers as less competent. High-achieving kids who felt confident of their abilities had mothers who shared that view. In other words, what parents think of their children, the children will think of themselves.

Fathers are a very important influence for girls who later become successful in fields that are traditionally masculine. It seems that fathers are less likely than mothers to view their children's abilities in stereotyped ways. Mothers of daughters thought their girls had to exert more effort to be competent in math compared with mothers of sons. Mothers overestimate their daughters' abilities in English and underestimate their sons' abilities. Fathers showed no bias.

School:
Rejected by Classmates

In the wake of the tragic school shootings in such places as Littleton, Colorado and Jonesboro, Arkansas, there has been a keener concern about why some students become social outcasts. It has been known for years that children who are rejected by classmates are at higher risk for problems later on. Research shows that a snowball effect occurs whereby rejected kids are either more aggressive or withdrawn, which further leads to rejection. As someone involved in the care of children, you should know the following dozen facts:

➢ Rejected children show higher rates of criminal activity, substance abuse, and behavioral problems in school.

➢ Children rejected by peers in the third grade were three times more likely than nonrejected students to have poor adjustment in middle school.

➢ Peer rejection at age ten is associated with involvement in a deviant peer group at age twelve. Deviant peers are more likely to abuse drugs, engage in criminal activity, and drop out of school.

➢ Middle-school boys abused by peers (bullied, rejected) were depressed and had poor self-esteem ten years later.

➢ The single best predictor of peer rejection is aggressive or disruptive behavior.

➢ However, many rejected children are not aggressive at all. They are oversensitive, submissive, unassertive, and viewed as easily pushed around.

➤ Being viewed as shy by peers is not the same as being viewed as easily pushed around. Shy children were viewed as quiet, nondisruptive, and hesitant in social interaction but not viewed as oversensitive and easily bullied.

➤ Peers view well-liked students as being not too aggressive or disruptive, average in assertiveness, and especially kind, cooperative, and trustworthy.

➤ Well-liked students are viewed as capable of handling good-natured teasing. Aggressive children view teasing as an attack; submissive children view teasing as ridicule.

➤ Whether or not peers rejected an aggressive child or a withdrawn/submissive child seemed to be based on the child's ability to also show friendliness, cooperation with peers, and supportiveness toward others. The more positive behaviors children displayed, the more likely they would be accepted by peers even if they also acted aggressively or submissively.

➤ In a study of grades K–2, children relied heavily on teachers' comments about other children to form their opinions about their classmates. Thus, a disruptive child who was put down and not merely corrected by the teacher ("Billy, can't you ever sit still!") was more disliked by students. When teachers praised the good behavior of disruptive students ("Good, Billy. You're paying attention"), the other students had more favorable opinions of that child. Negative behavior that was corrected by a teacher (for example, "Billy, stop making paper airplanes and get back to work") had no effect on opinions.

➤ Boys who tend to be victimized often have overprotective mothers who treat them as younger than their age and who overcontrol the boys' spare-time activities. Victimized girls tend to have mothers who are hostile and critical of them, who threaten to leave, or who threaten to withdraw love if the girls misbehave. Fathers tend to be absent or uninvolved. Boys who are overprotected don't develop the kind of social skills respected by a peer group (rough play, autonomy, risk-taking, and acceptance of teasing). Girls who are rejected or criticized (with hostility) by mothers have a harder time developing the necessary social skills of empathy, cooperativeness, and sharing.

How to Say It

- Inquire as to the extent of the rejection. "Who is putting you down? Is it just one child, or do several kids do this?" The more children involved, the more likely the rejection will be harder to handle.

- "What do you say or do when these children do these things to you?" An overly submissive child is more likely to continue to be victimized. An aggressive child may be rejected but not bullied. Peers may later accept a child who can laugh it off and not withdraw.

- "How long has this been going on?" It is easier to change classmates' perceptions earlier than later. Asking a teacher to find ways to praise your child may also help, especially in the earlier grades.

- **EMPATHIZE.** "It really must hurt your feelings when that happens."

- "I imagine it makes you angry or sad."

- **TEACH** more socially desirable behaviors such as cooperativeness, use of humor, and kindness. These tend to counterbalance the negative views of others enough to end rejection. "I don't blame you for not wanting to be nice to the kids who mistreat you. But it has been shown that if your classmates view you as kind or cooperative, they will like you more. Want to try?" You must practice this daily until your child is adept.

- "How about twice a day for a week you say something kind to some of your classmates? You don't have to say it to the meanest ones just yet. Maybe you could tell someone he has a nice jacket or she asked a good question in class. What other things could you say?"

- If your child is aggressive, he is likely to interpret socially ambiguous acts (being bumped while standing in line, good-natured teasing) as having hostile intent. If he then acts with hostility, he is more likely to be rejected by peers. **TEACH** alternative ways of responding. "Let's pretend you're in the cafeteria line and someone bumps you. Instead of bumping back, what else could you do?"

- If your child is very sensitive to criticism, he may view good-natured teasing as ridicule. **TEACH** alternative ways of reacting. "For example, if someone laughs at the ink mark on your face, you could just smile and laugh."

- "I remember not being liked by some of the kids." Offering stories of hope can help. Give advice on how you coped while emphasizing how your child means the world to you.

How Not to Say It

- "Just join the crowd even if they don't like you. They'll learn to like you." Not necessarily. If your child lacks the social skills to handle criticism or to act his age or to initiate conversation appropriately, he will continue to be rejected. Teach him the necessary skills and remind him of his many good qualities.

- "You don't need them for friends. You have me. I love you and always will." This is well intended but not realistic (and it may be a clue that you are overprotective of your child which can be part of his problem). Kids still need to feel accepted by at least some of their peers. Minimizing that fact only informs your child that you really do not understand.

- "I'm going to talk to those other kids' parents!" Be careful, or you may do more harm than good. Older children may end up being even more disliked. You may get the other kids to stop teasing or bullying your child, but you won't make them like him. Teaching positive social skills is your best bet.

Finally, it can be helpful for rejected children to feel very accomplished in some area outside of school such as music, theater, gymnastics, or martial arts. Martial arts can improve a child's sense of physical competence (submissive children view themselves as weak) while the philosophy of martial arts also teaches physical restraint (so your child is less likely to use his skill aggressively). A class outside of the school setting can validate your child's worth and can help him cope with rejection from schoolmates.

School Safety Concerns

Olivia and her brother Pete couldn't help but watch the videotapes being replayed by the newscasters. The school shootings were a national story that had parents, teachers, and experts shaking their heads and wondering "Why?"

"Will that happen at our school?" Pete asked his mother.

"I'm afraid," Olivia said.

Fortunately, most schools are safe, especially in kindergarten through eighth grade. Still, many children get apprehensive when they hear news reports that undermine their sense of security.

Things to Consider

➢ The school shootings that made national headlines were newsworthy because the killers were themselves children or adolescents and because such killings are extremely rare. According to Richard Gelles, director of the Center for the Study and Prevention of Intimate Violence at the University of Rhode Island, fewer than one hundred homicides are committed annually by children under fourteen.

➢ Some elementary and middle schools do contain students in gangs or who use drugs.

➢ Unless steps are taken to make parents feel more confident about school safety, it will be hard for parents to reassure their children.

➢ There is always uncertainty. While experts can isolate the factors associated with an increased incidence of violence, it is very difficult to predict ahead of time who will commit a violent act. It is especially difficult when predicting homicide by children since the rates of occurrence are already so low.

➢ There can be no significant learning in an environment where safety is at risk and children are apprehensive.

➤ If you have any questions or concerns, talk to the school principal about the school's policy regarding student violence. Are violent acts immediately punished? In what way? What does a school do with repeat offenders?

➤ A nationally representative sample of eighth graders commented about the frequency of being victimized at school, about getting into trouble for bad behavior, and about concerns regarding school safety. The fascinating result: Those three conditions were significantly higher in schools that had only grades 6 to 8 or 7 to 9, compared with schools that had grades K to 8 or K to 12. If your child attends a middle school with no lower or higher grade levels, inquire more about school safety and policies regarding bully behavior.

➤ Does your school have school resource officers available? According to John Coleman and Bonnie Ryan-Spanswick, housemasters at John F. Kennedy Middle School in Enfield, Connecticut, an SRO can make a huge contribution to school safety. The SRO is a sworn police officer who is assigned to a specific school on a daily basis and spends most of the day interacting with students, teachers, and staff. The SRO is visible and available not merely to respond to a crisis but to discuss any concerns and, it is hoped, prevent a crisis. Parents also can feel free to discuss problems with the SRO and learn about such things as parents' rights and the legal consequences of certain troublesome behaviors by students.

How to Say It

- Don't be quick to reassure your child without finding out exactly what her worries are. Your child may be unconcerned about a possible shooting but still very concerned about being bullied, for example. "You seem more nervous about going to school. What do you think about that makes you nervous?"

- "When did you last feel comfortable and safe in school? How long ago? What has happened since then to change your mind?"

- "If you had the power to make your school completely safe, what would you be sure to do?"

- **EMPATHIZE** without quickly trying to reassure your child all is well. Hasty reassurances might halt further conversation and leave you in the dark about hidden worries. "I imagine when you watched the news report on TV, you wondered what you would do if that happened at your school."

- "It's very frightening and sad when something violent happens at school."
- **TEACH** what your child can do to help protect herself. "If you have any suspicion that a student wants to hurt somebody, it is okay and important to tell an adult."
- "If you think you are in danger, go quickly to a teacher."
- **REASSURE.** "I love you so much that I would never, never, *never* put you in a place where I believed you would be hurt."
- "School shootings are scary, but they also almost never happen. Your school is going to take some precautions to make sure nothing like that ever happens there."
- "If I thought you were at risk, I wouldn't let you go."
- "Let's say a prayer for the people who died and their families." Don't miss an opportunity to demonstrate your religious faith. Belief that God can and will offer comfort and that prayers can make a positive impact on the future course of events is a powerful tool.
- Don't hesitate to bring up the topic weeks later even if you think your child has forgotten the news story. You will not add to your child's fears, and you will have an opportunity for further discussion if your child still seems worried. "Remember a few weeks ago we talked about violence in schools and you were worried? You don't seem worried anymore. Is that true?"

How Not to Say It

- "Oh, that happened in another state. You don't have anything to worry about." Dismissing your child's worry may not alleviate it. He just may choose not to bring it up anymore. Furthermore, what if another school incident makes headlines? Your believability will be compromised.
- "You shouldn't watch that news report. Now, what would you like for dinner?" If your child knows about a frightening incident, it is best to discuss it, even briefly, to find out what your child thinks.
- "The world is a scary place." Your child will probably take your words to heart. Emphasize how bad things can happen but they are infrequent. Show him that you are not daunted.

78

Improving Self-confidence

Nine-year-old Meredith is seated at the dining room table working diligently on her math homework. Her mother peeks over Meredith's shoulder, studies her daughter's answers, and proceeds to tell her how amazingly intelligent she is. Mom often praises her daughter's intellect. A while later Meredith's father checks up on her. He watches how she erases a mistake and how intense her concentration seems. "You sure put in a lot of effort in your work, sweetheart," he says.

Whose comment, Mom's or Dad's, is more likely to increase Meredith's self-confidence? Would it surprise you to learn that one of the comments could increase Meredith's tendency to worry about failure?

Professional opinion about children's self-esteem has been a confusing mess of late. As the smoke has started to clear, the only consensus is that self-esteem may not be as vital a component of mental health as once thought. It is important but overrated. In the above example, Meredith might indeed feel self-confident about her intelligence if her mom praises her for being smart. But she is also likely to see intelligence as a fixed trait and may not persevere if a task seems difficult. Kids praised for being bright fear failing more than kids who are praised for their genuine hard effort to meet a challenge. And kids consistently praised for hard effort persevere when the going gets tough.

The self-esteem bandwagon resulted in many fundamental changes in schools over the past two decades. Failing students were often promoted to protect their esteem. Coaches refused to keep score in intramural games of basketball and baseball so as not to make the losing team feel bad. Many schools instituted a revised version of "Student of the Week" and made sure every student had a turn regardless of performance. In the science fair, everybody got a trophy. The upshot is that parents and teachers may feel better for trying, but children are less adept at handling failure.

Furthermore, numerous studies now suggest that many aggressive children have an overly positive view of themselves and their competence.

Smart Talk

Praising a child has always been a powerful tool in child-rearing and in helping kids feel good about themselves. But studies show that praise is effective because it is a part of a larger, more important factor called "Parental Responsiveness." A responsive parent does more than praise. He or she is actively involved and talks to a child about a wide variety of topics (and in a TENDER way). Praise is great, but it doesn't replace time together, affection, and other ways that parents show involvement and caring.

Things to Consider

➤ Think of self-confidence in specific, not just global, ways. A lower-than-average self-esteem may hide the fact that a child feels very proud in specific areas. Conversely, a child with high esteem can feel lousy about herself in areas not obvious to a parent.

➤ Since nobody is perfect, children (and adults) need to develop confidence in their ability to withstand disappointments and personal failures. *Resilience,* or the ability to bounce back from a letdown or be able to accept certain personal limitations (how tall a child is compared with peers, how athletic, how smart, etc.), does more to enhance esteem in the long run.

➤ One prominent researcher discovered after years of scientific study that teaching a child self-control is more important than broad attempts at self-esteem building. A child who masters self-control will not act or speak impulsively, will learn to persevere at a task despite feelings of anxiety or inadequacy, and will be more likely to resist peer pressure. The skill of self-control increases that child's chance of achieving meaningful goals—an outcome that will profoundly affect his or her self-confidence.

➤ Self-esteem, like love, may not be easily or precisely defined, but most people report greater self-confidence when they have reason to feel proud of themselves. That usually happens with a combination of knowing they are truly cherished despite their imperfections and by accomplishing difficult or challenging tasks. Love without accomplishment or accomplishment without love doesn't quite cut it. (Note: Youths in violent gangs feel appreciated by their group and often show mastery at violent or illegal behaviors. Their esteem can be quite high. Teaching the proper values cannot be overlooked.)

How to Say It

As your child grows, your level of overall responsiveness will act as an inoculation against many of the ups and downs that children experience. Just as a combination of good diet and exercise enhances our immune system's ability to fight disease, a supportive, loving family life enhances your child's psychological immune system. Global comments like "You are wonderful . . . the best kid in the entire world," etc., are terrific but must be balanced by more specific praise and encouragement such as:

- "You started tae kwon do eight months ago, and even on nights when you didn't feel like attending class, you showed up anyway. Now you've earned your orange belt. You should be proud of yourself for sticking to it."

- "Social studies has been a hard subject for you, yet you studied and let me ask you questions even though it was sometimes frustrating. That shows effort, and I'm impressed."

- "How about we go on a hike today? Just you and me." (Communicating that you simply want to spend time with them—and actually spending that time—conveys that they are truly special.)

- "Your friends wanted you to stay out longer than you should have, but you came home on time anyway. Going against your friends' wishes isn't always an easy thing to do. That took some courage."

- "What you just did [or said] showed patience. Good for you!" (Praise any of the virtues such as persistence, kindness, a sense of fairness, a willingness to share, or obedience.)

Rule of Thumb: Spend time with your child in meaningful activities. Self-worth can be enhanced whether or not the activity leads to an accomplishment.

If your child's self-confidence has been shaken recently, **EMPATHIZ-ING** is your best first move. Preface your remarks by briefly **REPORTING** what has prompted you to start the conversation.

- "You dropped the fly ball and your team lost. Now you can't seem to get that picture out of your head. Have I got that right?"

- "You look so unhappy. Tell me about it."

- "I've noticed you are keeping very quiet since your friends went bike riding without asking you to join them. It makes me think that your feelings were hurt."

- "I remember that you felt the same way two weeks ago when you didn't get chosen for a part in the play. That felt unfair, too." (Connecting the current hurt to a past hurt may help the child understand why her reaction is particularly intense. If the past hurt had healed, the child may begin to think that the current problem will be temporary.)

How Not to Say It

- Don't automatically ask, "Do you want to talk?" Your child may instinctively say no even though she might find the idea appealing.

- Asking "How do you feel?" can be a turnoff when your child is obviously upset. You may get a snippy response such as "How do you think I feel?" It is better to report your observations ("You're walking with your head down," "You just slammed the door," "Your eyes are red") and then state your interpretation ("so I think you're still very sad," "and that tells me you're very angry," or "It's hard to think about Grandpa and not cry").

- Don't ask what happened. Say, "Tell me what happened."

- Whenever possible, don't give any advice without getting clear acknowledgment that you have first understood what the problem is and how your child truly feels.

Often, children whose egos are bruised will use phrases that reveal global negative comments about themselves ("I'm stupid," "I can't do anything right," or "Nobody likes me") or global comments about others ("Everybody else is smart except me," "Nobody feels the way I do," or "All the boys know more than I do"). After you have demonstrated empathy, it is extremely important to **TEACH** your child how to think more rationally:

- "You're not stupid. You didn't study as hard this time."
- "I've watched everybody on your team make an error. You aren't the only one."
- "Remember how you played that video game and kept increasing your score? That shows me that you can improve over time if you work at it."
- "Yes, you made a mistake. That doesn't mean you'll never get it right. You've done well in the past, and you'll continue to do well most days."

It is very important that you not say the above examples before you've understood the real problem and expressed empathy. Otherwise, a sincere effort to get your child to appraise himself realistically ("You've made friends before, you'll make them again . . .") can sound as if you are dismissing his hurt feelings ("You shouldn't feel that way because . . ."). If he does not really believe you understand, he'll tune out your pep talk.

79

Self-critical Child

"I can't do it!" eight-year-old Audrey said. She threw the bat on the ground and walked away. "I'm just not good enough. I don't do anything right!"

Her older brother turned to the neighborhood kids who were standing nearby. "She gets that way a lot," he said.

"Come on back, Audrey," one of the other girls cried.

Audrey walked back into her house and shut the door.

Just about everybody can be self-critical at one time or another. "I can't believe I did that!" is a phrase many people mumble. But self-criticism can be extreme. When that happens, put-downs become all encompassing. Instead of saying "I'm not that good of a baseball player, but I still do okay," a strongly self-critical child will say, "I never do anything right!" Extreme self-criticism cuts to the core of the person. He or she is stupid, lazy, bad, weak, or ugly—qualities that define the whole person instead of commenting only on aspects of oneself.

Self-critical children are at risk for depression. Believing themselves incompetent, worthless, or bad, they never feel good about themselves even when they succeed. They tend to be perfectionists and pessimistic, striving for standards that are hard to maintain and feeling guilty or shameful when they can't live up to them.

Things to Consider

➤ Self-criticism tends to remain a stable quality of female adolescents through early adulthood. Self-critical teenage boys tend to feel more inner anger than depression when they reach adulthood.

➤ Younger children (especially preschool) tend to feel responsible for problems that are not their doing. They can feel blameworthy just by their existence. "It's my fault that Mom and Dad are unhappy."

➤ Guilt can be healthy if it leads to appropriate self-evaluation, reparation, and correction of one's behavior. The ability to empathize is strongly correlated with the ability to feel guilt. Children with chronically depressed parents often have a more complicated form of guilt where they assume an inappropriate level of responsibility for the events at home.

➤ In a study that began in 1951 and examined nearly four hundred children for decades (Caucasian, from two-parent families), it was found that five-year-old kids with very strict, demanding, unaffectionate parents were self-critical and depressed by age twelve.

➤ The behavior of the same-sex parent seems particularly important in the development of depression-prone children.

➤ Parents who often claim "It's my fault!" tend to have children with that same style of self-blame.

➤ Still, even in homes with chronically depressed parents or parents who are critical and cold, some children develop with a reasonably healthy ability to relate to others and avoid depression. There are no simple answers.

How to Say It

- First, be on the lookout for a child's self-criticism that seems harsh and overstated. Listen for words that are all-encompassing such as *never, nobody,* or *always,* as in "I'll never get it right," "Nobody likes me," or "I'll always be stupid." Then ask for more information. "I heard what you just said. Tell me what makes you say that."

- Challenge the overstated language your child uses. "It's not true that nobody likes you," "It's not true that you'll never learn how to play," or "It's not true that everybody thinks you are stupid. You are exaggerating."

- "When do you say those things to yourself? At school? With friends?"

- **TEACH** more appropriate self-evaluation by pointing out exceptions to your child's opinions. "You say you are stupid, but you get mostly A's on your report card. To me that means you are bright." Make these corrections as soon as possible after you hear your child's negative self-evaluations.

- "It isn't true that nobody likes you. I watch you on the playground, and I know the other boys play with you and enjoy being with you."

- "Just because you have to practice the piano a lot doesn't mean you are no good at it. In fact, the only way to be real good at it is to practice."

- "Yes, that girl preferred to play with someone other than you. Sometimes that happens, but it doesn't mean she hates you."

- Encourage your child to challenge his negative views. "What other examples can you give me that show you are much better than you think?"

- If you tend to be a more strict, demanding parent or uncomfortable with big shows of affection, it is important for you to loosen up. Start by allowing your child to get away with some messy activity. Be less concerned about neatness or being on time, act goofy, make mud pies or snow angels, or go haywire with modeling clay. "How about we rake the leaves into a big pile and then take turns jumping in them?"

- Again, the very strict or perfectionistic parent might want to ease up on expectations. "You don't have to clean up your room right now. It's okay to have it stay messy once in a while. This weekend would be a good time."

How Not to Say It

- Don't place any high-maturity demands on your child and watch out for all-encompassing language. "Your room must *always* be spotless," "You must *never* hurt anybody," "There is *no* reason you cannot get straight A's," "You should *never* undress where people can see you," or "*Nobody* will like you if you don't share."

- "You are a bad child." Don't label the child. Criticize specific actions, not the whole person.

- "If you feel guilty, then you must be guilty." This is not always true. Self-critical children assume guilt when it is not realistic.

- "If you continue to act this way, I just may leave for good" or "I won't love you anymore." These types of threats are very damaging. They undermine trust in others as well as any self-worth.

80

Sexuality and Reproduction

"Mom, what's sex?" seven-year-old Alex asked.

His mom turned away from the computer monitor, composed herself, and answered, "It's the difference between boys and girls," she said.

"Oh. What's for lunch?"

Mom's answer was sufficient for now. But soon her responses will necessarily be more detailed. She returned to her computer but couldn't concentrate very well.

Things to Consider

➤ It's a good idea to always be prepared to answer children's questions about sex. Questions occur unexpectedly and are best answered right then and there.

➤ "The talk" is a misleading concept. It suggests that the discussion, once completed, will be final. If you have a one-time only discussion about sex, it is not because you answered all questions satisfactorily, it is because your child would rather not raise the issue with you again.

➤ Take your cue from your child as to what constitutes a satisfactory answer. If your child is restless or inattentive, perhaps you have said enough for now.

➤ Take advantage of "teachable moments." Authors Charles Schaefer and Theresa Foy DiGeronimo point out that television shows make occasional sexual references that could be explained, or you and your children may happen to observe animals mating. These are perfect moments to teach a quick lesson and convey that the topic is one you can be comfortable with.

➤ Children will learn from their peers, usually before you think they are ready. But some of what they learn is incorrect. Don't take comfort knowing that your kids will learn about sex "from the streets."

How to Say It

- Use proper terminology. Words like penis, vagina, intercourse, semen, ejaculate, and sperm are accurate and leave no room for misunderstanding. The term "make love" may also be suitable, but be prepared to explain it. "How does a woman become pregnant? A man and woman get undressed. When they want to get pregnant, the man's penis gets larger and is put inside the woman's vagina—that is an opening between her legs. Sperm comes out of the penis and stays inside the woman. If the sperm reaches an egg, the egg grows and becomes a little baby."

- If you are uncomfortable talking about sex, say that up front. Otherwise, your child will detect your reluctance and may decide not to ask you more questions in the future. But admitting your discomfort shows that despite your feelings, you want to talk about sex. "My parents didn't talk about sex with me, so I'm a bit uncomfortable. Bear with me. Still, I'd much rather talk to you about it than say nothing."

- "What does having sex mean?" "Sometimes it means having intercourse which is how to make a baby. Sometimes it means touching each other in ways people ordinarily do not do unless they are married. A man will touch the woman's breasts and vagina and bottom. A woman will touch the man's penis and bottom."

- "How does a man's penis get big?" "The penis is made of spongy material. Blood flows into the penis and the spongy material swells up. That's called an erection."

- **ENCOURAGE** future questions. "I'm really glad you asked that question. It was a good question. Please come to me anytime you want to know more."

How Not to Say It

- "Where did you hear that word? Who told you those ideas? We don't talk about such things in this house." You are implying that anything which suggests sex is bad or dirty or a shameful topic. It is a natural act that children need to be properly educated about.

- "You are too young to know the answers to those questions." Sorry, you're wrong. Your answers can be short and sweet and age-appropriate. If your child is asking, it means he has heard things—usually in school or from siblings or friends—and deserves accurate and honest answers.

- "Well, in the woman are organs called ovaries, and they contain tiny eggs. Each month an egg is released into a long tunnel called the fallopian tube. The egg passes through this tunnel on its way to the uterus where it becomes fertilized. . . ." Accurate, yes. Necessary? Probably not. Does it sound like a classroom lecture? Definitely. It's best to keep answers short and sweet. If your child is keenly interested, you can add more details.

81

Sex Play with Other Children

Kevin was in third grade. "Guess what," he said to his father as he put his glove and ball in the garage. "Margo and I made out today!"

Dad's jaw fell.

"What's French kissing?" Kevin asked. "Margo said it's okay to kiss, but it's not okay to French kiss."

"Hey, shortstop," Dad said. "What else did you two do?" He was afraid to ask but felt he had little choice. His little shortstop was now in triple-A, on his way to the big leagues.

Most children will experiment with sex. It may be with siblings or friends or on themselves. Some children, like Kevin, are open about their endeavors because they haven't figured out that parents usually freak out (at least on the inside) over such things. Others know they are doing something their parents won't like and will be very reluctant to confess when confronted.

Things to Consider

➤ A recent study showed that nearly half of all parents reported that their child had engaged in some type of sex play with another child by the time their child was six. Follow-up revealed that such an activity had no bearing on functioning when the child was interviewed at age eighteen.

➤ While normal, such sex play should be gently discouraged.

How to Say It

- **TEACH** about personal privacy. "I don't want you to touch other children's private parts, and I don't want other children touching your private parts. Okay? That is why they are called private."

- "Many kids like to play those kissing games. It makes them feel more grown up. You are too young, and I don't want you playing them."
- If your child denies he did anything and you know he is lying, don't push him to confess. "I saw you behind the garage playing doctor, but I don't want you playing doctor. Your body is not to be used as a game."
- **EMPATHIZE**. "Many kids are curious about their bodies. It's normal to want to see other people's bodies, but I don't want you taking off your clothes as part of a game."
- "What you did is not something children should do. Okay? You aren't bad for doing it, but you shouldn't do it again."
- "If another child wants you to take off your clothes or to show your private parts, what will you say and do?" Rehearse strategies to say no.

How Not to Say It

- "Tell me what you did! You're not leaving here to play until you tell me!" If your child is not forthcoming about what happened, he already realizes it is not a subject you can handle well. It is better to state matter-of-factly what you know and teach your child proper behavior. Punishment is not necessary.
- "You did a horrible thing." Lighten up. It is not evil but a normal curiosity.
- "Stop touching yourself there! That's bad." Masturbation or rubbing oneself may occur in children. Gently **TEACH** your child that such behaviors are not appropriate in public and try to occupy his hands with some other toy.

82

Sex:
Child Reading
Adult Magazines

Steve came up to his wife in the kitchen holding a magazine.

"I found this under Jimmy's bed when I was looking for his socks," he said.

Christine looked at the cover of the *Playboy*. "It's six months old," she said. "Do you think he's had it all this time?"

Steve shrugged. "What should we do with it? Put it back and act as though we never found it?"

The couple decided it would be best to talk with Jimmy.

Things to Consider

➤ It is normal for preteens and teens to be interested in adult magazines, boys especially. As a parent you have the right to keep the magazines out of your house, but that won't keep your child from scanning them when they are available.

➤ Pornographic magazines can range in content from nudity to explicit sexual acts. Men's magazines often contain sexual acts between women. These topics should be discussed with your child if you discover he has been reading these magazines.

➤ You may want to discuss the difference between sexual curiosity, which is normal, and pornographic material, which views people (usually women) as purely sexual objects—an attitude that is harmful.

How to Say It

• It may be hard not to lecture, but do your best. Begin by **EMPATHIZING** to put your child at ease. If he thinks he's going to get into trouble, he won't listen to the important things you have to say. "A lot of boys like to read these magazines. It is normal to be curious about naked women and sex. But I noticed you were trying to hide the magazine. My guess is you figured out there may be something wrong about these magazines, too."

- If you have books on art that contain some nudity or if you and the children have visited a museum where there were statues or paintings of nudes, you can **TEACH** how nudity by itself is not bad or wrong. "Some of the greatest paintings have people with no clothes on. The human body is very beautiful to look at. It's understandable that you would be interested. But the pictures in these magazines are there for a different purpose. They make what can be a loving act between people into a purely sexual one, without the love that belongs there."

- "Slavery is wrong because slaves were viewed not as people but as objects to be owned and used for whatever purposes the slave owners wanted. Pornography is wrong because the people in the pictures are viewed by others as sex objects only. If someone cares about you only because of your body or your appearance, what happens when you get older and your body is less attractive?"

- "You have a mother and a sister. Would you want people not to care about them and only take advantage of them?"

- "Some of these pictures show homosexual acts. Have you heard the word *homosexual* before? Some people find it exciting to watch two people who are both men or both women have sex. But sex for the sake of sex cheapens human dignity."

- "I hope you'll decide to remember what I've told you the next time you see a magazine like this. For now, I'm going to throw this magazine away. I don't want it in our home."

How Not to Say It

- "Where did you get this trash? Did you buy it with your own money or did someone give it to you?" He now knows you object. But you probably lost the opportunity to teach him anything about why pornography is wrong.

- "I can't believe you would look at such things! Didn't I raise you better than this?" His behavior is really normal curiosity. Teach your values in a manner that will make it easier for him to listen.

- "If you're going to read that stuff, don't let me see it around the house." What values are you teaching? Giving permission shows that you recognize it is a normal curiosity to read such magazines, but you have a responsibility as a parent to teach your child your values.

- "That's disgusting!" What's disgusting? The sexual act portrayed or the fact that it is depicted in a manner devoid of love? Your child might want to know.

83

Sex:
Child Walks In on
You and Your Mate

Eleven-year-old Sam had been outside cleaning his bike and fixing the chain. But when he couldn't find his bicycle pump, he ran inside to ask his father.

"Dad?" he called out just as he opened the bedroom door.

The next thing he saw was his parents scrambling to find the blankets and hide themselves, but doing a pretty poor job of it.

Sam closed the door quickly behind him and paused for a moment. His eyes bugged out and his heart pounded. *Did I just see what I thought I saw?*

Things to Consider

➤ These moments are not traumatic but can be acutely embarrassing for everyone involved.

➤ You may be tempted to pretend it never happened, but don't. Your child may be scared, confused, or laughing hysterically. You're better off finding out his or her reaction and doing your best to clarify any misunderstandings.

➤ Young kids will be confused. Older kids will probably know what you were doing but still may be shaken or afraid they did something wrong.

➤ In the future: When in doubt, lock your door.

How to Say It

- Immediately get out of bed and put a robe on or get dressed. Don't wait until later to have the discussion. Don't ask, "Why didn't you knock?" By now your child is wishing he had knocked. "I'm sorry you came in when you did. Mom and Dad were making love. We should have made sure we had privacy, but we forgot."

- A child who hasn't had any formal sex education may be confused or scared. She may understand to some extent what she saw but will also be puzzled. Be calm, soft-spoken, and reassuring. "Moms and Dads make love like that as a way of showing their feelings toward each other. It is something that grown-ups do. You look a little nervous. I hope we didn't scare you."

- "Do you have any questions about what you saw?" A much older child probably understands what he saw, though he never actually witnessed it before. A little humor can ease the tension. "Well, this isn't the way I had planned to teach you about sex. I'm embarrassed, but I'll get over it. What questions do you have?"

How Not to Say It

- "Don't you know you're not supposed to barge into our room? Don't ever do that again." True, he should have knocked, but don't make that the issue. Believe me, from now on he'll give you plenty of warning. He doesn't ever want to see you two at it again.

- "What exactly did you see?" While you may be hoping she saw very little, don't ask this question. It can be embarrassing to have to give details. Presume she saw everything and do your best to correct any misunderstandings.

Single or divorced parents may be in bed with someone they are not married to. If your child catches you in the act with someone you have been dating, you have much more to explain than sex and anatomy. Children ages six and up will regard your relationship as serious. Older kids may feel you have betrayed their other parent. Read the chapters on introducing children to a new partner and how to handle matters when kids do not like the new person.

Rule of Thumb: Don't sleep with a new partner when your children are anywhere around unless that partner is living with you and you are in a committed relationship (married, or about to be). Anything less and you run the risk of your children getting confused, hurt, or angry.

84

Promoting
Sexual Abstinence

Karen, a divorced mother of a pubescent eighth-grade girl, spoke to her therapist about what had happened.

"I came home from work early because I wasn't feeling well. When I opened the door, I heard a rush of activity in my bedroom. Who did I find but my daughter and her boyfriend in my bed. Of course she is grounded. But I was proud of the way I handled the situation later on. I told my daughter all about condoms and safe sex. Can you believe she didn't have any condoms? We were calm and open. I really felt as if I was doing a good job as her mother."

Single parents have a tough job, but it is made tougher when society and the media claim that teenage sexual activity is inevitable, that abstinence is an old-fashioned, you-got-your-head-in-the-sand virtue, and that education about safety is paramount. Karen believed the propaganda that good parents teach good information about safe sex and that abstinence has gone the way of the typewriter.

Things to Consider

➤ Early sexual activity among children and teens is associated with early use of alcohol, drugs, criminal activity, and poorer social adjustment several years later.

➤ Once a teenager has had intercourse, frequency of church attendance declines. Grades fall significantly the year after the first sexual experience.

➤ Poor family relationships predict early sexual activity.

➤ Sexual experimentation does not cause experimentation with drugs or alcohol, but the three go together. A sexually active preteen or teen has probably experimented with these substances.

➤ Data from 1989 and 1992 show clearly that abortion rates are significantly lower for girls ages fifteen to seventeen in states with parental involvement legislation. This means that sexual activity is also lower in those states. Contact your legislator if you live in a state that overrules parental involvement.

➤ Statistics vary, but by twelfth grade more than half of all teens have engaged in sexual intercourse. In poor urban areas the statistics show that by age fourteen more than 80 percent of teens have had sex. A study in Iowa showed that 19 percent of seventh-grade students and 64 percent of twelfth-grade students had engaged in intercourse at least once.

➤ A sizable minority of students are able to postpone sexual intercourse beyond twelfth grade. Will your child be one?

How to Say It

- For preteens especially, make your values clear and explicit. Leave no room for doubt as to how you feel about teenage sexual experimentation. "Yes, sometimes children or teenagers have sex, but it is wrong to do that. It is a huge mistake. It increases the chance that the girl will get pregnant, but she will be too young to properly care for the baby. It's important to wait until you are grown up and able to provide a home and two parents for your baby before you have sex."

- **EMPATHIZE** but be clear about **DO'S & DON'TS.** "Many teenagers try to have sex. You will want to when you are a teenager, or someone else may want you to have sex. While it can be hard to say no, I want you to say no. The longer you wait to have sex, the better off you will be."

- "I will always want you to talk to me if you are tempted to have sex. I will not punish you for those feelings, but I will help you resist them because it is safer for you to resist them."

- "Another problem with having sex before you are grown up is that you have an increased chance of getting what is called a sexual disease. Many of these diseases can be treated with medications, but they can cause much pain and possibly some damage. Diseases like AIDS are not curable." (A report in the *New England Journal of Medicine* indicated that the strongest factor for cervical cancer was the human papillomavirus, one of the more prominent sexual diseases among younger women.)

Smart Talk

The Role of Nonverbal Communication

A study by Melody Graham at Mount Mercy College in Iowa showed that teens were less likely to engage in sex if:

They turned to their parents first for any problem.

Parents were available. Some parents communicate well but are too busy. They were less effective in helping their kids postpone sex.

They believed their parents would be very upset if they had sex. Interestingly, some parents were poor verbal communicators, but their teens got the clear message that sex was not allowed. Good communication was not effective in hindering sexual activity per se. A stronger factor was the teenagers' own values. Teens who thought having sex was okay and who had friends who engaged in sex were more likely to have sex themselves.

The message for parents: Your children are likely to postpone sexual activity if they believe you value abstinence, if they feel they can talk to you about anything, if family harmony is good, and if their friends are not sexually active.

How Not to Say It

- "You shouldn't have sex during high school, but if you do, please be sure you use a condom." While teaching that condom use reduces risks of pregnancy (but does not by any means eliminate that risk) is important, it is far more important to make a clear statement that premarital sexual activity is wrong and harmful. Saying "You shouldn't, but if you do . . ." is really saying that you accept the idea. It is a weak opinion. Kids need clear statements of your values. Teaching safe sex is important. Teaching abstinence is vastly more important.

- "Everybody has sex in high school eventually, so I expect that you probably will, too. Just be careful." You are really giving your permission. And you are telling your child that you have no faith in his or her ability to resist peer pressure or to make a mature decision regarding sex.

- "If I ever find out you had sex, I'll make your life a living hell." No question, your values are clear. But the best combination is clear values *plus* open lines of communication. This comment may teach your child never to approach you when peer pressure to have sex is high.

85

Sexual Abuse: Alerting Your Child

Jim was listening to the local television news while preparing dinner. He wasn't paying close attention, but seven-year-old Alyson was. When he finally realized that the reporter was discussing the arrest of a man who had sexually abused children, he quickly shut off the television. Alyson looked up at him but didn't say anything. Later, he asked his wife if he should have spoken to his daughter about what she might have overheard.

"Probably," his wife said. "But I sure feel uncomfortable about the idea."

Most parents do. But according to best estimates, between 12 percent and 25 percent of children will experience some form of sexual abuse. The most vulnerable time is between the ages of eight and twelve. Girls are more vulnerable than boys. Abuse can be a single incident but typically occurs many times over the course of weeks, months, or years. Some sexual abuse may not involve touching; instead, the adult wishes to become sexually aroused by exposing himself or by showing erotic material to children. At a minimum, the child can be very uncomfortable. Psychological trauma is possible in more severe cases.

When Alyson heard the news report about a child molester, she didn't say anything to her father. While some children will ask parents, "What's sexual abuse?" or "What's a child molester?" many—perhaps a majority—will not. It is up to parents to inform their children because sexual abuse is common and is usually perpetrated by people children know—not strangers.

Things to Consider

➤ Much sexual abuse occurs before a parent has had an opportunity to explain the facts of life to their children. Parents are therefore compelled to warn their children about sex abuse using language and concepts they hadn't expected to say until a few years later. Before children can make sense of the concept of sexual abuse, they will need to understand some of the basics about human sexuality. That will include the names of a person's private parts (it really is best to use the actual terms: penis, vagina, anus, breasts).

➤ Next, it will be necessary to describe the idea of inappropriate touching, or any touching that can make a child feel uncomfortable, and distinguish it from acceptable touching (hugs, frolicking, visits to the doctor, etc.). Be matter-of-fact, and try not to sound frightened. You simply want to explain that certain kinds of touching are not allowed and that people do not have a right to touch children any way they wish.

➤ It is a good idea to give your child examples of ways they might be approached by a molester: the stranger in a car; someone who offers gifts or candy; someone who pays attention to her but then asks if she wants to play doctor; someone who asks for help searching for a lost animal. Remind your child that molesters are often friendly and try to entice children by giving them gifts or spending extra time with them. Role-playing effective ways to recognize and get away from a potential molester is also a very good idea.

➤ Girls are sexually assaulted at twice the rate of boys. The rate of assault for girls does not increase as the girl gets older—which means younger girls are at as great a risk as teenage girls.

How to Say It

- "The part of your body that your underwear covers we call your private parts. We call it that because nobody needs to see those parts of your body except sometimes your parents or a doctor. That is why you don't see people walking on the street without clothes on."

- "Some people want to touch your private parts. They might want to touch your bottom or your penis [vagina]. No one has a right to do that unless it is a doctor and I have given the doctor permission. Anytime you think someone wants to touch your private area, you can scream or say 'no' real loud and run away. You can tell me what happened."

- "No one has a right to even look at your private parts. That is why we call them private."

- "Sometimes the people who want to touch you in your private area first try to show you pictures of people with their clothes off. You might be curious about that but you should not trust that person."

All of the above is a form of **TEACHING**. Don't hesitate to make an **EMPATHIZING** remark if you think your child has a strong reaction.

- "You look worried, Molly. Are you wondering if something like that could happen to you?"
- **ENCOURAGE** your child to come to you with questions. "If you think this has happened to you before, or if someone touches you in a way I've just described, you must talk to me. You will never get in trouble for that. It is a good thing to talk to me."

What Else to Say

- If you are obviously ill at ease with the topic and think your child senses that, say, "It is a difficult topic because I don't like to think about someone hurting you or touching you in the wrong ways." If you give the impression that sex is an uncomfortable topic, your child may think twice about talking to you about it in the future.
- Follow up the initial conversation with your child, perhaps with your spouse also present. A husband might say to his wife, "I spoke to Molly today about that report on the radio about a child molester. I explained how some people might want to touch her in ways that could make her uncomfortable and how she should always come to one of us if she has any concerns about that."
- Offer reassurances. "I will always do my best to protect you. Most children are not abused but too many are." But remind her that such things happen when loving parents aren't looking, so she must be ready to say "no" and run away even if the person is someone she trusts.

How Not to Say It

There is no need to be dramatic or graphic. Descriptions of intercourse or masturbation are unnecessary unless your child understands sexual reproduction and feels comfortable with those terms.

- "Let me know if someone gets too friendly with you." That comment is too vague and underplays your concerns. Children think very literally. Be specific and clear.

- "Stay away from strangers." Most child abusers are people your children know. Besides, your kids watch you exchange pleasantries with many strangers (the meter reader, a checkout clerk, people sitting next to you in church or on a plane) and will get confused.

- Don't make it a one-time-only discussion. There will be other opportunities to remind your kids about the importance of saying no to uncomfortable touching. "Remember when I spoke to you about bad people who want to touch your private parts? That story you just heard was about a man who was arrested for doing that. What do think about that?"

With as many as one in four children being sexually abused at some point during childhood or adolescence, parents need to be alert to situations where abuse occurs. While the vast majority of adults who volunteer time to work with kids as coaches are decent, pedophiles often look for situations where their access to children is easy and fairly unrestricted. Remind your children about inappropriate touching and their need to tell an adult if abuse occurs or is suspected.

86

Sexual Abuse:
After It Happens

The trip back from the doctor's office was surreal. Marjorie had all she could do to concentrate on her driving and keep her eyes from filling with tears. She tried to sound reassuring to her eleven-year-old daughter, Samantha. The girl stayed quiet and pressed her face against the passenger window.

"It's over now, Sam," Marjorie said. She rubbed the back of her hand against Sam's cheek. "He'll never do that to you again."

What made the revelation of sexual abuse even more shocking to Marjorie was finding out who the perpetrator was—Alan, a neighbor just a few doors down. Alan was a father and respected member of the town. He was even at their house for a barbecue two weeks earlier. No one ever suspected a thing.

Since parents are often traumatized themselves when their child suffers severe abuse, they sometimes minimize or exaggerate the harm done. Neither extreme is helpful. Pretending that their child will eventually "get over it" or being panic stricken at the thought of the child ever going anywhere unaccompanied will complicate the recovery process.

Not all children who are sexually abused show any symptoms. The most reliable indicator of abuse is age-inappropriate sexual behavior or knowledge. Children who rub their genitals frequently, masturbate compulsively, or expose themselves to other children are often signaling for help. Or a child may have her dolls engage in sex play. Still, according to Cynthia Monahon, author of *Children and Trauma: A Guide for Parents and Professionals,* 20 percent to 60 percent of sexually abused children do not show any behavioral disturbances. Monahon also states that most children under eleven may not talk at length about shameful or painful feelings.

Healing after sexual abuse can be strengthened when parents say the right things. Patience is also important, since there are no quick solutions to overcoming trauma.

Things to Consider

➤ Don't be surprised if a child's school performance slips temporarily. Nightmares, phobias, and clinging behavior (wanting to sleep with parents) are also not unusual.

➤ In the immediate aftermath, protect your child from exposure to stimuli, such as violent or sexually provocative television shows, that might trigger bad memories.

➤ Don't assume that your child must talk out her feelings. Some children can only talk about the trauma for brief periods, while others talk every chance they can get. According to trauma expert Cynthia Monahon, a problem occurs when there is a mismatch between how much a parent needs to talk about what happened and how much a child needs to talk. Look to your child for clues and go at her pace.

➤ Be prepared to hear details that might horrify you. Do your best to convey to your child that you can handle it.

How to Say It

In the immediate aftermath, be **ENCOURAGING**. Your child needs reassurance that she will feel better over time, that she is deeply loved, and that she is not bad or in any way at fault.

- "We will always be here for you. You will not have to go through this alone."

- "All children who are abused are innocent. No matter what they did, they are not at fault for what the grown-up did."

- "The man who did this to you is bad. You are not bad."

- "You will start to feel better, not all at once but a little each day. Just like finding pretty shells on the beach—every day you add to your collection."

In the weeks or months that follow (depending on the severity and duration of the abuse and whether or not the abuser was a close relative), you might need to help your child cope with specific fears or vague anxieties. Girls tend to withdraw more; boys may act out more.

- "You'd rather sleep with your sister [or parents] tonight instead of alone in your room. That's fine for now, but soon you won't have to be doing that." (Your words should indicate that you expect she will feel better.)

- "You're feeling nervous inside right now. I can tell by the look on your face. Let's talk about ways that can help you feel better right now."

- Use encouragement by reminding her of past fears she overcame. "Remember two years ago when we had the car accident in the rain? You were scared to be a passenger for a little while, but then you got over it. You'll feel less afraid about this, too."

- Reassure her that anxiety and other symptoms of trauma are normal. "I do not expect you to act brave. It's normal to feel scared or have nightmares. But I know you won't always feel that way."

- During a nightmare or disturbing flashback, refocus the child's thoughts on the present. "I'm here with you, and we are safe in the house. You aren't with that man."

- "It's over. That was in the past."

How Not to Say It

- "You're fine. There's nothing to be afraid of." She is not fine, and her fears are real to her. It is better to say you understand she's feeling the way she is and reassure her that it is in the past and she will feel better eventually.

- "You're young. You probably won't even remember this when you get older." False. She will remember, and so will you.

- "Going to the mall with all those strange people is scary for you. Fine, we don't have to go." That comment subtly implies that avoidance is always reasonable and that the fears may last a long time. It would be better to empathize by saying that the mall *feels* scary (but it's just a feeling), and that the two of you can go some other time.

- "Why didn't you tell me right away!" This implies that your child was wrong or made a mistake. Molesters often use fear tactics to keep children from informing on them. Never blame your child.

- "You know you're not supposed to let anybody touch your private parts!" Again, you are telling the child he was in some way responsible. If you catch yourself saying these types of things, immediately correct yourself. "I'm sorry. You are in no way to blame. That man did those things to you and it must have been scary and confusing for you."

The more severe or prolonged the symptoms, or if the child refuses to attend school, it is wise to seek professional help.

87

Sharing

"Artie, share with your friend," his mom said. "You have plenty of time to play with that when your friend isn't visiting."

"But I'm playing with it now," the seven-year-old answered. "He can have it later."

"You have to learn to share," Mom said. "Now give him that toy."

Artie obeyed, but unwillingly. Was Mom right to make him share?

Things to Consider

➤ Sharing is important if children are to learn to get along favorably with peers. Preschoolers have a harder time sharing.

➤ The older the child (especially ten or older), the more he is capable of seeing the benefits to sharing instead of seeing only the costs.

➤ Some studies show that if a child's peer owns a toy, the parent is more likely to tell her child to let the owner have it back. But if her child owns the toy, the same parent is likely to tell her child to share. That bias can make it harder for kids to see the value in sharing.

➤ Studies show that children are more likely to share after observing a peer share than if they observed an adult share.

➤ Children ages nine to thirteen with mild retardation or cognitive deficits shared about one-quarter as often as same-age peers without such deficits.

➤ Some toys are very special and difficult to share. (Would you be willing to share your new car with your neighbor?) Before a play date, have your child select some toys he is willing to share and place the others out of the way.

How to Say It

- When possible, discuss the expectation of sharing before the event occurs. Preparation may help your child cooperate. "When your cousins come over, they will want to play some of your video games. Even though the games are yours, I want you to let them play games even if you don't want to play."

- "Are there some games you'd rather not let anybody play?"

- "What do you think about sharing your baseball glove when your cousins come over? Chances are some of them won't have their own glove. Would you be willing to play some innings without using your glove?"

- **EMPATHIZE** when necessary. "It isn't always fun to share. I know it can make you feel upset. But sometimes it makes you feel good."

- **TEACH** consequences by letting your child make up his own mind. "You don't have to share if you don't want to, but I'm concerned that your friends won't want to share with you next time."

- **ENCOURAGE** sharing by praising it. "I noticed you let your neighbor ride on your bike when his was broken. It was no fun for you because you had to stand around, but I'm proud of you for sharing. That was very kind."

- "I noticed that your friend shared his candy with you. That must have made you feel good. How would you have felt if he didn't want to share?"

- If your child refuses to share, consider that there may be underlying issues. "I wonder if not wanting to share your toys now has anything to do with the fact that our cat died a few days ago."

- "I notice that you especially don't like to share with Johnny. Is there something about him that bothers you?"

How Not to Say It

- "It's not nice to be selfish." You don't need to call names to make your point.

- "You have to share." Older children (budding attorneys) will tell you they do not have to; younger kids won't understand why, if they have ownership, they must give it up. Sometimes the fair thing is to let the other child wait. (Be aware that sometimes parents urge sharing so as to avoid making an unfavorable impression on other adults. When that happens, you may be inconsistent in your guidelines.)

- "If you don't share, I'm going to punish you." Is it really important that your child share right then and there? You may get compliance, but you may worsen the problem. If your child feels he has nothing to call his own, he may become even more withholding in the future. Sometimes natural consequences work better. If your child doesn't share, perhaps later his sibling won't share with him; that will have more of an impact than a threat from you.

- "Actually, since I paid for the toys, they are mine, not yours. And I'm saying to share my toys." That won't fly—especially later when you want your child to clean up *his* toys.

88

Shyness

"What did you do in school today, Billy?" Uncle Ray asked.

Billy shrugged his shoulders.

"He's shy," Billy's father said. "Billy, tell Uncle Ray about your field trip. Tell him where you went."

"To the zoo," Billy said.

"Tell him what your favorite animal was."

"The giraffe."

"You had a great time, didn't you, Billy? Didn't you say you also liked the monorail because it took you all around the zoo? Tell Uncle Ray about the monorail . . ."

When a child is shy, conversations with unfamiliar people can be short and sweet. Parents often try to coax their shy children into becoming more involved. It is a good idea if done right.

Things to Consider

➤ About 10 percent to 15 percent of all children are shy or "slow to warm up." By adolescence at least a third of these children are no longer shy.

➤ Shyness can be painful when extreme, but it has its benefits, too. Shy children are less likely to take impulsive, fearless risks. Shy children are the least likely to act aggressively or criminally. Sensitive, they can develop empathy more easily.

➤ Peers do not necessarily dislike shy children. However, it may take shy children longer to make friends.

➤ The children who tend to overcome shyness have parents who do two things: Set clear rules and limits (the more vague the rules, the more likely a shy child can fade into the background) and help their child rehearse appropriate risk-taking.

➤ Don't force a shy child to perform.

➤ Don't answer questions for a shy child.

➤ Don't take over for a shy child when he could do it himself. Otherwise, shy children learn to become even more passive.

➤ Research shows that shy boys tend to marry later than non-shy boys. Not so for shy girls, who also tend to drop out of the workforce more in order to stay at home with their children.

How to Say It

- "Tell me what you did in math and science class today." These "Tell me" questions are better than "Did you . . ." or questions that can be answered briefly.

- **TEACH** assertiveness. "Let's practice talking loud on the phone." Shy children speak softly, which makes it more likely that others will stop speaking to them.

- "Let's practice what you can say when your aunt and uncle arrive. How about 'Hi, Aunt Mary. Did you eat at any fun restaurants on the drive down here?'"

- "Let's practice what you can say to a kid at school who is by himself."

- **ENCOURAGE** assertiveness by praising it. "You went right over to that group of kids and asked if you could play soccer with them. Good for you!"

How Not to Say It

- "Just go over there and introduce yourself. It's no big deal." Saying that is like telling someone who is claustrophobic to sit inside a closet. Practice ahead of time, then encourage.

- "No one will like you if you're shy." That won't help. In fact, it may make her more self-conscious. Besides, shy kids can be well liked once they make friends.

- "There's nothing to be afraid of." Not to you, maybe. It is better to say, "It isn't easy to speak up more, but it doesn't have to be hard all the time, either. Practice makes perfect."

- "C'mon. Please? Pretty please?" If you have to beg your child to be more assertive, you don't understand shyness. It is better to ask him what would make it easier for him to try.

89

Sportsmanship

The tae kwon do instructor watched as his team of eight- to ten-year-olds went down to defeat in the sparring competition. He congratulated the kids on their good effort and then gave them one more instruction.

"Go over and shake hands with the team that beat you. They taught you some things, and it's important to be a good sport."

Sportsmanship is a key ingredient to getting along well with other children. Plus, learning to lose gracefully and hope for the best the next time is a mark of a resilient, optimistic child.

Things to Consider

➤ Your influence is important, but so is the influence of the gym teacher and the athletic coach. Be sure to talk with them about their approach to teaching.

➤ Children with low self-esteem do very well with coaches who are supportive, who use positive words of encouragement, and who teach specific skills. High-self-esteem children can fare well with a coach who tends to be critical, but their low-esteem counterparts do not. If you place your child in a class such as martial arts to improve his esteem, make sure the instructor does not use criticism as a teaching technique.

How to Say It

- **TEACH** what you mean by sportsmanship. "Being a good sport means that even if you lose, you won't complain and you won't get angry at the player who beat you. It also means not making fun of any player you beat."

- "It isn't always easy, but good sportsmanship means trying harder the next time instead of giving up. That way you can inspire your team."

- **EMPATHIZE** after a loss or if your child feels he let the team down. Don't try to cheer him up without empathizing first. "It's normal to feel bad when your team loses."

- "All those who don't score a goal feel bad about it, especially if their team doesn't win."

- "It feels lousy when you are the only one who doesn't get a hit."

- **ENCOURAGE** sportsmanship by praising it. "I like the way you shook hands with the other player after the game and said, 'Good job.'"

- **TEACH** by asking questions about popular sports figures who misbehave. "That famous basketball player just got arrested" or "That baseball player was caught doing drugs. How do you think that affects his team?"

- "Someone is always watching you play. Maybe it's your family, maybe it's a big crowd, maybe it's just your opponent. But when the game is over, people will have an impression of you. Will it be positive or negative? . . . Why do you say that?"

How Not to Say It

- "Don't be a baby. Nobody can win every time." Name-calling won't help. It's better to empathize and show optimism. It simply will take a little time (usually a day) before your child feels better about a loss.

- "Hey, Coach, what's wrong with you? Why'd you take my kid out of the game so soon?" Questions for the coach are best asked privately. It can be disturbing for your child to see two people he (hopefully) respects—his parent and his coach—arguing.

- "If you played harder, you might have won that game." Your child knows that. If you really think your child was showing poor effort, you could inquire without making it sound like a criticism. "You seemed a little sluggish on the court today. Was that my imagination or was something on your mind?"

- "If you play your best, we can go for ice cream later." Do you really think that ice cream will be the main motivation? Not likely. Go out for ice cream whether she wins or loses and make it a fun time, regardless of the outcome of the game.

- "You really creamed your opponent," "You showed no mercy," "You were a killer on the court," or "Did you see his face when you beat him? Ha!" Tone it down. Be enthusiastic but don't encourage annihilation of the opposing team. **TEACH** having respect for the opponent.

Stealing

Joanne's parents told their daughter's teacher that some new felt-tip pens were missing from Joanne's desk, along with a brand-new notebook with a unique cover. The teacher investigated and found the pens and notebook in the possession of another little girl, who denied she had stolen them.

"I know that the girl stole them from your daughter," the teacher told Joanne's parents. "But her mother said she thinks she bought them. No one saw her take them, so we couldn't accuse her of stealing."

The teacher was in a dilemma. Circumstantial evidence showed the girl to be guilty, but there was no hard proof. What should parents and teachers do?

Things to Consider

➤ Most children will steal at least once. But a few will steal regularly and with increased sophistication. When first discovered, parents shouldn't overreact. Most children learn that stealing is wrong and will learn not to take other people's belongings.

➤ Frequent stealing among children ages ten to twelve is a predictor of court-recorded offenses later on. Frequent stealing is a sign of serious emotional problems.

➤ One study showed that a significant number of children who were referred for psychiatric assessment because they had been accused of stealing came from families where there was little parental warmth or personal attention.

➤ Stealing is hard to detect as kids get older. When stealing becomes a noticeable problem, you are better off taking the approach where your child has to prove his innocence rather than you prove his guilt. The little girl in the opening story who stole felt-tip pens got away with it because the teacher believed a child is innocent until proven guilty. Give children the benefit of the doubt at first. But if they are repeat offenders, you will make more headway if you make them prove their innocence.

How to Say It

- Younger children who are otherwise good kids are best taught that stealing is wrong (**DO'S & DON'TS**) without traumatizing them. "This toy doesn't belong to you. It is wrong to take things that are not yours."

- "It is called stealing when you take something that you did not pay for. Put it back."

- Use normal events to model honesty. "I just noticed that the woman at the checkout register overpaid me. Let's go and return the money to her."

- "This money on the table is for the waiter. The people who sat here before we did left it. Someone else might have taken this money and kept it. Let's make sure that the waiter gets his money."

- **EMPATHIZE** when your child really wanted something, but be sure to state that stealing is wrong. "You have the balloon in your pocket that we saw at the store. I know you really wanted it, but stealing is wrong. We'll go back to the store and return it."

- If infractions are more frequent and serious, consistent negative consequences are needed. If the child gets away with stealing even once in a while, it will become harder to break the habit. "This is the third time this week I've noticed money missing from my wallet. The first two times we found out that you stole it. Now I cannot trust you, and I have to believe that you stole the money again this time. Unless you can prove to me you were innocent, you will have to wash all the windows as a punishment."

- **ENCOURAGE** honesty by rewarding it with praise. "These cookies were on the counter all afternoon. I know you wanted some, but you didn't take any because you knew they were for the party. That shows honesty and trustworthiness."

Smart Talk

Signs That Your Child May Be Headed for Disaster

Prominent psychologist Jerome Kagan has outlined five categories to predict adolescents who are at risk for criminal behavior (such as stealing), teen pregnancy, or substance abuse. If your child fits even one of the categories, he or she is at risk.

Child has had chronic school failure.

There is a history of family abuse or neglect.

Child is easily vulnerable to peer pressure and peer values.

Child wants to prove he is fearless and is willing to take dangerous risks.

The child comes from a family that regards criminal behavior, teen pregnancy, and substance abuse as normal.

How Not to Say It

- "You're a thief!" Stealing is something all kids do at least once. Labeling them is an overreaction. Firmly tell them that what they did was wrong and why.

- "What am I going to do with you? Huh? Go to your room." If stealing is very infrequent and minor, you are overreacting. If the stealing has become more frequent and you are worried, try not to come up with arbitrary, spur-of-the-moment punishments. Instead, make the consequences clear and punitive, and apply them consistently.

- "If you keep that up, you'll get into real trouble someday." What you are saying is true but ineffective. Kids for whom stealing will become a problem do not think about long-term consequences.

Strangers

The mother leaned closer to the car window and began giving the driver directions. The driver had just pulled over, rolled down the window, and asked her if she knew where Prospect Street was. She held her child's hand while she spoke to the strange man.

When parents do these reasonable things, it can be confusing to kids who've been told not to talk to strangers. Evidently, parents can talk to them, but children shouldn't. When a parent casually says "hi" to a passerby, is that person still a stranger?

One man called a coworker at home. "Is your dad there?" he asked.

The little girl on the other end of the line spoke hesitantly. "Uh, no. He's . . . in the shower."

An hour later the man called back. "Is your dad there?" he asked again.

"Uh, no," the girl said. "He's in the shower."

"Can I speak to your mom then?"

"Uh, no. She's in the shower, too."

Parents try to teach their kids how to handle contact with strangers. It's just not that simple.

Things to Consider

➤ In 1988, 200 to 300 children were kidnapped by a stranger (taken more than fifty miles or ransomed, or murdered). Between 3,200 and 4,600 children were abducted by a stranger (taken, lured, or detained—usually to be sexually victimized). There were 115,000 reported unsuccessful abduction attempts. The rate of abduction by family members is much higher. A survey of children ages ten to sixteen in 1995 revealed that 3 percent reported having been abducted.

➤ Smaller children up to about age nine tend to think in black-and-white terms. Trying to teach them to distinguish between a safe and unsafe stranger can get confusing. It is better to talk about safe and unsafe *situations* and *behaviors* (inappropriate touching no matter who the person is, answering a door when you are home alone, etc.).

➤ Even familiar faces pose a potential danger. In most cases of sexual abuse the victim knows the perpetrator.

➤ Limit any unnecessary safety risks. Don't leave kids in a car unattended for any length of time. If no adult is home, let the answering machine pick up, not your child.

➤ Review, review, review. Kids can't remember all the rules. To pass the time, go over the rules while driving.

➤ Abductions by a parent during litigation are increasing. Studies show that such abductions are more likely to occur when a parent has a concern about an abusive or criminal environment for the child; when a parent has no respect for the law; when a parent is reluctant to seek help from the court; when the parent was not married to the other parent, was poorly educated, and had low income.

How to Say It

- **TEACH** about the danger posed by some people (not necessarily strangers). "There are people—grown-ups—who can act very friendly or as if they need your help. But really they are bad and might want to hurt other people. Most people are good, but it can be hard to tell the difference, so I don't want you speaking to people you don't know or standing close to them unless somebody you trust is there."

- Review a list of "nevers," such as:

    "Never get into a car with somebody you don't know even if it's raining or you are tired from walking."

    "Never tell anybody on the phone that you are home alone."

    "Never answer the door if you are home alone. If the other person says it's an emergency, call 911."

    "Never accept any food from somebody you don't know."

- Quiz your children on how they might handle certain situations. "What if a stranger asked you to go into the woods and help him find his dog? What would you do?" "What if somebody told you that I gave him permission to pick you up? What would you do?"

- "If you are not sure what to do, you can run away and you can scream. Then go to a place where you know somebody."

- "If you are at a mall or parking lot and feel threatened, yell out loud that the stranger is *not* your parent. Otherwise, some people will think you are just being a disobedient child."

- Offer reassurance if kids get too frightened. "As I said, most people are good and would not want to hurt you, but in order to be safe you must not trust many people. When you get older, you'll learn how to tell the difference better."

Smart Talk

How Best to Educate Your Child About Safety

Research shows that verbal instructions alone are inadequate. Four additional steps are essential.

Modeling. Demonstrate to your child what to say and do in a variety of unsafe situations.

Rehearsal. Have your child rehearse what to say and do, much like a child would rehearse a scene from a play.

Corrective feedback. Tell your child what he did well and what he did that was not helpful.

Practice. Review these methods frequently. Don't presume that as your child gets older (preteen or adolescent) he is prepared. *For reported cases of sexual assault, the majority of victims are teenagers.* (However, when asked retrospectively about prior victimization, 64 percent of adults claim they were sexually assaulted before the age of twelve.)

How Not to Say It

- "Be careful whom you speak to" or "Watch out for strange-looking people." Kids require very specific information, not vague, ambiguous rules. Saying "Be careful" is not the same as teaching a child to run away or scream.

- "Why didn't you answer the phone? It was an important message for me" or "Why didn't you accept the package when the mail carrier knocked on the door? Now I have to wait until tomorrow" or "Why didn't you act friendly to the adults at the party when they spoke to you?" Unless you give children specific *prior* instruction ("It's okay to answer the door if the mail carrier knocks. I'm expecting an important package"), don't criticize them for taking safety precautions.

- "Strangers sometimes kidnap little kids, take them away from their parents, hurt them, and kill them." Don't overly frighten your child. What if your child needs help and has only strangers to ask? All trustworthy people were strangers at one time.

Rule of Thumb: The best approach is to emphasize self-protective behaviors instead of emphasizing the negative consequences of failing to protect oneself.

Swearing

Mark and his sister, Melanie, were arguing about hogging the computer. Fourth-grader Mark ended the argument by calling his sister a bitch. Their mother was nearby and came running into the room.

"Mark! How dare you call your sister such a name!"

"Oh, it's not that bad, Mom. I only called her a female dog."

Mom was slightly taken aback, partly because she figured out that Mark must have looked up the word in a dictionary—perhaps the only time in his life he did that for something other than a homework assignment.

What should a parent do when his child swears?

Things to Consider

➤ Cursing and use of foul language have become a rite of initiation for many preteens and teens. You won't be able to prevent your child from swearing if his peers swear and he wants to fit in. But you can keep him from swearing at home.

➤ If you or your partner swears in front of the kids, even infrequently, your effort to prevent them from swearing will be seriously hindered.

➤ If you don't swear in front of your children, they will not swear in front of you.

➤ Frequent swearing by an adult (especially when aggravated) can actually increase anger. That can cause an increase in swearing. Teaching kids how to cope with frustrations without excessive anger or cursing is a wonderful thing to do.

How to Say It

- **TEACH** your values regarding swearing. "You don't hear me swear because even though it is common, it is like spitting on the sidewalk. It also offends many people, and we should show respect."

- If your child asks if you ever swear, **REPORT** the truth. "Yes, I do swear once in a while, but only if I'm alone or with somebody I know won't be offended. Frankly, swearing is a bad habit."

- Your preteen may object that curse words are just that—words. "But words have meaning, and they can offend people. If I called somebody stupid or made a racial remark, it is true that I'd be saying only words, but they would be hurtful words, offensive words. It would be wrong to say them."

- **EMPATHIZE** with a preteen's need to fit in. "Using bad words makes many kids your age feel cool. They want to fit in with their friends. That's understandable, but I'll be glad when you feel you can fit in without having to do things that are offensive."

- **DO'S & DON'TS.** "I still don't want to hear you swearing at home."

- **ENCOURAGE.** On occasion let your child know that you appreciate her use of proper language. "Some kids your age use curse words even at home. I'm proud of you for not doing that."

How Not to Say It

- "If you curse, I'll wash your mouth out with soap." You shouldn't have to take it that far. If you don't swear and your home life is reasonably happy, your children will respect your wishes. If they happen to swear in your presence, a firm reprimand will suffice.

- "Just because I swear doesn't mean you can." True. But don't expect compliance when you are modeling inappropriate behavior.

- "Jesus Christ!" Any swearing does not help you teach values such as patience, tolerance, or respect. Using a religious profanity also degrades God and your child's view of God. Since most Americans do have religious beliefs, you are undermining your efforts to teach religious values and love for God by using such language.

Tattling

"Mom!" cried eight-year-old Sabrina. "Ben is sneaking a cookie!"

"We don't like tattletales, Sabrina," Mom said.

Later on a neighbor knocked on the door and informed the mother that Ben was playing on the roof.

On the roof!

Mom ran upstairs to Ben's bedroom and found the window wide open. Sabrina was playing in the hallway. "Sabrina!" Mom said. "Why didn't you tell me that Ben was on the roof!"

"Because we don't like tattletales," she said.

Things to Consider

➤ Tattling is a quality most parents object to. However, parents still take action about the information the tattler gives. Consequently, parents give a mixed message.

➤ Tattling tends to be more frequent among kids up to age six.

➤ Children who tattle are rarely reprimanded, though tattling is discouraged.

➤ Parents seem to want the information a tattler reveals but dislike the (usually) self-serving motives of a tattler (to feel important, to get a sibling in trouble, etc.).

➤ Most kids outgrow tattling. Unnecessary tattling is sometimes punished by the one reported on—who gets even (often by finding something to tattle about). That natural consequence can curtail excessive tattling.

How to Say It

- You want to discourage your young children from being spies, police officers, and miniature parents, and learn to report on only serious or dangerous situations. Expect your child not to make the fine distinctions you would. "Anna, I know you like to tell me when your brother is doing something he shouldn't. Please tell me only if he is hurting someone or is in danger."

- "If you tattle just to get your sister in trouble, I won't appreciate it."

- "If you aren't sure whether to tell me, it's okay to tell me."

- "If you tell me something that I don't think was your business, I will say 'thank you,' but I probably won't do anything about it."

- Probe for underlying reasons for tattling. "Sometimes children like to tattle because it makes them feel good or they are mad about something. Tell me all your reasons."

- "You just tattled on your brother when he gave the dog his ham sandwich. What was your reason?"

- ENCOURAGE appropriate tattling. "Thank you for telling me that your brother went on the canoe without a life vest. It might have saved his life."

How Not to Say It

- "No one likes a tattletale." This really doesn't teach a child to properly discriminate between appropriate and inappropriate tattling.

- "Only little kids tattle. You should know better." Actually, an older child is more likely to learn the difference between safe and unsafe situations and when "telling" is appropriate.

- "I'm so glad you told me that your brother didn't brush his teeth." Encouraging tattling of minor infractions is not a good idea. You will create a monster.

- "You're a good helper for telling me the things your brother is doing wrong." Don't encourage her.

Being Teased

The neighborhood kids were tossing the football around. Occasionally, one of them would run for a pass or try to intercept a throw. At one point Jerry Scott grabbed the ball.

"Hey, don't let Scotty have it," a boy called out. "He doesn't know whether to dribble it or kick it!"

Everybody laughed. Jerry Scott took the ribbing good-naturedly. Later, he intercepted a throw and turned to the boy who just missed catching it. "Sorry, lady," he said. "Maybe next time."

Some teasing remarks are clearly mean-spirited and meant to ridicule. Some are obviously meant to be fun. However, much teasing can be hard to interpret unless one is keenly aware of the social context. A ribbing by a good friend is overlooked. The same comment by a new kid on the block might result in a war of words.

At some point everyone gets teased. Boys and men often define their friendships as one of good-natured but sometimes vicious put-downs. Insulting a buddy is a man's way of saying "I care about you."

Handling teasing among children is not always straightforward. Sometimes telling kids not to let teasing bother them is like telling a swimmer not to get wet.

Things to Consider

➢ Younger children regard teasing as hurtful most of the time.

➢ Eighth-grade boys rate teasing and being teased as a positive experience.

➢ According to reports, teasing is more a part of boys' lives than girls' lives.

➤ Teasing is a paradox. It can bring people closer together or create emotional distance.

➤ Children who were rejected by peers for being overly aggressive or submissive were often criticized for being unable to tolerate teasing. Coping with teasing and the ability to distinguish teasing from ridicule is a major task of children, especially as they get older. Rehearsing with them how not to overreact to teasing is crucial. They won't learn it by verbal instruction only.

How to Say It

- If your child is hurt by a teasing remark, your first response should be one of **EMPATHY**. "When your friend said that to you, it felt like he was making fun and that must have hurt."

- "It isn't fun when somebody teases you."

- "You felt sad when the kid on the bus laughed at your dress. It wasn't a very nice thing to do." (Often, an empathic remark makes the child feel understood and reassured that she is loved and cared about. That may be all that is required to help her get over the hurt.)

- If you believe that your child is taking it too hard or has misinterpreted a teasing remark, **TEACH** about alternative ways to interpret. "Remember how Uncle John and I tease each other a lot? We don't do that to be hurtful. It is our way of saying we love each other. I know that sounds strange, but it's true. I wonder if the boy who teased you really likes and admires you. Is that possible?"

- "Some kids make fun of other kids because they are jealous. Sometimes they are unhappy about things in their life, so they strike out at others with mean words. Is it possible that Jeffrey could be unhappy about things?"

- Get your child to imagine how other children successfully cope with teasing. "Have you ever seen a kid at school get teased and *not* feel bad about it later? Why do you think that was?"

- "I remember when Jason from next door teased you, but you didn't seem to be bothered. Why was that?"

- "There is a magic formula to handling being teased. If you smile and say nothing, the teaser will probably stop teasing. If he teased you because he likes you, then he also liked it that you smiled. If he teased you because he wanted to be mean, he won't like it that you smiled and will probably stop teasing."

- **TEACH** by distinguishing good-natured teasing from ridicule. "Kids who want to be mean usually make mean faces when they tease you. Someone who likes you usually won't do that."

- "Someone who wants to hurt your feelings might show off in front of others by laughing at you and trying to get others to laugh at you. Someone who is just making a small joke may say it only to you and not try to get others to laugh at you."

- "If a good friend teases you, she probably doesn't mean to be hurtful. But if it bothers you, talk to her about it later. If she is really your friend, she'll stop teasing you that way."

- Tell stories about how you were teased when you were young. That often takes the sting out of it for your kids. "Oh, sure I remember being teased. When kids in my class thought it was cool to play the guitar, I took violin lessons. They teased me about that. But it didn't last long, and today I'm a pretty good violinist."

- A child who overreacts to teasing may well be troubled by other things. He may be feeling inadequate or unhappy or scared. Probe for possibilities. "How about we go for a ride and get an ice cream cone. I want to talk. I'm thinking that some things are bothering you and hoping you'll tell me what they are."

- A child who is very troubled by teasing may be someone who is being cruelly and repeatedly teased. This can be extremely harmful to your child and can result in severe behavioral disturbances. A loving, supportive family is crucial. You must also take steps to protect your child. "What those other kids are doing is very cruel. I will talk to the school principal and I will also speak to one of the parents whom I know. In the meantime, I want to rehearse with you how you can act when kids tease you. And remember, I love you with all my heart."

- "This may not help much, but I want you to know I think you are terrific. Every day for me is a happy one in large part because of you."

Rule of Thumb: If the home life is happy and secure, your child will most likely learn to handle being teased.

How Not to Say It

- "Hey, everybody gets teased. You'll get over it." This "don't worry, be happy" approach isn't necessary. Yes, your child probably will get over it (unless he is being mercilessly teased), but you can help by showing some **EMPATHY** first. "It sounds as if you had a rough time on the bus ride home."

- "Oh, quit your whining." You are coming perilously close to teasing your child because she is upset about being teased. You are validating her belief that there is something wrong or inadequate about her.

- "Stop teasing him. You're being mean." You may be right, but you may not be. Remember, the words themselves are less the problem than the context. If the kids still play together and enjoy each other's company, their teasing may be good-natured.

- "Oh, come on. I was just teasing you. Stop crying. Can't you take a joke?" Sometimes a parent teases a child hoping to get a laugh, but it backfires. When that happens, never add insult to injury ("Can't you take a joke?"). Apologize instead and offer comfort. When your child is less upset, you can try to explain what your intentions were.

- "How would you like it if someone teased you!?" This effort to instill empathy may not work if your child is eleven or older. Chances are he has begun to learn how to handle teasing. If he answered your question honestly, he'd probably say, "I wouldn't mind it if I got teased."

Trading Cards and Mild Gambling

"I didn't think those pocket monster trading cards would be such a big deal to my kids," one mother said. "But they've taken over my children's lives. They're all they think about. When we're at the store they want me to buy them more cards. Then there is the issue of trading. It seems as though I'm watching young warriors at the stock market, the way they go at it. Should I be concerned?"

Kids have been trading cards ever since the first baseball card was printed a century ago. But today the characters being traded also have their likeness printed on hundreds of merchandising products and are the subject of movies and video games. It is hard to escape them. Like many things, it can get out of hand if parents are not observant.

Things to Consider

➤ For most children, trading cards will not become an obsession that interferes with their lives. But research suggests that children who tend to be more impulsive by nature do not foresee negative consequences and do not halt their actions quickly despite these consequences. They may be more likely to take some games to the limit.

➤ Trading has a gambling component. Kids are not always sure they made the best deal and may in fact lose out. Popular cards often have a limited printing that causes kids to keep purchasing more in hopes of finding the elusive ones.

➤ Many schools have banned trading cards because they pose too much of a disruption in schoolwork.

➤ High-frequency video game players gamble more than low-frequency video game players do. They also report that gambling makes them feel important.

➤ Gambling at age twelve predicts later substance abuse.

➤ Research has shown that parents overestimate the age at which their children first gambled and underestimate the probability that their child has already gambled.

➤ Trading cards can be fun and not dangerous. Parents can no longer presume it is completely innocent fun when in fact these items are marketed to entice kids to purchase more and more cards. Use common sense.

How to Say It

- Learn about your child's interests. It will help you decide whether any parental intervention is required. "Tell me all about these cards you have. What makes them interesting?"

- "How many cards do you get in a pack? How many different cards are there in all?"

- "Which friends have these cards? Do you trade with them?"

- **TEACH** about gambling. "When you buy a pack of cards, you may end up getting the same cards you already own, so you may waste your money. That's gambling. You are taking a chance with your money."

- **DO'S & DON'TS**. Parents must limit their children's involvement in activities that can get out of hand. "You can buy a new pack of trading cards every week [two weeks, etc.]."

- "No trading cards or talking about it with friends until your homework is done and corrected."

- "No looking on the web for more trading cards."

- **EMPATHIZE**. "It can be fun to collect as many cards as possible. Sometimes it gets frustrating when no matter how hard you try, you still can't collect them all."

How Not to Say It

- "I don't want you trading any cards." Trading is not a problem unless it becomes an intense preoccupation. Most kids outgrow the desire to collect the objects.

- "Buying trading cards is a complete waste. It's silly." You are probably right, but what are you achieving? If you don't want your child spending money on such things, say so. If you intend to let him purchase cards, then explain your concerns in a manner that doesn't sound insulting.

Trauma from an
Accident or Natural Disaster

Kenny is a six-year-old admitted to a pediatric hospital in Boston. While his injuries after a bike accident were not life-threatening (350,000 children are injured each year from bicycle accidents), he had something more interesting to report: He had recently witnessed a stabbing. According to the *Journal of the American Medical Association*, 10 percent of hospitalized children (ages six and under) in Boston reported witnessing a shooting or stabbing. A study of sixth, eighth, and tenth graders in New Haven, Connecticut, revealed that 40 percent of these students had witnessed at least one violent crime in the past year. Almost all eighth graders knew someone who had been killed.

Three months after Hurricane Andrew devastated parts of Florida, one-third of children affected by the hurricane had significant symptoms of post-traumatic stress. After seven months many children improved except for those who had been more anxious and inattentive prior to the hurricane.

Too many children witness violence in the home or in their community. About 7 percent of children are regularly teased or bullied by peers. Odds are that by the time your child is ready to leave the nest, she will have witnessed or experienced some violent act, serious accident, or emotional trauma.

Things to Consider

➤ The impact of an extreme event can be reduced if the child lives in a loving, supportive home environment. But esteemed researcher and trauma expert Dr. Ronnie Janoff-Bulman at the University of Massachusetts in Amherst warns that the negative effects can be magnified if the child resides in an uncaring, abusive home.

➤ A caring family is not sufficient to help a child cope with disaster or trauma. Unless the parents or caretakers are willing to talk about the trauma on a regular basis, the barrier to communication will be a barrier to health. Parents should not conclude that discussing an upsetting event would retraumatize their child. Children need to talk about (or draw or playact) the painful events.

➤ Common symptoms after experiencing or witnessing a traumatic event include: bed-wetting, sleep difficulty, separation anxiety, intrusive thoughts about the event, physical complaints, and increased dependency. Girls tend to complain more about anxiety and depression than boys do, but boys may experience troublesome memories.

➤ Extreme symptoms are likely if the child experienced distress that was either life threatening, included scenes of grotesque destruction (mangled bodies, etc.), or involved serious injury to self or a family member.

➤ Greater effort to suppress upsetting thoughts or memories is associated with more severe symptoms.

➤ Children can exhibit intense symptoms when they have experienced mild trauma or mild symptoms when they have experienced extreme trauma. Don't judge the emotional impact on the basis of the seriousness of the accident alone. How parents react to the trauma has tremendous bearing on how the child reacts.

How to Say It

- Reassure your child that she is safe now and that the event has passed. "You are okay now. I am here with you, and all is safe. What happened was awful, but it's over. It's done. It's all gone." Be prepared to remind your child frequently that she is safe and that the event has passed.
- Speak calmly. Allow your child to say what he needs to. Encourage opening up. "When you are ready, you can tell me what happened."
- "I want to hear what happened . . ."
- "I want you to tell me what it was like for you . . ."
- "Even though it's over, I want you to be free to talk to me anytime about it."

- If your child shows symptoms that are upsetting to him (bed-wetting, fear of losing you, nightmares, etc.), reassure him that these are normal. "Children who go through what you went through usually wet their bed or have fears about doing certain things. The fears will go away soon."

- Guilt is a common aftereffect of surviving or witnessing trauma. Sometimes children believe they caused or could have prevented the event or injury. "These things happen. It was not your fault. The people who were injured were doing what they normally do, and yet they ended up getting hurt."

- "If you feel you'd like to do something for the people who were hurt, there are many things you can do. You can pray for them. If you'd like, we can stop in at church and say a special prayer. You can make a card. You can write a note. You can plant some flowers for them . . ."

- Observe your child at play and notice if she is trying to cope with the trauma by drawing or playing with dolls, etc. Use it as a springboard for a discussion later. "I noticed you were playing with the Barbie doll and you had her go to the hospital. Maybe you were thinking about the car accident . . ."

- **ENCOURAGE** dialogue. "I'm so glad you are talking about it with me. It's important to talk. Talking is like medicine. It will help you feel better."

Rule of Thumb: Initial signs that your child is okay can be misleading. Symptoms often occur many weeks or months later. Also, symptoms can reemerge on "anniversary" dates, especially if the event is shown on TV (a tornado, hurricane, flood, etc.).

How Not to Say It

- "Try to forget about it." Suppression of memory leads to more complications. If it is upsetting for you to talk about it, let your child talk to others or to a professional. (You should, too.)

- "I warned you not to go there," "I told you to wear a seatbelt," or "You knew better than to go with those other kids." If your child has experienced or witnessed some violent event, these comments will add to guilt and perhaps result in his not wanting to talk further about the event.

- "Oh, don't worry. You'll be fine. You'll get over it." You may be right, and your intent to be reassuring is good. However, be careful you don't give your child the impression that you do not want her to talk about it with you. Plus, really listen to her concerns before you start telling her to cheer up.

- "Oh, every time you talk about it, I shudder. I hate thinking about it." This is not a good idea because he may choose to keep quiet.

- "If you keep talking about it, you'll never get better." False. The opposite is true.

Violence and Sexual Material in Television and Movies

Wanda was careful about what she let her children watch on television. She was well aware that the sexual content of "family" programs had risen sharply. Still, she was surprised at how the objectionable material slipped into the television viewing. While watching an "allowed" show with her kids, a commercial came on advertising a show that was to air later that evening. In the preview two teenage girls were discussing their prom night. One lamented that she'd had a miserable time. "Why?" her friend asked. "Because my mom ended up sleeping with my boyfriend."

The line was supposed to get a laugh from the audience. Wanda was shocked, and she didn't know what to say to her eight- and ten-year-old children watching with her.

Television, movies, and video games play a huge role in the lives of most kids—even larger when the kids become teenagers. American kids watch between three and four hours of TV a day. Many movies try to attract preteens by using popular actors. Movies such as *Men in Black, Titanic, Ace Ventura,* and others boast a PG-13 rating, luring many kids younger than thirteen to more mature sexual or violent displays.

Things to Consider

➤ According to the research on the effects of television violence, there is overwhelming evidence of a link between TV violence and aggressiveness in children. The link is circular. Aggressiveness promotes the watching of violent programs, which fosters more aggressive tendencies. Obviously, media violence is just one of many links to aggressive behavior.

➤ Media violence puts some children at greater risk, particularly children with established emotional or behavioral disorders or children from homes where violence already exists.

➤ TV viewing adds to mindless daydreaming and detracts from a child's use of creative imagination.

➤ In a study of fourth and fifth graders, the students watched a low-grade violent film *(Karate Kid)* or a nonviolent sports program. They were later asked to monitor two children (shown on videotape) and ask for help if the two children needed assistance. Kids who watched the more violent film took longer to ask for help when the kids were fighting aggressively; in other words, they had a greater tolerance for watching real-life violence.

➤ Television news is downright frightening to children. It is best that they limit any viewing of news.

➤ One study in the journal *Pediatrics* showed that the onset of teen drinking was strongly related to the viewing of TV, music videos, and movie videos. The more they watched in ninth grade, the more likely they began drinking within the year. While it is not accurate to state that TV viewing caused drinking (perhaps teens who are inclined to drink like to watch more TV and videos), excessive viewing is a warning sign that drinking may follow.

➤ TV shows, music videos, and movies tend to show teen sexual behavior or partying as normal and risk free. Yet half of all teenage deaths due to injury are alcohol related, and 10 percent of teenage girls get pregnant each year.

Rule of Thumb: Parents must monitor and severely limit their children's TV viewing. It will improve the children's academic scores and reduce any effect TV violence or inappropriate sexual material may have.

How to Say It

- DO'S & DON'TS. "From now on you can watch TV only between the hours of . . ."

- "From now on you can watch only these programs . . ."

- "From now on the TV stays off during the week on school nights unless it is a special educational program or one I give you permission to watch." (You may want to unplug the TV after each use. It will help curtail impulsive TV viewing.)

- **TEACH** your values when objectionable material is shown. "That program showed two unmarried young people going to bed. I think that is a dangerous message for young people. Sex without love and commitment can increase the risk of unwanted pregnancy or disease."

- "That program makes fun of religion. Religion is very important to me and to many people. What are your thoughts?"

- "That racing-car video game shows women in two-piece swimsuits standing on the sidelines and cheering on the competitors. Why do you think that is?"

- **TEACH** younger children the difference between reality and fantasy. (One research study revealed that children with emotional or behavioral problems tended to prefer aggressive TV characters and more often believed fictional material to be true.) "Could somebody really jump out of a plane without a parachute and land on his feet?" or "Is it likely someone can drive that fast and dangerously and not get into an accident? Could that happen in real life?"

- **ENCOURAGE** alternatives to TV and video games. Even a half hour less of TV per night devoted to school or a family activity would pay huge dividends. **EMPATHIZE** with your child's initial frustration at having less TV time. "I know that not having the TV on as much can be boring. I know reading books is not something you look forward to. But I'm hoping you can spend some of the time playing games, learning new things, or with me."

How Not to Say It

Don't say anything that weakens your authority, sounds wishy-washy, or abandons your role as parent.

- "Why are you watching that junk?" Your sentiment is well taken, but what precisely do you mean? Do you want the TV off? Then say so. Did you want to explain why you don't like the show? Do that. Don't ask open-ended questions. Preteens and teens have answers for everything and are genetically programmed to be great defense attorneys.

- "I wish you wouldn't watch that show." Why be a wimp? You have the authority to enforce your views.

- "Are you sure that movie is okay for someone your age?" He's sure. But it still may be inappropriate and against your values. Don't ask his opinion. He thinks purple hair and body piercing are cool, too.

- "How long are you going to be playing that video game? Don't you have homework to do?" You sound so reasonable and fair, but it is okay to set a time limit for games. You don't have to let your child play as long as she wants. As a general rule, homework before pleasure makes sense. "When the show is over in ten minutes, please turn off the TV and start your homework. I know you have a test tomorrow."

Whiny and Demanding Child

"But why can't I see that movie? Everybody in my class saw it already!" Steve said.

"I doubt everybody saw it. It's rated PG-13, and you're only ten," Dad answered.

"They did see it! That's all they talk about."

"Well, just because other kids can do something doesn't mean it's right for you."

"It's not fair!" Steve plopped himself on the couch and sat like a statue, arms folded, face contorted with anger.

"It may not seem fair but—"

"How do you know I shouldn't watch it? Just because it's PG-13 doesn't mean I'm not old enough!"

The discussion continued a long while. Steve's form of whining was typical of older kids—complaining, debating, sulking, and facial expressions that could scare away a grizzly bear. Younger children like to stretch out their syllables ("Mommm! Pleeeease!) with a tone of voice as soothing as a dentist's drill.

Things to Consider

➤ All kids whine occasionally. Those who whine more have been rewarded for it.

➤ Many parents are guilt ridden because they have careers, are too busy, were previously divorced, or don't make enough money. Consequently, they overindulge their children just enough that the kids believe the world revolves around them.

➤ Spouses often don't deal with a whiny child in exactly the same way. One parent may be firm; the other may give in. That increases the likelihood of whining (not just by the child but by one of the frustrated parents, too).

➤ Sometimes kids whine because they have a legitimate complaint that the parent is ignoring. They may be overtired, very bored at an adult function, or frustrated by some other problem.

How to Say It

- Children can benefit from a four-step procedure. First, **TEACH** why whining bothers you:

    "It is as if you are hitting me with your voice."

    "Whining is not polite."

    "Whining is something younger children do, and you are older."

    "Whining after I say no to something is like disobeying me."

    "Whining gives me a headache."

- Next, demonstrate how to talk without whining. "If you want something and I say no, you could say, 'But I really want that. Can I talk to you about it again after lunch?'"

- "You could say, 'Mom, I'm tired and I want to go home please,' instead of whining, 'I want to go home right now!'"

- "You could say, 'I'm upset that other kids can see a movie and I can't. Please think about ways I could see it.'"

- Next, have your child rehearse speaking or complaining without whining. "Pretend you want something and I'm not agreeing to it. Talk to me in a way that is polite instead of whining."

- Finally, praise and **ENCOURAGE** appropriate behavior. "I like the way you asked me that. You weren't whining. You were being polite. I'm impressed."

- Anticipate whining situations and discuss it ahead of time with your child. "When we are in the supermarket, I know it will take us longer to shop than you would like. I'll do my best to hurry. Remember how you learned ways to talk to me without whining? Please practice them in the store." While shopping, periodically praise your child for not whining. Don't wait until the trip is over to praise. By the way, an occasional treat (ice cream cone, etc.) is fine as a reward, too.

- If your child is being polite and reasonable but you still must say no to a request, be careful. Your child may have no choice but to whine. It is better to **EMPATHIZE** and try to meet your child's legitimate needs at least partly. "You're right. It is hot and we have stayed here too long, but I can't leave yet. I don't blame you for being tired and upset. What could happen now that would make it easier for you to stay just a while longer?"

- Even if your child stops whining, he won't necessarily get his way. Be sure to **EMPATHIZE** then and thank him for cooperating. "I know it is upsetting that we can't drive to your cousin's house this weekend. You were looking forward to it. Let's figure out when we can go again. I appreciate it that you are being good about this."

How Not to Say It

- "Stop whining!" By itself this is not an effective technique. Perhaps you've noticed. If you've caved in to whining in the past, you helped create a monster. Stop rewarding unpleasant behavior and have your child rehearse better ways to try to manipulate you—er, I mean, better ways to converse with you.

- "If you don't stop your whining, I'll . . ." Threats may work for the moment, but you'll have a sulking, resentful child on your hands who will probably continue his whining later. It is better to approach this problem more systematically: Assess whether you've rewarded whining in the past and **TEACH** your child better ways to speak.

- "Grow up!" She will someday. She'll be dating boys with fast cars, an overabundance of testosterone, and God knows what kind of jewelry hanging from what parts of their bodies, and you'll wish she was seven again and whining like crazy. Parents are sure fickle.

- "You're driving me crazy!" That is what your child intended. Ignoring her is better than admitting she got to you.

Working Parent
(When You Used to Stay at Home)

Sylvia was a stay-at-home mom until her youngest child, Paula, entered first grade. The family could use the extra income, and Sylvia went back to work as a computer programmer—a job she gave up after the birth of her first child. But Sylvia had some concerns. Would she have enough energy at the end of the day to handle her home responsibilities? Would her husband help out more? Would the kids be at an emotional disadvantage because they had gotten used to having her around at all times? What happens when the kids get sick and have summer vacation? Could she handle the worry and stress that comes from trying to please a boss and a family at the same time?

Things to Consider

➤ More than half of all mothers are now in the workforce.

➤ There are spillover effects. A miserable job can add to family tension, though a happy family life can often make it easier to cope with a difficult job. Women who work at exciting or challenging jobs often report a greater ability to cope with the ups and downs of parenting than women with tedious jobs.

➤ Employment status is not the essential factor when assessing children's coping. The quality of home life overall is a more potent force.

➤ Extra income can add to a child's quality of life. However, research shows that if the frequency of shared parent-child activities is lessened due to employment, children may have poorer adjustments and show a decline in school performance.

➤ Working parents in a crunch for time spend more of it with younger kids. (Don't overlook the older kids.)

➤ Some evidence (though controversial) shows that infants in day care more than twenty hours per week for their first year of life have weaker attachments to parents and are more aggressive and noncompliant in school.

How to Say It

- Much depends on whether the parent is happy or unhappy about returning to work. **REPORT** by giving your child a clear idea of how your job will affect him. "I expect to leave for work after you get on the school bus and be home about an hour after you get home. That means you will be cared for by [Dad, yourself, your older sibling, Grandma, a neighbor, day care, etc.]."

- "I'll have less time to do housework, so I'll need you to do these extra chores to help out."

- "It is important to me that you and I still have time every day to share things like singing, reading books, homework, going for walks . . ."

- If you are looking forward to working, discuss why. If you are forced to work due to finances, try to sound optimistic. "The extra money will help pay for a new car that we really need. And we hope to save for a nice family vacation."

- **EMPATHIZE**. "I'm wondering if you feel worried about my working. Some kids do, some don't."

- "You seem excited. I'll have some interesting stories to tell about my day, won't I?"

- For a few months after you begin work, ask your child periodically how he is doing with the changes. Be careful not to ask leading questions. "I've been working for a week now. How was it for you?"

- If your child has relevant objections or concerns, do everything you can to fix things. The main objection will be that you have less time available. It is a reasonable objection with no easy answers for some people. "You're right. I do spend less time with you, and I hate that part. I have to work because I need the money. But I promise to try to plan my schedule a little differently. Do you have any ideas of how we could spend more time together?"

How Not to Say It

- "I'm taking a job, but I'm sure we'll all pitch in and do just fine." Don't be so reassuring just yet. Take time to spell out what the impact will be on your kids and listen to their responses. Otherwise, a child's uneasiness may be overlooked.

- "I can't help it if I have to work! You'll just have to get used to it. Other kids can handle it, so you should, too." It sounds as if you feel a little guilty for working and are lashing out at the kids. (Research shows that professional women don't feel they're doing enough for their kids even when they are doing more than their husbands.) Speak more tenderly to the kids (it's not their fault), look objectively at what you and your mate each do to help out at home, and get a grip.

- "You don't like it that I work, do you?" or "You like that I work, don't you?" Don't ask leading questions. Children may give you the answer you want to hear and not the answer they are really thinking about.

Rule of Thumb: You can't do it all. If both partners work, something will suffer. You will lose couple time, alone time, time for the kids, or time to do household chores. Research shows that couple time is usually sacrificed, which is a mistake. Ease up on housework, hire someone to mow the lawn, and spend the extra time with your mate.

Worried Child

Grandma's upcoming visit all the way from Michigan was on Hillary's mind. She was excited but worried, too.

"What if there's bad weather and the plane can't fly?" Hillary said. "Or what if the plane flies, but the pilot makes a mistake and the plane crashes?"

Mom tried to reassure her young daughter. "There's no need to worry," she said. "Grandma has visited many times, and she always has a safe trip."

"But what if . . ."

Hillary was off and running. She worried about everything: her grades, her health, the health of her family, and the future in general. About 3 percent of kids have anxiety severe enough to warrant a clinical diagnosis sometime during their childhood. But over 70 percent of kids ages eight to thirteen worry every few days to the point where it is hard for them to manage their concerns.

Things to Consider

➢ Highly anxious parents pose an obstacle to the successful treatment of highly anxious children unless the parents get treatment, too.

➢ Surveys indicate that school-age children worry frequently about school matters, dying, and social relationships. One study showed that global issues (pollution, starvation, and war) were high on the list of concerns for sixth graders.

➢ Parents underestimate the amount of worrying their children do.

How to Say It

- Probe for hidden concerns. "If I were to ask kids your age to list their top three worries, what do you think the answers would be?"

- Probe for coping skills. "If a child who was two years younger than you was worried about school grades [bullies, making friends, health, etc.], what advice would you give?"

- "A few weeks ago you were worried about the camp sleepover. What helped you to feel better? What did you do that made a difference?"

- **EMPATHIZE.** "You seem worried about your appearance. Some people worry about that. Do you think your friends are just as worried as you, or are they more worried?"

- "It must be hard for you to relax when you get so worried about things."

- **TEACH** alternative ways of viewing situations. "What is the evidence that people won't like you if you don't wear the right clothes? You've made many friends. Would they abandon you? Really?"

- "What is the evidence that you'll do poorly on that test?"

- "Once you think about the possibility that something bad could happen, you start to believe that the possibility is a strong likelihood. It's like seeing a small cloud and believing there will be a hurricane."

- "Make a list of everything you worry about for next week. Then we'll check off everything that comes true. I bet most of what you worry about never happens."

- "Next time you worry about something, tell yourself, 'My worry is like a balloon that I keep blowing into. It looks bigger and bigger, but it really is small when all the air is out of it.'"

- "Let's practice. I'll think of a few things to get nervous about and you try to show me why I'm exaggerating or worrying about something I can't control."

- "Tell yourself, 'I'm just having thoughts. Just because I think them doesn't mean they will happen.'"

- Find ways to praise and **ENCOURAGE** your child for reducing her worrisome thoughts. "You were worried about Grandma's safety, but then you told yourself she will be fine. Good for you."

How Not to Say It

- "It's silly to worry about those things." It isn't silly to your child. Help him to challenge his beliefs rather than dismiss his concerns as silly.
- "Don't worry about it." Nice try, but it probably won't work. Involving your child in some interesting activity may help.
- "You're just going through a phase." This is dismissive and doesn't help your child think more objectively about his concerns.

Smart Talk

At dinner or while driving in the car, practice being optimistic with your children. Ask, "What went right today? Let's think of as many things as we can." Later, have a discussion about things you can look forward to. Immediately challenge any pessimistic or fearful expectations with upbeat beliefs. The more positive expectations you possess, the easier it will be for your overly worried child to think positively. Tell your worried child to "turn your worry inside-out," and then give examples of how she can do that successfully. Praise her efforts.

When You Say It Right (but Things Still Go Wrong): Ten Winning Tips for Troubleshooters

Your world is probably filled with examples of "solutions" that used to work but don't anymore, or that work for other people but not you. Some solutions actually make the problem worse. For example:

A medication you take no longer is effective. You need something stronger.

Your dog follows the commands of a neighbor, but you can't get him to sit.

Your cold tablet stops your sniffles but makes you drowsy and unable to do your job.

You work longer hours to provide for your family, but now you rarely have time to see them.

You withdraw from an argument for fear of making it worse, only to grow increasingly resentful and distant from your spouse.

There are no perfect formulas to solve every child problem, but when common-sense solutions fail and creative solutions fail, chances are you have misidentified the problem. Giving your car a tune-up to make it run better won't help if the problem is bad gasoline. Wearing a sweater to keep warm is fine, but it doesn't fix the furnace.

Family life is complicated. People seek professional help because their efforts to resolve certain problems have failed and they don't know why. When reasonable efforts to parent your children backfire, something fundamental to the situation is being overlooked. This chapter will help you locate the culprits and fix them.

Reason #1: A Child Problem Is Really a Disguised Marital Problem

This takes many forms. One form occurs when a parent complains about a child's behavior (sloppy, inattentive, unappreciative, disrespectful, etc.) but the parent is hurt most by the belief that his spouse acts those ways, too. Thus, a man who is annoyed with his wife's inability to handle menial household chores by herself (such as a burned-out bulb or a tire with low air pressure) may yell at his daughter when she acts helpless. He is really angry with his wife. A wife who thinks her husband takes her for granted may find it difficult when the kids are whining while she's trying to eat lunch. She may mishandle that situation because her frustration with her husband is not being addressed.

When anger is misdirected at the children, yelling at them is often done within earshot of the spouse. "Will you kids please clean up your mess? How many times do I have to tell you!" may be a wife's way of yelling at her mate to help out more around the house.

Sometimes a child's behavior problem serves a hidden purpose. It gives a spouse an excuse to blame the mate for something. "See, I told you that you are too lenient [or harsh] with discipline. Now look at what he's done." When marital differences are annoying but unresolved, parents may have less flexibility when dealing with their children's problem behaviors, and those behaviors might then continue.

Finally, if a child's actions distract an unhappy couple from focusing on their relationship, the actions may persist despite reasonable efforts to resolve them. For example, a child who has many unrealistic fears and anxieties may keep parents from discussing (arguing about) an area of conflict. Instead, they may focus on the child. By bringing the parents together in a common cause, the child may subconsciously learn to develop symptoms.

If you want to assess your marriage, take the Argument Audit found in the Appendix. High scores may indicate that marital issues are interfering with your ability to effectively parent your child.

Reason #2: You Are Overly Involved or Underinvolved with Your Kids

Experts sometimes use the word *enmeshed* to describe an overly involved parent. Such parents mean well but actually tend to overprotect, smother, and stifle normal growth. They become uneasy with a child's growing independence because their own role is threatened. These parents use empathy a great deal and try to reason with their kids. This is not so bad, but usually they are trying to reason in ways that overprotect. Children in these cases tend to become more dependent and therefore require more involvement with their parents, so it is a self-perpetuating cycle. Some kids rebel and pull away from the smothering. Efforts to persuade them may fail—not because the words are ineffective but because the reason for the rebellion is being overlooked. Until Mom pulls back some (most enmeshed parents are mothers), nothing will change.

Underinvolved parents are referred to as "disengaged." They may care, but it takes a lot to get their attention. It will take a bloodcurdling shriek from a squabbling child before the parent (often a father) steps in and tells the kids to break it up. These parents admire autonomy and give their kids plenty of room. But, unfortunately, the kids receive less supervision and less affection as well. Such dads are good at giving orders but poor at affection or empathy.

You can see how these patterns can make it hard to communicate effectively. Imagine that the kids are fighting frequently (sound familiar?). An enmeshed mother jumps in to arbitrate, reason with the kids, and maybe tells them to be quiet. Ten minutes later the kids are at it again. A disengaged father may intervene if the fighting gets serious. But as soon as he goes back to the newspaper, the fight may resume, though at a slightly lower decibel level.

The mom is ineffective because instead of letting the kids work out their own squabbles, she teaches them that they can count on her to settle their differences for them. Dad is ineffective because if the only attention he gives the kids is negative attention, the kids will opt for that. Until Dad is more involved in the kids' lives overall (not just when they are fighting) and until Mom backs off a bit and lets the kids have a life without her, beautifully phrased communications will have no long-term effect.

Reason #3: You Are Depressed or Overwhelmed

When a parent's ability to take control is hampered by illness or depression, that parent's listening skills deteriorate. A depressed father will tune out the kids or limit his interactions with them. He may also interpret a child's misbehavior more harshly. The more overwhelmed a mother feels, the less capably she will handle any child situation.

Since dissatisfied couples are twenty-five times more likely to become depressed than are happy couples, it is important for a depressed person to look closely at the state of the marriage. Antidepressant medications can be very helpful. Support from other adults is also necessary when a person feels overwhelmed. Single parents have a very difficult task because they are on the job constantly.

Reason #4: Are You a Walking Contradiction?

When you teach "do as I say, not as I do," your credibility diminishes. You may want your children to obey rules, to put things back where they belong, to clean up their mess, and to show consideration, but you may act in the following ways:

> You change your mind about a supermarket item and place it back on the wrong aisle shelf for the sake of convenience.
>
> You find an expensive item on the ground and keep it instead of trying to locate the owner.
>
> You remark at a restaurant how the waiter forgot to charge you for something, and you say, "That's his problem, not mine."
>
> Your car is a mess.
>
> The top of your dresser is a mess.
>
> You routinely speed on the highway.
>
> You are frequently impatient with other drivers or when standing in a checkout line.
>
> You postpone work projects until the last minute.
>
> You are often late.

Children watch their parents carefully. As kids mature they are more likely to adopt a more casual set of values when their parents have done the same. Parenting will become more difficult.

Reason #5: You Overly Identify with Your Children

If your child is experiencing some difficulty that you once experienced, your background may help you understand—but it might also interfere. If you presume too much, you may stop listening to your child and miss some key elements of his concerns. For example, Fred was shy as a child, and he knew that his son, Danny, was shy, too. Not wanting Danny to feel bad about being shy (as Fred once did), Fred gave Danny encouraging pep talks but never really listened to any of his son's concerns. As a result, Danny was reluctant to talk to his father about the issue. Some parents are so convinced that their child is "just like me" that they overrule their spouse's opinions about the child, thereby setting the stage for spousal resentment.

In the book *Parenting by Heart,* psychologist Ron Taffel says that over-identification means you are reacting to your child but not truly connecting. Consequently, parenting may become more complicated because you think you know what is best when in fact you might not. You have to consider the possibility that you are not being objective. Ask for opinions from trusted friends or loved ones.

Reason #6: You Say, "I *Never* Want to Be Like My Parents!"

The more adamant you are about this, the more it usually backfires. For example, if your parents were frequently angry and you want to avoid feeling angry, you may become an ineffective disciplinarian. (Predictably, your spouse will be stricter, and you will yell at him for being harsh when in fact he is only balancing out the system.) If your parents were inattentive, you will want to give your children attention—but you may overdo it. Thus, your kids may become more dependent, or you may feel overwhelmed with time and work pressures but feel afraid to limit your time with the kids. (It's okay to do that sometimes. Kids need to learn patience and self-sufficiency.) Or you'll spend lots of time with the kids but have no time left over for yourself or your mate. It's funny but true: The parents who didn't raise you properly were trying to overcome factors present when their parents didn't raise them properly. If you take matters to extremes, you will lose perspective and effectiveness.

Reason #7: Your Expectations Are Self-fulfilling

A group of mothers who were convinced that their sons acted negatively when given sugar were divided into two groups. One group was told to play with their sons after the boys were given a sugary drink. The other mothers played with their sons when the boys were given an artificial sweetener. The boys had ankle and wrist "actometers" that measured their physical activity. In truth, none of the boys were given sugar, but the mothers who believed their sons had a sweet drink rated them as more active and difficult—despite the fact that their actometers revealed the boys to be less active than the other group.

Once you have labeled your child, that label will stick in your mind. A child who routinely delays doing his homework might prompt a parent to scold him when he is watching television instead of inquiring what the homework status is. That parental approach may cause more negative feelings on both sides and interfere with cooperation.

Reason #8: You Are Part of a New Stepfamily

Stepfamilies can run smoothly, but it usually takes time. Sometimes the adults are living together but unmarried, and that can be even more complicating because the nonparent has even less legitimate authority. Also, in some of these arrangements each party pays their individual bills, which further diminishes the sense that it is one big happy family. Generally, stepfamilies should follow these guidelines:

The stepparent should help make rules but should not be the main enforcer.

The stepparent should not try to replace the absent biological parent.

The stepparent should find some quality one-on-one time with each of the kids. It is the best and fastest way to build rapport.

Problems should be handled in family meetings until the stepparent is treated as a legitimate authority.

Don't expect a stepparent to automatically love the stepchildren. Depending on the child's age, stepparents may never quite love their stepchildren the way they do their biological children, but treatment of all kids should be fair.

Reason #9: You Allow Stereotypes to Intrude in Your Family

Fathers who won't change diapers and mothers who won't play catch with their kids are not only missing out, they are messing up. It may seem small, but when you limit your activities with a child and let your mate take over, you limit your role in other ways, too. Eventually you will be a two-dimensional parent—very involved in your area of expertise but uninvolved in other areas. This can have far-reaching effects. One study showed that couples with one child, a girl, were 9 percent more likely to divorce than couples who had only a boy. Couples with two girls were 18 percent more likely to divorce than couples with two boys. Why? Evidently fathers spend more time in child-care activities with sons than with daughters. A dad's greater involvement usually improves marital satisfaction and reduces the risk of divorce. (Another study showed that if a girl had brothers, her father was more involved in her life than if she had no brothers.) While it is true that some parents are better skilled at some child-focused tasks than their mates, the less-skilled parent shouldn't abandon efforts to be useful in those areas.

Reason #10: You Don't Give New Approaches a Fair Shot

Ironically, frustrated parents have a tendency to overuse parenting approaches that haven't proved useful but give up on helpful approaches quickly. For example, parents who have found that taking away privileges from a child doesn't stop some unacceptable behavior will continue to take away privileges. They don't question the technique but just assume that their child is obstinate or extra difficult. But maybe they have misidentified the problem. Maybe the punishment is actually making matters worse. These same parents may try a new approach, but the first time they don't get the desired response, they abandon it and go back to the old standbys. If you have reason to believe that a different approach makes sense, try it for at least two weeks. If there is improvement but no resolution, then there is something about the approach that is working. Don't abandon it.

The happier and more stable your marriage, the more likely that parenting will be mostly a joy although certainly worrisome at times. A troubled marriage, however, can create problems with your children and in your ability to manage those problems effectively.

The Argument Audit below will give you clues about the status of your marriage. It will tell you if conflicts are minimal, if they are a bit troublesome but manageable, or if they have become seriously threatening to the marriage. The higher your score, the more you may want to consider marital counseling.

THE ARGUMENT AUDIT

Please mark your scores in the space provided at the end of each item. Use the following scale:

Rarely 0

Sometimes 1

Often 2

Much of the time 3

When you complete the items, tally the individual scores. Compare your final score with the key presented at the bottom.

1. Do you feel you must assess your mate's mood before you feel free to speak to him/her? _____

2. Do the same arguments/conflicts occur repeatedly? _____

3. Do you feel out of sync with each other emotionally (for example, when he's ready for lovemaking, you're not, and vice versa)? _____

4. Are you accused of overreacting or underreacting to his or her behaviors or attitudes? _____

5. When the relationship seems to be going well, do you anticipate problems on the horizon? _____

6. Are you more invested in your spouse's changing some aspect of his/her behavior than he/she is? _____

7. When you believe that some problems are improving, do you view a setback as "back to square one"? _____

8. When you and your mate disagree, do you react more to his manner (tone of voice, attitude) than to the specifics of the disagreement? _____

9. Do you get defensive or offensive with your mate? _____

10. Do you anticipate (correctly or incorrectly) what your mate will say or do before it happens? _____

11. Do you act on those assumptions before checking them out with your mate? _____

12. Do you feel threatened that your mate has (or might be interested in having) some separate interest or hobbies? _____

13. Does one or both of you avoid discussing areas of conflict, or does at least one of you withdraw from that discussion prematurely? _____

14. Do you feel responsible for your mate's feelings/actions to the extent that if he/she is feeling blue, you wonder what you might have done to cause it? _____

15. Do you feel disowned by your parents or cut off from them emotionally? _____

Score

0–10   No problems. Any future problems will be avoided or caught early enough to resolve.

11–25   Some problems are developing but can be nipped in the bud.

26–35   Some problems have become difficult or unmanageable. Solutions do exist. Children may be affected.

36–45   Many unresolved problems. Marital satisfaction is low. A committed effort to resolve issues is absolutely essential.

A QUICK TEST FOR MARITAL HAPPINESS

If you are unsure whether your mate is happy in the marriage, there is a quick way to get a fairly accurate measurement. (Of course, talking with your mate about it is also a good idea.) This method is very reliable, assuming you and your mate are in good physical health.

1. Calculate the number of times you made love during a certain time frame (say, the past two weeks).

2. Calculate the number of arguments you've had during that same time period. (An argument is defined as any time you or your mate was "uncooperative.")

3. Subtract the number of arguments from the number of times that you made love.

4. If the difference is a positive number, you and your mate are probably happy. If the difference is a negative number, you and your mate are probably not happy.

Sources

Introduction: Smart Talk: The Six Ways We Speak to Our Kids

Hofferth, Sandra L. Changes in American children's time, 1981–1997. In *Brown University Child and Adolescent Behavior Letter* 15 (3), (March 1999).

Chapter 1: Adoption

Sharma, A., M. McGue, and P. Benson. The psychological adjustment of U.S. adopted adolescents and their non-adopted siblings. *Child Development* 69 (1998): 791–802.

Chapter 2: Angry Child

Donovan, Denis, and Deborah McIntyre. *What Did I Just Say?: How New Insights into Childhood Thinking Can Help You Communicate More Effectively with Your Child*. New York: Henry Holt, 1999.

Viscott, David. *The Language of Feelings*. New York: Pocket Books, 1976.

Chapter 3: Apologies

Krevaus, Julia, and John Gibbs. Parents' use of inductive discipline: Relationships to children's empathy and prosocial behavior. *Child Development* 67 (1996): 3263–77.

Chapter 4: Arguments Between Two Adults

Cummings, E. M., and P. Davies. *Children and Marital Conflict: The Impact of Family Dispute and Resolution*. New York: Guilford, 1994.

Davies, P., and E. M. Cummings. Marital conflict and child adjustment: An emotional security hypothesis. *Psychological Bulletin* 116 (1994): 387–411.

Chapter 5: Bed-wetting

Houts, A., J. Berman, and H. Abramson. Effectiveness of psychological and pharmacological treatments for nocturnal enuresis. *Journal of Consulting and Clinical Psychology* 62 (1994): 737–45.

Chapter 7: Bullies

DuRant, R., D. Krowchuk, and P. Kreiter. Weapon carrying on school property among middle school students. *Archives of Pediatric and Adolescent Medicine* 153 (1999): 21–26.

Chapter 15: Comforting the Dying Child

Mulhern, R. K., M. E. Lauer, and R. G. Hoffman. Death of a child at home or at the hospital: Subsequent psychological adjustment of the family. *Pediatrics* 71 (1983): 743–47.

Chapter 17: Divorce: Telling the Children

Ulrich, David N. Mobilizing family resources for constructive divorce. In Mark Karpel (ed.), *Family Resources: The Hidden Partner in Family Therapy*. New York: Guilford, 1986, p. 401.

Chapter 18: Divorce: Introducing Your Child to Your New Partner

Neuman, M. Gary. *Helping Your Kids Cope with Divorce the Sandcastles Way*. New York: Random House, 1998.

Chapter 20: Divorce: When One Parent Abandons the Children

Booth, Alan, and David Johnson. Premarital cohabitation and marital success. *Journal of Family Issues* 9 (1988): 255–72.

Bumpass, Larry L., James A. Sweet, and Andrew Cherlin. The role of cohabitation in declining rates of marriage. *Journal of Marriage and the Family* 53 (1991): 913–27.

Margolin, Leslie. Child abuse and mother's boyfriends: Why the overrepresentation? *Child Abuse and Neglect* 16 (1992): 541–55.

Chapter 25: Fostering Empathy and Emotional Intelligence

Azar, Beth. Our siblings teach us how to read people's emotions. *APA Monitor* (September 1995): 29.

Goleman, Daniel. *Emotional Intelligence*. New York: Bantam Books, 1995.

Chapter 31: Fears of Harm or Injury

Swedo, Susan Anderson, and Henrietta L. Leonard. *Is It Just a Phase? How to Tell Common Childhood Phases from More Serious Problems*. New York: Golden Books, 1998.

Chapter 32: Teaching Forgiveness

Enright, Robert. Helping el nino to forgive. In *The World of Forgiveness*. Madison, WI: International Forgiveness Institute, 1998.

Chapter 33: God: Common Questions

Coleman, Paul. *The 30 Secrets of Happily Married Couples*. Holbrook, MA: Adams, 1992.

Gellman, Marc, and Thomas Hartman. *Where Does God Live? Questions and Answers for Parents and Children*. Liguori, MO: Triumph Books, 1991.

Glenn, Norval. Inter-religious marriages in the U.S.: Patterns and recent trends. *Journal of Marriage and the Family* 44 (3) (1982): 555–68.

Chapter 34: God: Prayer

Bel Geddes, Joan. *Children Praying: Why and How to Pray with Your Children*. Notre Dame, IN: Sorin Books, 1999.

Princeton Religion Research Center. *Religion in America: Will the Vitality of the Church Be the Surprise of the 21st Century? Princeton, NJ: Gallup Poll, 1996.*

Chapter 35: God: "I Don't Want to Go to Church"

Greeley, Andrew. *Faithful Attraction: Discovering Intimacy, Love, and Fidelity in American Marriage*. New York: Tor Books, 1991, p. 190.

Chapter 37: Hitting

"Is your kid a killer?" *Psychology Today* (October 1999): 16.

Perozynski, L., and L. Kramer. Parental beliefs about managing sibling conflict. *Developmental Psychology* 35 (1999): 489–99.

Chapter 38: HIV/AIDS

Whalen, C., B. Henker, J. Hollingshead, and S. Burgess. Parent-adolescent dialogues about AIDS. *Journal of Family Psychology* 10 (1996): 343–57.

Chapter 39: Home Alone/Latchkey Kids

Galambor, N., and J. Maggs. Out-of-school care of young adolescents and self-reported behavior. *Developmental Psychology* 27 (1991): 644–55.

Kelly, P., M. Weir, A. Atkinson, and R. Lampe. Latchkey: Three voices with one message. *Clinical Pediatrics* 25 (1986): 462–65.

Messer, S., K. Wuensch, and J. Diamond. Former latchkey children: Personality and academic correlates. *Journal of Genetic Psychology* 150 (1989): 301–9.

Mulhall, P., D. Stone, and B. Stone. Home alone: Is it a risk factor for middle school youth and drug use? *Journal of Drug Education* 26 (1996): 39–48.

Chapter 44: Lying

Goleman, D. "Analyzed: Mental disorders or normal growth?" *New York Times,* May 17, 1988, p. 19.

Chapter 45: Manipulative Behavior ("But Mom Said I Could!")

Christensen, A., G. Margolin, and M. Sullaway. Interparental agreement on child behavior problems. *Psychological Assessment* 4 (1992): 419–25.

Shinnar, Shlomo. Epilepsy treatment in the 21st century. *Exceptional Parent* (October 1999): 64–74.

Chapter 47: Medical: Hospitalization

Barakat, L. P., A. Kazak, A. Meadows, R. Casey, K. Meeske, and M. Stuber. Families surviving childhood cancer: A comparison of post-traumatic stress symptoms with families of healthy children. *Journal of Pediatric Psychology* 22 (1997): 843–59.

Chapter 48: Medical: When a Child Has a Chronic Illness

Allen, K., and M. Shriver. The role of parent-mediated pain behavior management strategies in biofeedback treatment of childhood migraines. *Behavior Therapy* 29 (1998): 477–90.

Bock, Steven J., Kenneth Bock, and Nancy P. Bruning. *Natural Relief for Your Child's Asthma.* New York: HarperPerennial, 1999.

Gartland, H. J., and H. D. Day. Family predictors of the incidence of children's asthma symptoms: Expressed emotion, medications, parent control, and life events. *Journal of Clinical Psychology* 55 (1999): 573–84.

Johnson, Robert Wood, Sale Johnson, Casey Johnson, and Casey Kleinman. *Managing Your Child's Diabetes*. New York: Master Media, 1992.

Shinnar, Shlomo. Epilepsy treatment in the 21st century. *Exceptional Parent* (October 1999): 64–74.

Chapter 49: Medical: Talking to Siblings of Children with Chronic Illness

Walker, L., J. Garber, and D. Van Slyke. Do parents excuse the misbehavior of children with physical or emotional symptoms? An investigation of the pediatric sick role. *Journal of Pediatric Psychology* 20 (1995): 329–45.

Chapter 50: Medical: When a Parent Has a Serious Physical Illness

Armistead, L., K. Klein, R. Forehand, and M. Wierson. Disclosure of parental HIV infection to children in families of men with hemophilia: Description, outcomes, and the role of family process. *Journal of Family Psychology* 11 (1997): 49–61.

Chin, D., D. Schonfield, L. O'Hare, S. Maynes, P. Salovey, D. Showalter, and D. Cicchetti. Elementary school-age children's developmental understanding of the causes of cancer. *Journal of Developmental and Behavioral Pediatrics* 19 (1998): 397–403.

Chapter 54: Nagging

Brown University Child and Adolescent Behavior Letter 15 (7) (1999): 2.

Chapter 55: New Baby

Druckman, Amanda. Commitment crowded out. *Psychology Today* (November/December 1999): 21.

Chapter 57: Increasing Optimism

Evitt, Marie Faust. Comeback kids. *Child* (September 1999): 55–58.

Seligman, Martin E. P. *Learned Optimism*. New York: Pocket Books, 1990.

Chapter 58: Parental Emotional Problems: Depression, Fears, Compulsions

Beardslee, W. R., E. M. Versage, E. J. Wright, P. Solt, P. C. Rothberg, K. Drezner, and T. Gladstone. Examination of preventive interventions for families with depression: Evidence of change. *Developmental Psychopathology* 9 (1997): 109–30.

Chapter 62: Perseverance

Diener, C., and C. Dweck. An analysis of learned helplessness II: The processing of success. *Journal of Personality and Social Psychology* 29 (1980): 940–52.

Chapter 63: Pets

Van Houtle, B. A., and P. Jarvis. The role of pets in preadolescent psychosocial development. *Journal of Applied Developmental Psychology* 16 (1995): 463–79.

Chapter 64: Concerns About Physical Appearance

Drotar, D., R. Owens, and J. Gotthold. Personality adjustment of children and adolescents with hypopituitarism. *Child Psychiatry and Human Development* 11 (1980): 59–66.

Field, A., L. Cheung, and A. Wolf. Exposure to the mass media and weight concerns among girls. *Pediatrics* 103 (1999): 36–44.

Holmes, C., J. Karlsson, and R. Thompson. Social and school competencies in children with short stature: Longitudinal patterns. *Journal of Developmental and Behavioral Pediatrics* 6 (1985): 263–67.

Holmes, C., R. Thompson, and J. Hayford. Factors related to grade retention in children of short stature. *Child Care, Health, and Development* 10 (1984): 199–210.

Skuse, D. The psychological consequences of being small. *Journal of Child Psychology, Psychiatry, and Allied Disciplines* 28 (1987): 641–50.

Chapter 66: Quarreling with Siblings

Perozynski, L., and L. Kramer. Parental beliefs about managing sibling conflicts. *Developmental Psychology* 35 (1999): 489–99.

Chapter 68: Refusing to Talk

Leaper, C., K. Anderson, and P. Sanders. Moderators of gender effects on parents' talks with their children: A meta-analysis. *Developmental Psychology* 34 (1998): 3–27.

Chapter 69: Running Away from Home

Schaffner, Laurie. Searching for connections: A new look at teenage runaways. *Adolescence* 33 (1998): 619–27.

Chapter 72: School: "My Teacher Is Mean!"

Bennett, William, Chester E. Finn, and John T. Cribb. *The Educated Child: A Parent's Guide from Preschool Through Eighth Grade.* New York: The Free Press, 1999.

Madon, S., L. Jussim, and J. Eccles. In search of the powerful self-fulfilling prophecy. *Journal of Personality and Social Psychology* 72 (1997): 791–809.

McLoyd, Yonnie. Socioeconomic disadvantages and child development. *American Psychologist* 53 (1998): 185–204.

Murdock, Tamera. The social context of risk status and motivational predictors of alienation in middle school. *Journal of Educational Psychology* 91 (1999): 62–75.

Tal, Z., and E. Babad. The teacher's pet phenomenon: Rate of occurrence, correlates, and psychological cost. *Journal of Educational Psychology* 82 (1990): 637–45.

Chapter 74: School: "I'm Afraid to Ask a Question in Class"

Neuman, Richard. Children's help-seeking in the classroom: The role of motivational status and attitude. *Journal of Educational Psychology* 82 (1990): 71–80.

Chapter 75: School: Poor Report Card

Frome, P., and J. Eccles. Parents' influence on children's achievement-related perceptions. *Journal of Personality and Social Psychology* 74 (1998): 435–52.

Phillips, D., and M. Zimmerman. The developmental course of perceived competence and incompetence among competent children. In R. J. Sternberg and J. Kalligian, Jr. (eds.), *Competency Considered*. New Haven, CT: Yale University Press, 1990, pp. 41–66.

Wentzel, Kathryn. Student motivation in middle school: The role of perceived pedagogical caring. *Journal of Educational Psychology* 89 (1997): 411–19.

Chapter 76: School: Rejected by Classmates

Coie, J., J. Lochman, R. Terry, and C. Hyman. Predicting early adolescence disorders from childhood aggression and peer rejection. *Journal of Consulting and Clinical Psychology* 60 (1992): 783–92.

Finnegan, R., E. Hodges, and D. Perry. Victimization by peers: Association with children's reports of mother-child interactions. *Journal of Personality and Social Psychology* 75 (1998): 1076–86.

Hodges, E., and D. Perry. Personal and interpersonal antecedents and consequences of victimization by peers. *Journal of Personality and Social Psychology* 76 (1999): 677–85.

Ollendick, T., M. Weist, M. Borden, and R. Greene. Sociometric status and academic, behavioral, and psychological adaptation: A five-year longitudinal study. *Journal of Consulting and Clinical Psychology* 60 (1992): 80–87.

Parkhurst, J., and S. Asher. Peer rejection in middle school: Subgroup differences in behavior, loneliness, and interpersonal concerns. *Developmental Psychology* 28 (1992): 231–41.

White, K., and J. Kistner. The influence of teacher's feedback on young children's peer preferences and perceptions. *Developmental Psychology* 28 (1992): 933–40.

Chapter 77: School Safety Concerns

Anderman, E., and D. Kimweli. Victimization and safety in schools serving early adolescents. *Journal of Early Adolescence* 17 (1997): 408–38.

Gelles, Richard. Explaining the unthinkable: The Jonesboro tragedy. *Brown University Child and Adolescent Behavior Letter* (May 1998): 1, 5.

Ryan-Spanswick, B., and J. Coleman. Incorporating your school resource officer into the fabric of your middle school community. *Impact 1999*, 6 (1) (1999): 2–4.

Chapter 78: Improving Self-confidence

Baumeister, Roy F. Low self-esteem does not cause aggression. *APA Monitor* (January 1999): 7.

Chapter 79: Self-critical Child

Koestner, R., D. Zuroff, and T. Powers. Family origins of adolescent self-criticism and its continuity into adulthood. *Journal of Abnormal Psychology* 100 (1991): 191–97.

Zahn-Waxler, C., G. Kochanska, J. Krupnick, and D. McKnew. Patterns of guilt in children of depressed and well mothers. *Developmental Psychology* 26 (1990): 51–59.

Chapter 80: Sexuality and Reproduction

Schaefer, C., and T. DiGeronimo. *How to Talk to Your Kids About Really Important Things.* San Francisco: Jossey-Bass, 1994.

Chapter 84: Promoting Sexual Abstinence

Graham, Melody. *The Effects of Parent-Adolescent Communication on Adolescent Sexual Behavior.* Poster session presented at the Centennial Annual Convention of the American Psychological Association, Washington, D.C., August 1992.

Chapter 85: Sexual Abuse: Alerting Your Child

Finkelhor, D., and J. Dzuiba-Leatherman. Victimization of children. *American Psychologist* 49 (1994): 173–83.

Chapter 86: Sexual Abuse: After It Happens

Monahon, Cynthia. *Children and Trauma: A Guide for Parents and Professionals.* San Francisco: Jossey-Bass, 1997.

Chapter 87: Sharing

Owens, C., and F. Ascione. Effects of model's age, perceived similarity, and familiarity on children's donating. *Journal of Genetic Psychology* 152 (1992): 341–57.

Ross, Hildy. Negotiating principles of entitlement in sibling property disputes. *Developmental Psychology* 32 (1996): 90–101.

Siperstein, G., and J. Liffert. Managing limited resources: Do children with learning problems share? *Exceptional Children* 65 (1998): 187–99.

Chapter 88: Shyness

Kerr, M., W. Lambert, and D. Bem. Life course sequelae of childhood shyness in Sweden: Comparison with the U.S. *Developmental Psychology* 32 (1996): 1100–05.

Chapter 89: Sportsmanship

Smith, R., and F. Smoll. Self-esteem and children's reactions to youth sport coaching behaviors: A field study of self-enhancement processes. *Developmental Psychology* 26 (1990): 987–93.

Chapter 90: Stealing

Kagan, Jerome. Etiologies of adolescents at risk. *Journal of Adolescent Health* 12 (1992): 59–96.

Moore, D., P. Chamberlain, and L. Mukai. *Journal of Abnormal Child Psychology* 7 (1979): 345–55.

Seymour, F., and D. Epston. An approach to childhood stealing with an evaluation of 45 cases. *Australian and New Zealand Journal of Family Therapy* 10 (1989): 137–43.

Chapter 91: Strangers

Bovey-McCoy, S., and D. Finkelhor. Psychosocial sequelae of violent victimization in a national youth sample. *Journal of Consulting and Clinical Psychology* 63 (1995): 726–36.

Bromberg, D., and B. Johnson. Behavioral and traditional approaches to the prevention of child abductions. *School Psychology Review* 26 (1997): 622–33.

Finkelhor, D., and J. Dzuiba-Leatherman. Victimization of children. *American Psychologist* 49 (1994): 173–83.

Finkelhor, D., G. Hotoling, and A. Sedlah. The abduction of children by strangers and non-family members: Estimating the incidence using multiple methods. *Journal of Interpersonal Violence* 7 (1992): 226–43.

Johnston, J., L. Girdner, and I. Sagitun-Edwards. Developing profiles of risk for parental abduction of children from a comparison of families victimized by abduction with families litigating custody. *Behavioral Science and the Law* 17 (1999): 305–22.

Chapter 93: Tattling

Ross, H., and I. denBak-Lammers. Consistency and change in children's tattling on their siblings: Children's perspectives on the moral rules and procedures in family life. *Social Development* 7 (1998): 275–300.

Chapter 94: Being Teased

Keltner, D., R. Young, E. Heerey, C. Oemig, and N. Monarch. Teasing in hierarchical and intimate relationships. *Journal of Personality and Social Psychology* 75 (1998): 1231–47.

Chapter 96: Trauma from an Accident or Natural Disaster

Dollinger, S. Lightning-strike disasters among children. *British Journal of Medical Psychology* 18 (1985): 375–83.

Groves, B., B. Zuckerman, S. Marons, and D. Cohen. Silent victims: Children who witness violence. *Journal of the American Medical Association* 269 (1993): 262–64.

Janoff-Bulman, R. *Shattered Assumption: Towards a New Psychology of Trauma*. New York: The Free Press, 1992.

Kliewer, W., S. Lepore, D. Oskin, and P. Johnson. The role of social cognitive processes on children's adjustment to community violence. *Journal of Consulting and Clinical Psychology* 66 (1998): 199–209.

LaGreca, A., W. Silverman, and S. Wasserstein. Children's predisaster functioning as a predictor of post-traumatic stress following Hurricane Andrew. *Journal of Consulting and Clinical Psychology* 66 (1998): 883–92.

Marans, S., and D. Cohen. Children and inner-city violence: Strategies for intervention. In L. Leavitt and N. Fox (eds.), *The Psychological Effects of War and Violence on Children*. Hillsdale, NJ: Erlbaum, 1993, pp. 281–302.

Chapter 97: Violence and Sexual Material in Television and Movies

Comstock, G., and V. Strasburger. Deceptive appearances: Television violence and aggressive behavior. *Journal of Adolescent Health Law* 11 (1990): 31–44.

Godow, K., and J. Spratkin. Television violence and children with emotional and behavioral disorders. *Journal of Emotional and Behavioral Disorders* 1 (1993): 54–63.

Liebert, R., and R. Baron. Some immediate effects of television violence on children's behavior. *Developmental Psychology* 6 (1972): 469–75.

Molitor, F., and K. Hirsch. Children's tolerance of real-life aggression after exposure to media violence. *Child Study Journal* 24 (1995): 191–207.

Robinson, T., H. Chen, and J. Killen. Television and music video exposure and risk of adolescent alcohol use. *Pediatrics* 102 (1998): 54–66.

Valkenburg, P., and T. van der Voort. Influence of TV on daydreaming and creative imagination: A review of research. *Psychological Bulletin* 116 (1994): 316–39.

Chapter 98: Whiny and Demanding Child

Endo, G., H. Sloane, T. Hawkes, and W. Jenson. Reducing child whining through self-instructional parent training materials. *Child and Family Behavior Therapy* 13 (1991): 41–58.

Chapter 99: Working Parent (When You Used to Stay at Home)

Bryant, W., and C. Zick. An examination of parent-child shared time. *Journal of Marriage and the Family* 58 (1997): 227–37.

Moorehouse, Martha. Linking maternal employment patterns to mother-child activities and children's school competence. *Developmental Psychology* 27 (1991): 295–303.

Chapter 100: Worried Child

Cobham, V., M. Dadds, and S. Spence. The role of parental anxiety in the treatment of childhood anxiety. *Journal of Consulting and Clinical Psychology* 66 (1998): 893–905.

Gottlieb, D., and P. Bronstein. Parent's perceptions of children's worries in a changing world. *Journal of Genetic Psychology* 157 (1996): 104–18.

Muris, P., C. Meesters, H. Merckelboch, A. Sermon, and S. Zwakhalen. Worry in normal children. *Journal of the American Academy of Child and Adolescent Psychiatry* 37 (1998): 703–10.

When You Say It Right (but Things Still Go Wrong): Ten Winning Tips for Troubleshooters

Hover, D., and R. Milich. Effects of sugar ingestion: Expectations of mother–child interactions. *Journal of Abnormal Child Psychology* 22 (1994): 501–15.

Kerig, P., P. Cowan, and C. Cowan. Marital quality and gender differences in parent–child interactions. *Developmental Psychology* 29 (1993): 931–39.

Lindahl, K., M. Clements, and H. Markman. Predicting marital and parental functioning in dyads and triads: A longitudinal investigation of marital processes. *Journal of Family Psychology* 11 (1997): 139–51.

Taffel, Ron. *Parenting by Heart*. Reading, MA: Addison-Wesley, 1991.

Appendix

Coleman, Paul. *Getting to the Heart of the Matter*. Holbrook, MA: Adams Media, 1994.

Howard, J., and R. Dawes. Linear prediction of marital happiness. *Personality and Social Psychology Bulletin* 2 (1976): 478–80.

Index